Taxcafe.co.uk Tax Guides

How to Save Property Tax

By Carl Bayley BSc FCA

Important Legal Notices:

Taxcafe®
TAX GUIDE – "How to Save Property Tax"

Published by:
Taxcafe UK Limited
67 Milton Road
Kirkcaldy
KY1 1TL
United Kingdom
Tel: (01592) 560081

Twenty-fourth Edition, December 2019

ISBN 978-1-911020-51-6

Disclaimer
Before reading or relying on the content of this Tax Guide, please read the
disclaimer.

Disclaimer

1. Please note that this publication is intended as **general guidance** only and does NOT constitute accountancy, tax, financial or other professional advice. The author and Taxcafe UK Limited make no representations or warranties with respect to the accuracy or completeness of the contents of this publication and cannot accept any responsibility for any liability, loss or risk, personal or otherwise, which may arise, directly or indirectly, from reliance on information contained in this publication.

2. Please note that tax legislation, the law and practices of government and regulatory authorities (e.g. HM Revenue and Customs) are constantly changing. Furthermore, your personal circumstances may vary from the general information contained in this tax guide which may not be suitable for your situation. We therefore recommend that for accountancy, tax, financial or other professional advice, you consult a suitably qualified accountant, tax specialist, independent financial adviser, or other professional adviser who will be able to provide specific advice based on your personal circumstances.

3. This guide covers UK taxation only and any references to 'tax' or 'taxation', unless the contrary is expressly stated, refer to UK taxation only. Please note that references to the 'UK' do not include the Channel Islands or the Isle of Man. Foreign tax implications are beyond the scope of this guide.

4. Whilst in an effort to be helpful this tax guide may refer to general guidance on matters other than UK taxation, Taxcafe UK Limited and the author are not expert in these matters and do not accept any responsibility or liability for loss which may arise from reliance on such information contained in this guide.

5. Please note that Taxcafe UK Limited has relied wholly on the expertise of the author in the preparation of the content of this tax guide. The author is not an employee of Taxcafe UK Limited but has been selected by Taxcafe UK Limited using reasonable care and skill.

6. The views expressed in this publication are the author's own personal views and do not necessarily reflect the views of any organisation which he may represent.

About the Author

Carl Bayley is the author of a series of 'Plain English' tax guides designed specifically for the layman and the non-specialist. Carl's particular speciality is his ability to take the weird, complex and inexplicable world of taxation and set it out in the kind of clear, straightforward language that taxpayers themselves can understand. As he often says himself, "My job is to translate 'tax' into English."

Carl enjoys his role as a tax author, as he explains, "Writing these guides gives me the opportunity to use the skills and knowledge learned over more than thirty years in the tax profession for the benefit of a wider audience. The most satisfying part of my success as an author is the chance to give the average person the same standard of advice as the 'big guys' at a price which everyone can afford."

Carl takes the same approach when speaking on taxation, a role he frequently undertakes with great enthusiasm, including his highly acclaimed annual 'Budget Breakfast' for the Institute of Chartered Accountants.

In addition to being a recognised author and speaker on the subject, Carl has often spoken on taxation on radio and television, including the BBC's 'It's Your Money' programme and BBC Radio 2's Jeremy Vine Show.

Carl began his career as a Chartered Accountant in 1983 with one of the 'Big 4' accountancy firms. After qualifying as a double prize-winner, he immediately began specialising in taxation.

Having honed his skills with several major international firms, Carl began the new millennium by launching his own tax and accounting practice, Bayley Miller Limited, providing advice on a wide variety of taxation issues; especially property taxation and tax planning for small and medium-sized businesses.

Carl is a former Chairman of the Tax Faculty of the Institute of Chartered Accountants in England and Wales and a member of the Institute's governing Council. He is also a former President of ICAEW Scotland and has co-organised the annual Practical Tax Conference for the last 18 years.

When he isn't working, Carl takes on the equally taxing challenges of hill walking and creative writing – his Munro tally is now 104 and he has just completed his first novel.

Carl lives in the Scottish Borders and has four children.

Dedication & Thanks

For the Past,
Firstly, I dedicate this book to the memory of those I have loved and lost:

To my beloved mother Diana – what would you think if you could see me now? The memory of your love warms me still. Thank you for bringing me into the light and making it all possible; To my dear grandfather, Arthur - your wise words still come back to guide me; and to my loving grandmothers, Doris and Winifred;

Between you, you left me with nothing I could spend, but everything I need. Also to my beloved friends: Mac, William, Edward, Rusty, Dawson, and the grand old lady, Morgan. Thank you for all those happy miles; I still miss you all.

For the Present,
To the lovely lady Linda – thanks for bringing the sunshine back into my life; for opening my ears and putting the song back in my heart. How quickly and completely you have become my world – I owe you more than you will ever know.

For the Future,
I also dedicate this book to some very special young people:

Robert – the 'chip off the old block', who is both cursed and blessed to have inherited a lot of my own character; luckily for him, there is a lot of his mother in him too!

James – the intellectual of the family, a true twenty-first century gentleman and one of the nicest guys I have ever met;

And lastly, and furthest from least:

Michelle – my truly wonderful daughter, I told her when she was just sixteen that she was one of the most interesting people I had ever met: since then she has grown more interesting, and more amazing, with every passing year!

I am so very proud of every one of you and I can only hope that I, in turn, will also be able to leave each of you with everything you need.

I would like to thank my old friend and mentor, Peter Rayney, for his inspiration and for showing me that tax and humour can mix. Thanks also to Rebecca, Paul and David for taking me into the 'fold' at the Tax Faculty and for their fantastic support at our Practical Tax Conference over many years. Thanks are also due to Gregor for giving me a chance to see theory put into practice.

Contents

Introduction

This guide was first published in 2002, as a response to the huge demand for advice on property taxation issues we had been experiencing at Taxcafe.co.uk. That demand continued to grow at a phenomenal pace and is responsible for the fact that now, 17 years on, this guide is in its twenty-fourth edition, and has expanded to the eight chapters you have here.

People in the UK have invested in property for centuries, but substantial increases in personal wealth and disposable income over a number of decades prior to the banking crisis in 2008/9 combined with difficulties in other areas of investment and the pensions industry to make this a significantly important area of personal financial planning.

The first few years of this century, in particular, saw phenomenal growth in the property sector, not just in the amount of property investment activity but also in the sheer numbers of people entering the property market as investors, developers and dealers. While the big flotations of the 1980s acted to spread investment in stocks and shares into all sectors of society; the late 1990s and early years of this century witnessed a similar spreading of property investment.

'Property Investment' itself is a very wide term. A few years ago, the majority of new investors tended to be purely interested in the 'Buy-to-Let' market. As the property sector grew larger and more sophisticated, however, many other types of activity began to proliferate more widely, including 'Buy-to-Sell', 'Let-to-Buy' and, of course, a great deal of renovation, conversion and development activity. Beyond these, there also lie the fields of property trading and management.

When increasing property prices raised the barrier to entry, people found other ways to invest in property, such as investing abroad, or clubbing together to invest through joint ventures, syndicates or special purpose vehicles (often called 'SPVs').

All these different types of activity are subject to different tax regimes and establishing the correct tax classification for each property business can be quite tortuous. One of our first tasks in this guide is therefore to help you understand how your own business will be treated for tax purposes and this is something we will consider in depth in Chapter 2.

There are also many different reasons for becoming a property investor. Some fall into it by accident, finding themselves with a second property through marriage, inheritance or other changes in personal circumstances.

Others move into the property sector quite deliberately, seeing it as a safe haven providing long-term security and perhaps an income in retirement. Still others see the property market as a means to generate a second income during their working life.

An ever-growing proportion of landlords are choosing to enter the property business as a professional career.

In fact, given the ever-increasing volume of rules and regulations which the private rented sector has to contend with, a professional approach to property investment has now become essential: whatever reasons you may have for entering the property market in the first place.

This is no bad thing: a professional approach has always been desirable. Those who are prepared to devote substantial time and resources to their business are generally rewarded with better results – including those who plan their tax affairs carefully.

The last decade or so has seen enormous changes in the property market and in the economy as a whole and previously held views on the certainty of capital growth and the whole philosophy of 'you can't lose' have been questioned and found wanting.

While these changes have been disastrous for some, they have created opportunities for others and the lower level of interest rates enjoyed by many investors over the last few years have brought healthy rental profits to many.

In effect, the economic difficulties created by the 2008/9 banking crisis and its aftermath can be seen as part of an evolutionary process. The fittest property businesses have survived to become part of a stronger property sector.

Now, the property sector faces a new challenge: a challenge I can only describe as an unprecedented level of attacks via the tax system from a Government that would appear to be hell-bent on the sector's destruction. Quite where the Government expects to house all the former tenants that are likely to be made homeless as a result is a mystery to me!

Nonetheless, despite the difficulties it continues to face, I personally believe the property investment sector as we know it today is here to stay. Naturally, the sector will have its ups and downs, as any other business sector does, but the philosophy of property investment as a 'career move' is now so well entrenched it has become impossible to imagine it could ever disappear altogether.

Changes in both the economy and in tax legislation have always had a dramatic impact on the tax planning landscape for property investors and will continue to do so in the future. Before the banking crisis, Capital Gains Tax was many investors' biggest concern. Then, as capital growth slowed, or even stalled, and interest rates fell, Income Tax became increasingly important.

Now, with capital growth having returned to many areas, Capital Gains Tax rates on residential property still relatively high; and punitive Income Tax changes that deny proper tax relief for many landlords' biggest cost; planning for both these taxes together has become more crucial than ever.

Tax and tax planning are a vital part of every business's strategy. Property businesses are clearly no exception!

Whatever reasons you may have for entering the property investment market, and whatever type of property business you may have, my aim in this guide is to give you a better understanding of how the UK tax system affects you and show you how to minimise or eliminate your potential tax liabilities.

In the first two chapters, we will set the scene by looking at the different UK taxes you will meet as a property investor and how they apply to the various different kinds of property business.

Chapters 3 to 7 are then devoted to explaining in detail how the UK tax rules apply to property investment and other types of property business and how you can minimise your own tax burden. In Chapter 8 we will examine some more advanced tax planning strategies which will help to reduce your tax burden even further.

There are plenty of **'Tax Tips'** along the way to help you minimise or delay your tax bills, as well as **'Wealth Warnings'** designed to keep you away from some of the more treacherous pitfalls awaiting the unwary, and **'Practical Pointers'** to make the process of meeting your tax obligations as painless as possible.

I believe this guide is comprehensive enough to meet the needs of almost every property investor based in the UK and I hope, with its help, you will be able to enjoy a much larger proportion of the fruits of your endeavours.

Finally, I would just like to thank you for buying this guide and wish you every success with your property investments.

Scope of this Guide

This guide aims to help you understand the current UK tax system applying to property and also to help you plan for the future. We aim to cover as much as possible of the UK tax implications of investing in property, or running some other kind of property business.

While this edition primarily focuses on the current tax year and the future, we will generally continue to include the rules that form the basis for the preparation of tax returns for all years from 2017/18 onwards. (As explained in Section 3.6, tax returns for 2017/18 may currently still be amended.) Rules applying in earlier years will generally only be included where they continue to be relevant. For full details of the rules applying in earlier years, see previous editions of this guide.

There are three different types of property investor for whom UK tax will be an issue. These three types of investor may be summarised as follows:

(i)   UK residents investing in UK property
(ii)   UK residents investing in overseas property
(iii)   Non-UK residents investing in UK property

Obviously, the same person might have investments falling under both (i) and (ii) and we will cater for that situation also.

The UK tax position for non-UK residents investing in property is summarised in Section 2.15.

For tax purposes, the UK does not include the Channel Islands or the Isle of Man but comprises England, Scotland, Wales and Northern Ireland.

Wealth Warning
It is important to remember that both UK residents investing in property overseas and non-UK residents investing in UK property may also face foreign tax on their property income and capital gains. Each country has its own tax system, and income or gains which are exempt in the UK may nevertheless still be liable to tax elsewhere.

Additionally, in some cases, citizens of another country who are resident in the UK for tax purposes may still have obligations and liabilities under their own country's tax system. The USA, for example, imposes this type of obligation on its expatriate citizens.

It is only when talking about taxpayers who are both UK residents and UK citizens, who are investing exclusively in UK property, and who are neither residents nor citizens of any other country, that we can be absolutely certain that no other country has any right to tax the income or gains arising.

The tax-planning strategies outlined in this guide represent a reasonably comprehensive list of the main techniques available to individual property investors based in the UK.

This guide is aimed primarily at those who are running a property business personally, jointly with another individual, or through a partnership. While many of the principles will remain the same where another type of legal entity or investment vehicle is used, it should be noted that some of the points covered in this guide will not apply. Detailed guidance on the implications of using a property company is contained in the Taxcafe.co.uk guide *Using a Property Company to Save Tax'*.

Those who have the benefit of being non-UK resident or non-UK domiciled may be able to employ some more specialised tax-planning techniques, which are covered in the Taxcafe.co.uk guide *'Tax Planning for Non-Residents & Non Doms'*.

The Scottish Parliament has powers to vary the Income Tax rates applying to Scottish taxpayers (and has done so). We will look at Scottish Income Tax rates in detail in Section 7.21, together with some worked examples illustrating the differences arising in practice. Throughout the rest of this guide, unless stated to the contrary, I will refer only to the Income Tax rates applying to non-Scottish taxpayers. It is worth noting, however, that it is only the tax **rates** which are different and all other principles discussed throughout this guide remain equally relevant to Scottish taxpayers.

From 2019/20 onwards, the Welsh Assembly also has powers to vary the Income Tax rates applying to Welsh taxpayers. At present, however, Welsh taxpayers continue to pay the same overall rates of Income Tax as English or Northern Irish taxpayers. Furthermore, it is understood the Assembly does not intend to make any changes to Welsh tax rates in the immediate future. It is also important to note that, as with Scottish taxpayers, it will only be the tax **rates** which may be different in future and all other principles discussed throughout this guide will remain equally relevant to Welsh taxpayers. Further details of the Welsh Income Tax regime are given in Section 7.22.

Finally, the reader must bear in mind the general nature of this guide. Individual circumstances vary and the tax implications of an individual's actions will vary with them. For this reason, it is always vital to get professional advice before undertaking any tax planning or other transactions which may have tax implications. The author cannot accept any responsibility for any loss which may arise as a consequence of any action taken, or any decision to refrain from action taken, as a result of reading this guide.

A Word about the Examples in this Guide

This guide is illustrated throughout by a number of examples. Unless specifically stated to the contrary, it is assumed that all persons are:

- i) UK resident and domiciled for tax purposes
- ii) Not subject to the Child Benefit Charge (see Section 3.3)
- iii) Not claiming the marriage allowance (see Appendix A)
- iv) Not Scottish taxpayers (see Section 7.21 for the Income Tax rates applying to Scottish taxpayers)

In preparing the examples I have assumed the UK tax regime will remain unchanged in the future except to the extent of any announcements already made at the time of publication. Readers should understand, however, that some Government proposals are not yet law and may undergo alteration before being formally enacted. In extreme cases, it is not unknown for Government proposals to be abandoned altogether, especially when there is a change of government in the interim.

Furthermore, if there is one thing which I can predict with any certainty, it is the fact that change **will** occur. The reader must bear this in mind when reviewing the results of the examples in this guide.

All persons described in the examples are entirely fictional characters created specifically for the purposes of this guide. Any similarities to actual persons, living or dead, or to fictional characters created by any other author, are entirely coincidental.

For the sake of illustration, I have not checked whether dates in examples fall at the weekend or on a bank holiday. In reality, it will not be possible to enter into some transactions on a Saturday, Sunday, or bank holiday. Readers should take this into account when planning their affairs. Easter can be a particular problem, as it will often fall on or near to 5th April!

Finally, since 2020 is a leap year, the 2019/20 tax year ending on 5th April 2020 is a 'leap tax year' of 366 days': hence you may see the number 366 feature in calculations where you might normally expect to see 365.

Abbreviations Used in this Guide

Generally, at Taxcafe, we don't like using abbreviations or jargon because we want to keep our guides as simple as possible. To save some space, however, I have allowed myself a few abbreviations. I think they are fairly obvious ones, so they should not cause confusion. I will explain what each abbreviation means the first time I use it and they are set out again in Appendix D. Large numbers, such as £2,500,000 will be written as '£2.5m'.

Chapter 1

What is Property Tax?

1.1 KNOWING YOUR ENEMY

We will begin this guide with an explanation of how the UK tax system applies to property investment and other types of property business.

This is essential because you cannot begin to consider how to save property tax until you actually understand what property tax is. In other words, you must 'know your enemy' in order to be able to combat it effectively.

It is important to understand there is no single 'property tax', but rather a whole range of taxes which can apply to property. There is no point in avoiding one of these taxes only to find yourself paying even more of another!

Horror stories of this nature happen all too frequently, such as the taxpayer who managed to avoid 1% Stamp Duty on part of his new house, only to find he was stuck with a 17.5% VAT charge instead!

Worse still was the taxpayer who undertook some Inheritance Tax ('IHT') planning on the advice of his lawyer only to find himself with a £20,000 Capital Gains Tax ('CGT') bill without any cash sale proceeds from which to pay it.

If only they'd spoken to a real tax expert first!

In this introductory chapter we will therefore take a brief look at the taxes which can affect the property investor and give some consideration to the relative importance of each.

Later, when we begin to consider tax-planning strategies, it is vital to bear in mind that it is the overall outcome which matters most, not simply saving or deferring any single type of tax.

In fact, I would go even further than that...

Bayley's Law

The truly wise investor does not seek merely to minimise the amount of tax payable, but rather to maximise the amount of wealth remaining after all taxes have been accounted for.

If this seems like no more than simple common sense to you, then all well and good. However, in practice, I am constantly amazed at how often people lose sight of this simple fact and, in trying to save tax at any price, actually end up making themselves worse off in the long run!

1.2   WHAT TAXES FACE A PROPERTY INVESTOR?

There are a few UK taxes which are specific to property. These are:

- Council Tax (for residential property)
- Business Rates (for commercial property)
- Stamp Duty Land Tax ('SDLT') and its equivalents (see Section 1.4)
- The Annual Tax on Enveloped Dwellings ('ATED') (for residential property owned by companies and other 'non-natural persons')

However, as much as these taxes can be a painful 'thorn in the side', they are rarely as important as some of the other taxes which often apply. In fact, property investment is exposed to a huge range of UK taxes.

Tax is levied when property is purchased (SDLT), rented out (Income Tax) and sold (CGT). Property investors have to pay tax when they need to buy goods or services (VAT), when they make their investments through a company (Corporation Tax) and even when they die (IHT).

Those who are classed as property developers or property traders will pay Income Tax and National Insurance ('NI') on the profits derived from their property sales (or Corporation Tax if they use a company). Property developers must also operate and account for tax under the Construction Industry Scheme ('CIS') when using sub-contractors for even the most routine building work.

When the successful investor needs to employ help in the business, he or she will have to pay PAYE and employer's NI. Doubtless, the investor will also be paying Insurance Premium Tax, as well as Road Tax and duty on the petrol they buy as they travel in their business. They may even be paying Air Passenger Duty if their business takes them far.

Faced with this horrifying list, investors might be excused for turning to drink: only to find themselves paying yet more tax!

1.3   WHICH TAXES ARE MOST IMPORTANT?

For most property investors, two taxes comprise the vast majority of the tax burden they will face during their lifetime. These are Income Tax and CGT and they are covered in detail in Chapters 3 to 6.

The exact way in which these two very important taxes will actually be applied to your property business will depend on what type of property investor you are.

For tax purposes, there are a number of different categories into which a property business might fall and it is crucial that you understand how your business is likely to be classified before you can attempt to plan your tax affairs. I will return to this question in more detail in Chapter 2.

For some classes of investor, NI will form what is effectively an additional layer of Income Tax and we will examine this extra tax burden in Chapter 5. Other taxes that may also have a significant impact include VAT and the various forms of Stamp Duty. These are covered in Chapter 7.

For those investors using a company, Corporation Tax will become of equal, if not greater, importance to the two main taxes and IHT is also likely to be a major concern for most property investors. These two important taxes are covered in the Taxcafe.co.uk guides *'Using a Property Company to Save Tax'* and *'How to Save Inheritance Tax'*.

1.4   PROPERTY STAMP TAXES

There are different forms of Stamp Duty on purchases and transfers of UK property, depending on which part of the UK the property is located in, as follows:

England:	Stamp Duty Land Tax
Scotland:	Land and Buildings Transaction Tax
Wales:	Land Transaction Tax
Northern Ireland:	Stamp Duty Land Tax

The rules applying under each form of Duty are broadly similar and are explained in detail in Chapter 7. For the sake of simplicity, I will refer only to Stamp Duty Land Tax, or 'SDLT', throughout the rest of this guide, but readers should bear in mind that a slightly different tax will apply to purchases of property in Scotland or Wales.

1.5   THE EUROPEAN ECONOMIC AREA

Properties within the European Economic Area ('EEA') are subject to different tax treatment to other overseas property for a number of purposes, as we will see throughout this guide.

The EEA currently comprises the 28 member states of the European Union, plus Liechtenstein, Iceland and Norway.

Chapter 2

What Kind of Property Investor Are You?

2.1　INTRODUCTION

Before we begin to look in detail at exactly how property businesses are taxed in the UK, we must first consider what type of property business we are looking at. This is an essential step, as the tax treatment of a property business will vary according to the type of business activities involved.

While it would be possible to come up with a very long list of different 'types' of property business, I would tend to regard the following four categories as the definitive list as far as UK taxation is concerned:

- a) Property investment (including property letting)
- b) Property development
- c) Property trading (or dealing)
- d) Property management

Wealth Warning
Care must be taken here, because a great deal of what the layman would tend to call 'property investment' is, in fact, likely to be categorised as property development or property dealing for tax purposes.

Before we go on to look at the detailed tax treatment of these different types of property business, it is perhaps worth spending a little time to explain exactly what these different terms mean in a taxation context.

It is also important to understand these different types of property business are not exclusive to individual property investors and these different categorisations may also be applied to a property company, a partnership, or any other kind of property investment vehicle.

The reason we need to consider these different types of property business here is the fact that an understanding of what type of property business you have is crucial in determining which taxes will apply to your business and when.

The most fundamental issue is whether you are carrying on a property investment business (type (a) above), or a property trade (types (b), (c) and (d) above).

While each type of property business has its own quirks, the 'trading or investment' issue is by far the most important and I will be examining this in more detail in Sections 2.8 and 2.9.

To complicate matters still further, however, there is also a strange 'no-man's land' lying somewhere between a property investment business and a property trade, which is not regarded as a business at all and is taxed neither as a capital investment nor as a trade. For want of a better term, I will refer to this as 'casual property income' and we will look at it further in Section 2.7.

Further out, on the periphery of the property sector, there are other property-based trades such as hotels, guest houses, nursing homes and hostels, as well as activities in the commercial property sector such as serviced offices and warehousing.

These trades involve the provision of services far beyond that which the normal property investor would provide. We will look briefly at the tax treatment of these property-based trades in Section 2.12.

A property investor may, of course, be carrying on more than one type of property business, which could result in a mixture of tax treatments. We will look at the possible consequences of this in Section 2.11.

You will see there is no mention of SDLT in the remainder of this chapter. This is for the simple reason that this tax is generally unaffected by what kind of property business you have and the rules outlined in Chapter 7 apply equally to almost everyone.

The VAT treatment of the various different types of property business is also examined in Chapter 7.

2.2   DOES IT MATTER WHAT KIND OF PROPERTY YOU INVEST IN?

For tax purposes, there are two main types of property: residential and commercial.

Residential property, naturally, means people's homes, and covers flats, houses, apartments, bungalows, cottages, etc, etc. Also counted in this category are holiday homes, as we shall see later on in Chapter 4.

Commercial property covers a wide range of properties, including shops, offices, restaurants, pubs, doctors', dentists' and vets' surgeries, hotels, sports centres, warehouses, factories, workshops, garages, schools, hospitals, prisons… anything that isn't residential, basically.

It is important here to distinguish between:

a) Owning commercial property and renting it out to other businesses, (which is generally an investment activity), and,
b) Actually occupying and using the commercial property yourself, which is generally a trade.

Example
Basil owns a string of hotels which he does not run himself, but rents to a number of other businesses. Basil is therefore a property investor and is taxed as outlined in Section 2.3.

Sybil rents one of Basil's hotels and runs it as her own business. Sybil is therefore operating a hotel trade, which is taxed as outlined in Section 2.12. She is not a property investor.

Developing, or dealing in, commercial property is also a trade, but a very different one to occupying and using that property in your own trade. Naturally, it follows that the tax treatment of such trades is also very different.

How Does This Affect What Type of Business You Have?

Assuming you are not actually occupying and operating a trade from your properties, the type of property in which you invest has absolutely no bearing on which of the four main types of property business you have.

The guidelines set out in the remainder of this chapter therefore apply equally to both residential and commercial property investors. The question of what type of property business you have depends purely on the way you behave as an investor and not on the nature of the properties you own.

Naturally, though, there are many other important differences between the tax treatment of residential property and commercial property and, indeed, in the tax treatment of different types of residential and commercial property. We will examine these differences as we progress through the following chapters. Note also that it is quite possible to have both commercial and residential property within the same property business.

2.3   PROPERTY INVESTMENT (OR PROPERTY LETTING)

These are businesses that hold properties as long-term investments. The properties are the business's fixed assets, which are held to produce income in the form of rental profit.

While capital growth will usually be anticipated, and will generally form part of the investor's business plan, short-term property disposals should only take place in exceptional circumstances, or where there is a strong commercial reason, such as an anticipated decline in value in that particular geographical location or a need to realise funds for other investments.

The key point is that properties should be acquired with the intention of holding them as long-term investments producing income in the form of rental profit.

Where unexpected opportunities for short-term gains do arise, however, it would be unreasonable to suggest the investor should not make the most of them.

Example
Fletcher purchases three properties 'off-plan', intending to hold them as long-term investments. On completion of the properties, however, he sells one of them in order to provide funds for a new investment which he now wishes to make. Nevertheless, the other two properties are retained and rented out for a number of years. Although Fletcher sold one of the properties very quickly, there was a good commercial reason for doing so. Hence, he may still be regarded as having a property investment business.

Management

In many cases, the owner has a minimal level of involvement in the day-to-day running of the business and pays an agent to manage his or her property affairs. This is the model operated by many buy-to-let investors: who are thus generally regarded as having a property investment business.

There are also, however, many more 'hands on' property letting businesses where the landlord is much more involved in the management of the business on a day-to-day basis. For larger property letting businesses, the landlord's job even becomes a full-time one.

As long as the business still meets the overall long-term investment criterion outlined above, it remains a property investment business for tax purposes, regardless of the level of the landlord's involvement on a day-to-day basis. Managing your own properties does not, in itself, mean you have a property management trade.

Where the landlord begins to provide services way beyond mere management, the business could eventually become a property-based trade of the type examined in Section 2.12. Generally, this does require some fairly extreme steps but we will return to this issue and, in particular, some instances in which it may be beneficial, later in the guide.

For tax purposes then, we can generally regard 'property investment businesses' and 'property letting businesses' as one and the same. The only real difference lies in the level of administrative expenses that may justifiably be claimed, as we shall see in Chapter 4.

Tax Treatment

An investor with a property investment business must account for their rental profits under the specific rules applying to property income (see Chapter 4).

Property disposals are dealt with as capital gains (but see the 'wealth warning' below). Property held on death is usually fully liable to IHT (subject to the 'nil rate band' and the spouse exemption).

NI should not generally be payable on any property investment business, but we will return to this point in Section 7.17.

Is there any advantage in having a property investment business rather than one of the other types of property business?

Yes, there is often quite an advantage for an individual property investor (or a partnership, trust, etc.) in having a property investment business instead of one of the other types of property business that are classified as trades for tax purposes.

The main reason for this is the fact that property disposals are treated as capital gains, taxed under the CGT regime, and not income taxed under the Income Tax regime. This, in turn, enables the investor to benefit from CGT rates of just 28% at most, as well as providing the opportunity to utilise the many different CGT reliefs available (see Chapter 6).

However, this is far from the end of the story and we will return to the comparative advantages and disadvantages of property investment or property trading in Section 2.8.

Wealth Warning
It is always important to remember it is the way you carry on your business that determines the tax treatment – it is not a matter of choice!

Comparing the top CGT rate of 28% with effective combined Income Tax and NI rates on trading profits of up to 62% (or even more in some cases) means we can sometimes have differences of 34% or more between the tax applying to a capital gain and the tax applying to a trading profit. The tax on a property disposal could be over *twice as much* for a property developer or property dealer as for a property investor.

This makes it extremely important to take care that your business is classified correctly. With such a large differential applying to the tax at stake, you can be sure HM Revenue and Customs ('HMRC') is going to be vigilant!

Furthermore, recent changes in legislation mean more property disposals could sometimes now be subject to Income Tax rather than CGT. In Section 2.9 we will return to this issue and examine the borderline between investment and trading in greater detail.

2.4   PROPERTY DEVELOPMENT

These are businesses that predominantly acquire properties or land and carry out building or renovation work with a view to selling developed properties for profit.

The term 'property development' covers a wide range of activities, from major building companies that acquire vacant land and construct vast new property developments, to amateur property investors who acquire the occasional 'run-down' property to 'do up' for onward sale at a profit. No one would doubt that the former are correctly categorised as property developers, but not everyone realises the latter type of activity also means the investors are actually trading as property developers.

It is vital to understand here that even the most minor of conversion or renovation projects can lead to the investor being treated as a property developer if the property concerned was clearly acquired with the sole or main intention of realising a quick profit. This is what many of the characters we see on daytime television these days are actually doing.

Generally speaking with this type of business, a property will be disposed of as soon as possible after building or renovation work has been completed. It is the profit derived from this work that produces the business's income and the owners do not usually look to rent properties out other than as a matter of short-term expediency.

Example

Godber purchases three old barns in February 2020 and converts them into residential property. The work is completed in August 2021 and he sells two of the former barns immediately.

The third barn, unfortunately, proves difficult to sell. In the meantime, in order to generate some income from the property, Godber lets it out on a short six-month lease. The property is never taken off the market during the period of the lease and a buyer is found in January 2022, with completion taking place in March.

Although Godber let one of the properties out for a short period, his main business activity remained property development. His intention was clearly to develop the properties for sale at a profit. This was reinforced by the fact the property remained on the market throughout the lease. Godber therefore has a property development business.

Tax Treatment

A property development business is regarded as a trade.

The profits from property development activities, i.e. the profits arising from development property sales, are taxed as trading profits and subject to both Income Tax and NI (see Chapter 5).

Where, as in the example above, there is some incidental short-term rental income, it should be dealt with under the specific rules applying to property income. In practice, however, this is sometimes accepted as incidental trading income. Whether this is beneficial to the taxpayer or not will depend on a great many factors, as we shall see in Section 2.8.

The great disadvantage of being classified as a property developer is the fact that all profits are dealt with under the Income Tax regime and not the CGT regime. This means that reliefs such as the annual CGT exemption, principal private residence relief and private letting relief will not be available.

More importantly, it also means effective combined Income Tax and NI rates of up to 62% (or even more in some cases) will apply instead of CGT at no more than 28% at most.

On the other hand, the business itself, if it has any value (e.g. goodwill), may be eligible for both entrepreneurs' relief for CGT purposes (see Section 6.28) and business property relief for IHT purposes. The latter relief would even apply to any properties held as 'trading stock' at the time of death.

Capital gains treatment would apply to any disposals of the business's long-term fixed assets, such as its own offices, for example.

We will take a more detailed look at the comparative advantages and disadvantages of having a property trade, rather than being a property investor, in Section 2.8.

The Construction Industry Scheme ('CIS')

Property developers who utilise sub-contractors for any building work, even quite minor plumbing, decorating or electrical work, are required to operate CIS for tax purposes. This may involve having to deduct tax at a special rate particular to CIS from payments made to sub-contractors and then account for it to HMRC, rather like PAYE. The tax deduction rate currently applying to payments to registered sub-contractors is 20%. Payments to unregistered sub-contractors are subject to deduction at the higher rate of 30%.

2.5   PROPERTY TRADING (OR PROPERTY DEALING)

This type of property business used to be fairly rare, but has grown in popularity. A property trader generally only holds properties for short-term gain. Properties are bought and sold frequently and are held as trading stock. Such traders are sometimes known as property dealers.

Properties will not usually be rented out, except for short-term financial expediency. These investors derive their income simply by making a profit on the properties they sell. Property traders differ from property developers in that no actual development takes place on the properties. Profits are made simply by ensuring a good margin between buying price and selling price.

To be a trade, however, there does need to be some degree of serious intent involved. The investor must be undertaking the property trading activity in a reasoned and methodical manner. There is an important distinction, therefore, between a professional property trader and a casual investor. To be 'professional' in this context does not necessarily mean it must be a full-time activity; merely that it is more than casual. I will explain this concept further in Section 2.7.

Example
Over the last two years, Mr McKay has bought 30 different properties 'off-plan'. He has sold each property within a few months of completion. Since Mr McKay has neither developed any of the properties, nor held on to them as investments for any appreciable length of time, he is clearly neither a property developer nor running a property investment business. Furthermore, the frequency and scale of his activities clearly indicates that he is a professional property trader.

Tax Treatment

A property trader's profits from property sales should be taxed as trading profits within the Income Tax regime. Once again, these profits are also subject to NI (see Section 5.5).

As with a property developer, any incidental letting income should be dealt with under the specific rules applying to property income (see Chapter 4).

The value of this type of business is specifically not eligible for business property relief for IHT purposes. As for CGT, the theory is that a property trading business is still a 'trade' and hence the long-term assets (e.g. goodwill or office premises) should be eligible for entrepreneurs' relief (see Section 6.28).

> **Wealth Warning**
> The profit on a property disposal may sometimes be treated as trading income for Income Tax purposes even where an actual property dealing trade does not exist.
>
> This may catch some casual investors who are not professional property dealers but who are investing in property with a view to realising short-term gains. We will look at this issue in more detail in Section 2.9.

Is it always disadvantageous to be a property trader rather than a property investor?

No, not always; there are some situations where trading status is actually more beneficial overall, even despite the potentially higher tax rates.

We will take a more detailed look at the advantages and disadvantages of trading status in Section 2.8. Always remember, however, that it is the way you conduct your business that determines its status and not a matter of choice.

2.6   PROPERTY MANAGEMENT

These businesses do not generally own properties at all (except, perhaps, their own offices). Instead, they provide management services to property owners. If you have a property letting agent taking care of the day-to-day running of your properties, the chances are it is probably a property management company.

A property management business's income is derived from the management or service charges on the actual owners of the property.

Tax Treatment

A property management business is a trade for all tax purposes.

The long-term assets of a property management business are usually eligible for both entrepreneurs' relief for CGT purposes (see Section 6.28) and business property relief for IHT purposes.

The profits arising from property management activities will be treated as trading profits, subject to both Income Tax and NI.

Any incidental letting income should, as usual, be dealt with under the specific rules applying to property income.

2.7 CASUAL PROPERTY INCOME

Somewhere between property investment and property trading there lies a 'no-man's land', which I will term 'casual property income'.

As we have seen in previous sections, property investment businesses hold their properties as long-term capital assets, whereas property trades hold properties as short-term trading stock.

In this strange intermediate 'twilight zone', however, lie the property transactions that are neither long-term investments nor part of an organised trading activity.

The key features of casual property income are:

   i) Transactions are entered into with the expectation of short-term profit.
   ii) Profit is derived from a disposal of the investment, or an interest therein, rather than an income stream such as rent.
   iii) The investor plays a passive role in the transactions.

An 'investment' for this purpose may include an existing property, or interest in property, which becomes the subject of a 'casual property income' transaction. In these cases, the existing property effectively ceases to be a long-term asset as soon as the 'casual property income' transaction is entered into.

Example
Mr Barraclough is having a quiet drink in his local one night when he is approached by Mr Grout, a local builder. "That's a pretty big garden you've got there Barraclough; big enough for another house. Ever thought of developing it?"

"Well, I don't know really," replies Barraclough, "Mrs Barraclough is very fond of her garden you know."

Groutie won't take no for an answer and eventually persuades Mr Barraclough to give him half his garden in exchange for a quarter of the sale proceeds for the new house.

The part of the garden used for the development was worth £25,000 before construction began and the new house sells for £240,000, so Mr Barraclough makes a profit of £35,000 (£240,000 x ¼ - £25,000). Because Mr Barraclough's share was dependent on the eventual sale price of the new house, this profit will be treated as income in nature, rather than a capital gain.

On the other hand, however, Mr Barraclough's role was totally passive. Mr Grout sought him out. Barraclough did not have to 'get his hands dirty' in any way and did not participate directly in the development or sale of the new house. There is no way, therefore, that Mr Barraclough could be regarded as having a property trade and his £35,000 profit is casual property income.

Most people in Mr Barraclough's position would tend to prefer this profit to be treated as a capital gain, rather than as income, since £12,000 of 'profit' would usually be covered by their annual CGT exemption and the remainder would be taxed at just 18% or 28%. However, because Mr Barraclough effectively took a share in the development profit on the new house, his £35,000 profit cannot be treated as a capital gain and is taxed as 'casual property income'.

This type of transaction is also known as a 'slice of the action' contract and is probably the most common source of 'casual property income'. The 'investor' (i.e. Mr Barraclough) has a totally passive role, but profits indirectly from another person's property development trade.

It is worth noting that, if Mr Barraclough had simply sold his surplus land for a fixed price of £60,000, this would have been a capital gain. Furthermore, as we shall see in Section 8.13, if he had structured the sale correctly, it may well have been completely tax free! We will see some more examples of how to benefit from the existing development potential of your own property tax efficiently in Chapter 8.

Tax Treatment

Casual property income is not a trade as such but is treated as deemed trading income and is subject to Income Tax at normal rates.

Any **direct** costs incurred in earning the 'casual property income' may be deducted under the principles set out in Chapter 5, but this does not usually extend to interest and finance costs or other overheads.

Alternatively, the trading income allowance (see Section 5.13) may be claimed against this type of income. This would not have been appropriate in Mr Barraclough's case, as the £1,000 allowance would then have been given instead of the deduction for the value of the land prior to commencement of the development.

Where, as in our example, an existing property becomes the subject of a 'casual property income' transaction, any existing increase in the value of that property prior to that date will usually be a capital gain.

Hence, for example, if the original cost of the land Mr Barraclough gave to Mr Grout when it was worth £25,000 had been £8,000, Mr Barraclough would have had a capital gain of £17,000 in addition to his 'casual property income' of £35,000. (See Section 6.16 for details of how such a gain would be treated for CGT purposes.)

Any underlying assets held in the course of producing casual property income will not be eligible for business property relief for IHT purposes or entrepreneurs' relief for CGT purposes (see Section 6.28). Casual property income should not generally give rise to any VAT liabilities or any obligation to register for VAT.

The best thing about casual property income though is the fact that, since it is not an actual trade, it does not attract NI. For many people this means a saving of 9%. For most others there is still a saving of 2% - not much, but still better than a 'poke in the eye with a sharp stick'!

The only drawback, of course, is that to be 'casual income', there must be an absence of any serious trade-like intent. In other words, once you set out to make the income in any organised manner, it inevitably ceases to be casual and you will have a property trade. For this reason, this type of income is fairly rare.

Nevertheless, if you do meet a 'Harry Grout' in the pub and decide to participate in his venture, then at least you know you can avoid NI.

Any property rental income, no matter how transient or casual, will always be subject to the special rules for 'property income', as outlined in Chapter 4, and will never form 'casual property income'. Small amounts of rental income may however be covered by the property income allowance discussed in Section 4.17.

2.8   ADVANTAGES AND DISADVANTAGES OF INVESTMENT OR TRADING

As we have seen already, the most important issue is whether your property business is classed as investment or trading. The major difference is in the treatment of profits arising on property disposals, but there are many other differences. In this section, I thought it might be useful to set out a brief summary of the tax advantages and disadvantages of each type of property business.

Tax Advantages of Property Investment Businesses

- 'Profits' arising on property disposals are treated as capital gains. This means:
  - Tax rates of no more than 28% at most
  - Ability to claim CGT exemptions and reliefs, including:
    - The annual exemption
    - Principal private residence relief
    - Private letting relief
  - Most non-UK residents will enjoy exemption on gains arising up to April 2015 on residential property and up to April 2019 on commercial property
- No NI on rental income or capital gains
- No compulsory VAT registration of the business (in most cases)

Tax Disadvantages of Property Investment Businesses

- All business assets are usually fully exposed to IHT on death
- Abortive expenditure on property purchases (e.g. legal fees), or sales (e.g. advertising), may sometimes not be allowed for tax purposes
- Interest and finance costs may only be set against rental income and cannot be set against capital gains
- Further restrictions apply to tax relief for interest and finance costs relating to residential property
- Very limited scope for loss relief (both for capital losses and for rental losses)
- Accounting periods ended 5th April each year are generally necessary
- Difficulty in transferring business without incurring tax charges

Tax Advantages of Property Trades

- Greater scope for claiming indirect or abortive expenses relating to property purchases and sales
- Full relief for interest and finance costs
- Long-term assets of the business may be eligible for entrepreneurs' relief or rollover relief for CGT purposes
- Losses can be set off against any income arising in the same tax year or the previous tax year (subject to the limitations explained in Section 5.11)
- Any date may be chosen for the accounting year end
- The value of a property development or property management business will usually be exempt from IHT on death
- Businesses may usually be transferred (e.g. to a company or to another individual) without any significant tax charges

Tax Disadvantages of Property Trades

- Profits arising on property sales are subject to Income Tax and NI
- Non-UK residents are fully taxable on all profits derived from a property trade based in the UK and on any trading profits arising on the disposal of property located in the UK
- VAT registration becomes compulsory if annual turnover from taxable activities for VAT purposes exceeds £85,000

2.9   THE BOUNDARY BETWEEN INVESTMENT AND TRADING

After reading the previous section, you've probably got a fair idea of how you would *like* your property business to be treated for tax purposes. However, as I have already pointed out, it is not a question of choice, but is determined by how you conduct your business.

Furthermore, not only is it a matter of how you actually behave, very often it will hinge on what your intentions were at the beginning of any particular project.

Legislation states that the profit on disposal of UK property must be *treated* as trading income whenever the main purpose, *or one of the main purposes*, behind its acquisition is to realise a profit on disposal.

This broadens the scope of what might be considered *trading income*. It does not, however, alter the basic principles that determine when a *trade* actually exists. In other words, there is a middle ground where there is no actual trade, but where profits are simply *treated* as trading profits.

Categories of Activity

The situation can be summed up by defining three categories of activity, as follows:

1. **Where the sole or main purpose behind the acquisition was to make a profit on disposal:** a property trade exists, the profit on disposal is trading income subject to both Income Tax and NI, and the business will be taxed as set out in Sections 2.4 or 2.5 (depending on whether any development activity is taking place).

2. **Where one of the main purposes behind the acquisition (but not the only, or dominant, purpose) was to make a profit on disposal:** the profit on disposal will be treated as trading income and will be subject to Income Tax (but not NI).

For all other purposes, the business will be treated as a property investment business, as set out in Section 2.3.

3. **Where making a profit on disposal was not a main purpose behind the acquisition:** the profit on disposal will be a capital gain subject to CGT and, if a business does exist, it will be a property investment business, treated as set out in Section 2.3.

The principles used in determining whether a business falls under Category 1 are well established and have been discussed already in this chapter.

The dividing line between Categories 2 and 3 is dependent on recent legislation that has yet to be tested in court. It may be many years before the practical implications of this legislation are fully understood. The problem lies in understanding what '**a** main purpose' is. It is far easier to identify '**the** main purpose'!

Some commentators initially feared almost all property disposals would be treated as giving rise to a trading profit since, almost every time anyone buys a property, they hope to realise a gain on its disposal.

Personally, however, I do not think the simple **hope** of a long-term gain makes this a main purpose behind the acquisition. Fortunately, this view has been confirmed by HMRC guidance. In fact, the guidance suggests that very few disposals will fall into Category 2 and states the legislation should not apply to:

> *"transactions such as buying or repairing a property for the purpose of earning rental income or as an investment to generate rental income and enjoy capital appreciation,"* or

> *"straightforward long-term investment where the economic benefit arising to the owner is the result of market movement from holding that asset ...."*

The guidance also states that long-term capital growth may be a reasonable expectation without it necessarily forming a main purpose of the acquisition.

The general thrust of the guidance seems to suggest it is only where a profit can already be anticipated due to the property's **current** value at the time of purchase, or where a profit is anticipated due to some action to be carried out by the owner (typically developing the property), that the deemed trading provisions can apply. Even then, the profit on disposal will need to be a 'main purpose' behind the acquisition.

So it is clear that the mere hope or expectation of a long-term gain does not make this a main purpose behind the acquisition. There would need to be a more concrete strategy involving the realisation of a gain before this can be regarded as one of the main purposes behind the acquisition.

Nonetheless, it remains important for investors to be very careful about documenting their intentions when acquiring property.

What Are Your Intentions?

There are two things that the examples in Sections 2.3 to 2.5 had in common:

i) In each case, the taxpayer's intentions were clear
ii) They were all chosen to illustrate a position that quite definitely fitted the type of business in question

In reality, a taxpayer's intentions may not be so clear. When I ask my clients to tell me their plans for their property investments, I often hear answers like these:

> "I might sell it, or I might hang on to it for a while if I can't get a good price."
> "We think we'll rent it out for a few years, but we might sell if we get a good offer."
> "We'll probably sell a few and rent the rest out."

Naturally, any investor is going to do whatever produces the best result and if an unexpected opportunity comes along they would be foolish not to take it while they can.

For tax purposes though, we have to establish what the investor's main intentions were, at the outset, when the investment was made.

The trouble with intentions, of course, is they can be very difficult to prove. Who but you can possibly know exactly what was in your mind when you purchased a property? Looking at it from HMRC's point of view, the only evidence they generally have to go on is what actually transpired and this may be very different to what was intended.

Tax Tip
Document your intentions for your property business. This could take many forms. Some of the most popular are a business plan, a diary note, a letter to your solicitor, or notes of a meeting with your accountant. Remember to make sure your documentary evidence is dated.

Expect the Unexpected

A business plan that says "we will rent the properties out for five to ten years and then sell them" may not ring true if you actually sell all the properties very quickly. In other words, merely having a business plan (or other internal documentation) that purports to support your intention to hold properties as long-term investments may not be very persuasive if you actually start behaving blatantly like a property trader.

Example

McLaren buys ten properties off-plan in December 2019. He finances part of the purchase through a loan from a High Street bank. To support his loan application he draws up a business plan that states "I intend to hold properties in prime rental sites for a period of five to ten years."

Despite his business plan, in May 2020 McLaren sells all the properties; after having emigrated to Australia in March.

Any reasonably competent Tax Inspector is going to question McLaren's motives here and it is highly likely they would argue he was, in fact, a property trader, despite his business plan. But what if there is more to the story?

Example Part 2

McLaren protests that he had no intention of emigrating to Australia until the sudden and unexpected death of his great aunt Bunny in February 2020.

Bunny left McLaren a vast estate in Queensland and he had to move to Australia as quickly as possible in order to look after his inheritance. Running a UK property business now appeared impractical so McLaren sold the UK properties as soon as he could.

Now we can see that McLaren's behaviour was merely the result of an unexpected change in circumstances. His original business plan therefore regains more credence and might be sufficient to persuade HMRC that he did indeed have a property investment business and not a property dealing trade.

An occurrence as dramatic as the one in the example probably speaks for itself, but more often it is some more subtle shift in circumstances that causes an investor to change their mind.

Tax Tip

In such cases, documenting the reasons behind your change of plans is again the most sensible way to proceed. A diary note to the effect of "Johnny got a place at Glasgow University instead, so we sold the flat in St Andrews and bought one there," for example, could save you thousands of pounds one day!

Acceptable reasons for changing your mind could include:

- An unexpected shortage of funds
- An unexpected and exceptionally good offer
- Relocation due to work, family or other reasons
- Divorce or separation
- Bereavements and inheritance
- Health problems (yourself or a family member)
- Concerns over the property market in a particular location
- Funds are required for an investment opportunity elsewhere

Such changes leading to an early sale of a property do not mean you have changed your intentions, but rather that you have simply responded to a change in circumstances. Accordingly, the early sale of the property does not alter the nature of your property investment and any profit arising on the disposal will generally continue to be subject to CGT, and not to Income Tax.

Undertaking development work with a view to realising additional profit on a sale of all or part of your property is a rather different matter and represents a change of intention. We will look at the consequences of this in Sections 2.9 and 2.10. Even participating in a development profit could lead to a change in tax treatment, as we saw in Section 2.7.

But Life Isn't Always That Simple

The second common denominator in the examples in Sections 2.3 to 2.5 was the fact that they each fell so obviously into one type of business or another. Somewhere between these extremes there is the 'grey area' where investment meets trading. It's not always so easy to be sure which side of the line you're on.

It is almost impossible to give a definitive answer to explain exactly when investment becomes trading. Here, however, are some useful guidelines:

Renovation and Conversion Work
Activity such as building, conversion or renovation work may sometimes be indicative that there is a trading motive behind the purchase of land or property. However, the mere fact that this work takes place does not, in itself, necessarily make it a property development trade.

If you continue to hold the property for several years after the completion of your building work, it is likely that you still have an investment property.

On the other hand, however, if you sell the property immediately after completing the work, you may well be regarded as a property developer **unless** your original intention had been to keep the property and rent it out, but some change in circumstances led you to change your mind.

Frequency of Transactions

If you only sell a property once every few years, you are likely to be carrying on a property investment business. If you make several sales every year, representing a high proportion of your portfolio, you may be a property trader or developer.

Number of Transactions

As well as their frequency, the number of property transactions which you have carried out can be a factor in deciding whether you are trading.

Many people like to buy a house, 'do it up', then sell it and move on. If you do this once then you're probably nothing other than a normal homeowner in the eyes of HMRC. If you do it every six months for ten years, then I would suggest that somewhere along the way you have become a property developer.

Finance Arrangements

Long-term finance arrangements, such as mortgages or longer term personal loans are generally indicative of an investment activity.

Financing your business through short-term arrangements, such as bank overdrafts will be more indicative of a development or dealing trade. Short-term finance tends to indicate short-term assets.

Length of Ownership

There is no definitive rule as to how long you must hold a property for it to be an investment rather than trading stock. Like everything else, length of ownership is just one factor to consider. For example, many property developers hold land stocks for many years before commencing development (known as a 'land bank') but this does not alter the trading nature of their activities.

Where there is no obvious trading activity, I have heard it suggested that an ownership period of three years or more is generally regarded as being indicative of a property investment business: although there is no legal basis for this. This is not to say that ownership for any lesser period cannot represent an investment where the facts of the case otherwise support it and we have seen several examples of this already.

In practice, the longer you generally hold your properties, the more likely they are to be accepted as investments.

Renting the Properties Out

Renting properties out provides a pretty good indication that they are being held as investments and not part of a property trade.

Like everything else on this list though, it may not be conclusive on its own (see the example in Section 2.4).

Living in a Property

Living in the property is another useful way to evidence your intention to hold it as a long-term asset. Once again though, this may not be enough if the other facts of the case prove to be contrary to this idea. We will explore this area of planning in a great deal more detail later in the guide.

'Hands On' Involvement

Being actively involved in the renovation or development of a property makes you look like a property developer. Contracting all of the work out looks more like property investment.

Property Management

As mentioned in Section 2.3, managing your own properties does not mean you have a property management trade. Managing other unconnected investors' properties would almost always be a trade.

Managing a mixture of your own and other people's properties might, in some circumstances, amount to a trade. To be more certain of this treatment, the property management activities are better carried out through a separate entity, such as a company or partnership.

In Summary

Remember that each of the points examined above is just one factor in determining what kind of property business you have. Ultimately, it is the overall picture formed by your intentions, your behaviour and your investment pattern that will eventually decide whether you have a property investment business, a property trade, or both (see Section 2.11).

In many cases, this 'overall picture' will point to a fairly clear answer and the correct treatment of the business will be obvious.

In some cases, however, the position may be more borderline and the correct treatment will not be clear. This could create a risk that you might fall into the second of the three categories described at the beginning of this section, so that you could be subject to Income Tax on the profits arising on your property disposals.

In these cases, it may sometimes be beneficial to adapt your behaviour a little, bearing the guidelines set out above in mind, in order to produce a clearer picture of the nature of your business and secure a more beneficial treatment for tax purposes.

In Section 6.5, I have given some more detailed examples of cases that may be regarded as investment or as trading.

2.10 CHANGES OF INTENTION

All or part of an existing property held as a long-term asset, whether for business or personal use, may become a trading asset where there is a change of intention. We saw an example of this in Section 2.7, where Mr Barraclough participated in the development profit on part of his own garden.

In that case, Mr Barraclough's 'slice of the action' contract gave rise to deemed trading income falling under Category 2 of the activities defined in Section 2.9. We will return to look at how to benefit more tax efficiently from the development potential of your own home in Sections 8.12 and 8.13.

A property owner might also develop an existing investment property themselves with a view to realising additional profit on its disposal after the development is complete. Here again, the profit arising after the change of intention will be a trading profit, but any increase in value arising prior to that point will remain a capital gain.

Example
Louis bought a block of ten flats for £1m in 2014. He rented out the flats until 2020, by which time the property is worth £1.3m. He then redevelops the property into four luxury apartments at a cost of £400,000. He sells all of the apartments for a total of £2.4m.

The costs to be taken into account in calculating his development gain are the market value of the block before redevelopment, £1.3m, and the conversion costs of £400,000, a total of £1.7m. This gives him a development gain of £700,000 (£2.4m – £1.7m).

The treatment of this development gain will depend on a number of factors: the most important being Louis' intentions at the time the redevelopment commenced. If it is clear the redevelopment was carried out with a main purpose of realising an additional profit on the disposal of the property then the development gain will be a trading profit subject to Income Tax.

But, however the development gain is treated, the gain of £300,000 arising prior to the start of the development work will continue to be a capital gain subject to CGT.

In the case of a 'one off' development like this, it seems probable that Louis does not actually have a property development trade (see Section 2.4). Hence, even where his development gain is a deemed trading profit subject to Income Tax, it probably falls into Category 2 of the activities defined in Section 2.9 and is not subject to NI.

However, if Louis already has an existing property development trade, any trading profit will fall into Category 1 of the activities defined in Section 2.9 and will be subject to both Income Tax and NI, and indeed all the principles set out in Chapter 5.

This may also be the case where the development represents the first of a series of property developments, although the position here is less clear and will again depend on Louis' intentions at the commencement of the development work. It remains possible that he intended this to be a 'one off' development and only later decided to start a 'full on' property development trade.

2.11 'MIXED' PROPERTY BUSINESSES

"What if my business doesn't happen to fit neatly into one of the four types described in Sections 2.3 to 2.6?" you may be asking.

If you have a 'mixed' property business, involving more than one of the different types of property business described in this chapter, to a degree that is more than merely incidental, then, for tax purposes, each of the business types should be dealt with separately, in the usual manner applicable to that type.

Having said that, there is a great danger that any property development or property trading may effectively 'taint' what would otherwise be a property investment business, with the result that HMRC might attempt to deny you CGT treatment on all of your property transactions.

(Property management will generally stand alone without too much difficulty, as it does not involve any property ownership.)

> **Tax Tip**
> To avoid the danger of a property investment business being 'tainted' by development or trading activities, you should take whatever steps you can to separate the businesses, such as:
>
> i) Drawing up separate accounts for the different businesses
> ii) Using a different business name for the different activities
> iii) Reporting the non-investment activities as a different business in your tax return
> iv) Consider a different legal ownership structure for the non-investment activities (e.g. put them in a company or a partnership with your spouse, partner or adult children)

(On the other hand, it is also worth noting that combining a property investment business with a property development business may produce IHT savings: see the Taxcafe.co.uk guide *'How to Save Inheritance Tax'*.)

2.12 OTHER PROPERTY-BASED TRADES

As discussed previously, there are a number of trades that are inextricably linked with the business's underlying property, but which are quite distinct from simple property investment. Such trades include:

- Hotels and Guest Houses
- Nursing Homes and Private Hospitals
- Serviced Offices
- Holiday Parks

The key difference between these trades and the property businesses we have examined previously in this chapter is the fact that the property's owners actually occupy the property for use in their own trade.

Tax Treatment

The profits derived from running these business activities are treated as trading profits subject to Income Tax and NI.

Most of these businesses will need to be registered for VAT when their gross annual sales income exceeds £85,000.

Gains arising on disposal of the properties held by these businesses will be subject to CGT, with the full range of attendant reliefs available to business property, including entrepreneurs' relief and rollover relief (see Sections 6.28 and 8.27 respectively).

Most properties used in these types of business will also be eligible for business property relief for IHT purposes. Dangers arise, however, where the business confers some long-term rights of occupation to its customers, as is sometimes the case with nursing homes or caravan parks, for example.

2.13 SPOUSES AND CIVIL PARTNERS

Throughout this guide, you will see me refer to 'married couples', spouses, or husbands and wives. In each case, the treatment being outlined applies equally to:

- Married couples of opposite sexes,
- Married couples of the same sex, and
- Registered civil partners

Hence, any references to 'married couples' throughout this guide should be taken to also include registered civil partnerships; references to the taxpayer's 'spouse' will also include their civil partner where relevant; and references to 'husbands' or 'wives' will include spouses of the same gender and civil partners. References to widows or widowers also include surviving civil partners.

However, it remains important to remember that, unless specified to the contrary, the treatment being outlined applies to legally married couples and registered civil partners only. Unmarried couples are subject to entirely different rules.

2.14   JOINT OWNERSHIP & PROPERTY PARTNERSHIPS

Before we move on to look at the detailed tax treatment of property businesses, it is worth pausing to think about the potential impact of joint ownership.

The first point to note is that joint ownership itself does not alter the nature of your property business.

In England and Wales, joint ownership comes in two varieties:

- Joint Tenancy, and
- Tenancy in Common.

Don't be confused by the word 'tenancy' here, this is terminology only and doesn't affect the fact you jointly own the freehold, leasehold, etc.

In Scotland, joint ownership of property comes predominantly in one major form called 'Pro Indivisio' ownership and, as far as the tax position is concerned, this is more or less the same as a Tenancy in Common.

Joint Tenancy

Under a joint tenancy ownership of each person's share passes automatically on death to the other joint tenant. This is known as 'survivorship'. Furthermore, neither joint owner is normally able to sell their share of the property without the consent of the other.

Each joint owner under a joint tenancy is treated as having an equal share in the property. In effect, joint tenants are regarded as joint owners of the whole property.

Tenancy in Common

Under a tenancy in common, the joint owners are each free to do as they wish with their own share of the property and there is no right of survivorship. The joint owners' shares in the property under a tenancy in common do not necessarily have to be equal. In effect, tenants in common each own their own separate share in the property.

The same considerations apply equally to joint 'Pro Indivisio' owners in Scotland.

Tax Tip
A tenancy in common provides more scope for tax planning than a joint tenancy. We will see much more on the potential benefits of tenancies in common in the following chapters.

Property Investment & Joint Ownership

When it comes to a property investment business, all that joint ownership means is that each individual has their own property investment business, and is taxed on their own share of rental profits and capital gains accordingly. The joint ownership does not affect the nature of the underlying business.

Joint owners carrying on a property investment business will not generally constitute a business partnership unless they also formally create such a partnership.

Property Development

Joint owners engaged in property development will generally form a business partnership under basic legal principles. This is because two or more individuals engaged in the mutual pursuit of commercial trading profits are, in law, generally deemed to constitute a partnership.

Example
Ingrid and Lenny buy an old barn and some disused farm land as tenants in common. They convert the barn into a pair of semi-detached dwellings and build two new houses on the disused land. They then sell all of the newly developed properties and share the profit equally. Ingrid and Lenny are in a trading partnership.

It nevertheless does remain possible for joint owners of a property used in a property development trade to be engaged in a 'joint venture', rather than a business partnership, if the terms of the arrangements between the parties do not amount to the mutual pursuit of profit.

Example

Luke owns an old farm. At the edge of the farm there is a small field that Luke is no longer able to farm profitably.

Ives comes to Luke with a proposition that goes like this: "If you sell me a half interest in your small field for its current agricultural value, I'll get planning permission to build some houses and then, after I've built and sold them, I'll pay you the residential use value for your remaining half interest."

While this proposition does involve joint ownership of development land, it does not amount to a trading partnership, as Luke is not participating in Ives' development profit.

A property trading partnership may also exist without joint ownership.

Example

Norman holds a piece of land on which he has planning permission to build ten houses. Unfortunately, he does not have the funds or the expertise to carry out the development. Norman approaches Stanley, a wealthy property developer and suggests they carry out the development jointly and share the profit equally. While Norman is the sole owner of the land, his arrangement with Stanley may constitute a trading partnership.

In practice, the boundary between a partnership and a joint venture can be quite blurred and this is a subject that could easily take up a whole book on its own. Usually, in reality, the issue is resolved by the nature of the agreements drawn up between the parties.

The best principle I can provide is that a partnership usually exists where both parties share, whether equally or not, in the same risks and rewards. Where, however, one party's income is fixed, or determined without reference to the other party's overall net profit, this is more akin to a joint venture.

Where a joint venture exists, each party has their own business and it is even possible for one of them to have a property investment business while the other has a property development business. In fact, as we saw in Section 2.7, it is also possible for one of them to have no business at all, but to be merely receiving 'casual property income'.

Property Partnerships

In England and Wales, a partnership is not recognised as a separate person with its own legal status (like a company): except for Limited Liability Partnerships. This means that traditional style partnerships in England and Wales cannot own property in their own name.

This is reflected in the fact that it is not the partnership that has any capital gain on the sale of a property, but the individual partners.

The problem of legal ownership is generally circumvented through the use of nominees. Between two and four of the partners will usually own the partnership's property as nominees for the partnership. For legal reasons, it is wise to ensure there are at least two nominee interests, as a single nominee could claim to own the property outright!

In Scotland, a partnership does have its own legal status and can own property in its own name. The tax position remains the same, however, with the partners themselves being taxed on any capital gains made by the partnership.

The nature of the business carried on by a property partnership is determined under exactly the same criteria as we have examined earlier in this chapter.

For tax purposes, the partnership income is allocated to the individual partners in whatever shares have been established between them and continues to be treated as investment income or trading income, as appropriate. Hence, a partner may be in receipt of partnership trading income subject to both Income Tax and NI or partnership property rental income subject to Income Tax only. Or both!

The calculation of the tax due on each partner's share of the partnership income is exactly the same as if they had received an equal amount of the same type of income directly from their own individual business. The way in which the income must be reported does, however, get a little more complicated and we will return to this in the next chapter.

2.15 NON-RESIDENTS

The taxation of non-UK residents is subject to the terms of any double taxation agreement between the UK and their country of residence; although most agreements allow the UK to tax non-UK residents on income, profits or gains derived from UK property. Non-UK residents investing in UK property are therefore generally subject to most of the same UK taxes as UK resident investors, including:

Income Tax
UK Income Tax is payable on rental profits derived from UK property by non-UK resident individuals, trusts or companies (as noted below, companies will pay Corporation Tax instead from April 2020).

UK Income Tax is also payable by non-UK resident individuals or trusts developing, or trading in, UK property (non-UK residents are not subject to NI, however).

Where non-UK residents are subject to UK Income Tax, they pay at the main UK rates. Scottish and Welsh Income Tax rates do not apply, regardless of where the non-UK resident is from, or where their properties are located.

Corporation Tax
UK Corporation Tax is payable by non-UK resident companies developing, or trading in, UK property. From April 2020, non-UK resident companies will also pay Corporation Tax on rental profits derived from UK property.

For disposals taking place after 5th April 2019, non-UK resident companies are subject to Corporation Tax on capital gains on UK property. The element of the gain subject to tax is generally determined under the same principles as those applying to non-UK resident individuals paying CGT, as outlined below. However, for larger non-resident companies not defined as a 'close company', the exemption for the historic element of gains arising on residential property is extended to 5th April 2019.

See the Taxcafe.co.uk guide *'Using a Property Company to Save Tax'* for the definition of a 'close company', as well as further details on the UK tax position of non-UK resident companies investing in UK property.

Stamp Duty Land Tax (and its equivalents per Section 1.4)
These taxes currently apply in the usual way where the purchaser of a UK property is non-UK resident. See Chapter 7 for further details.

However, the Government is considering levying an additional SDLT surcharge on non-residents purchasing residential property in the future.

Inheritance Tax
Non-UK resident individuals generally remain subject to UK IHT on UK property. Non-UK residents who remain UK domiciled may be subject to UK IHT on all property worldwide.

VAT
Non-UK residents making taxable supplies in the UK are generally subject to UK VAT in the same way as UK residents (see Chapter 7).

The Annual Tax on Enveloped Dwellings ('ATED')
Companies and certain other 'non-natural persons' that own UK residential property not used for business purposes are subject to ATED. ATED applies equally to both UK resident and non-UK resident entities. Further details on ATED are included in Section 7.18

Capital Gains Tax
Non-UK resident individuals or trusts are subject to UK CGT on disposals of UK property. For residential property, the element of the gain arising after 5th April 2015 is taxable; for non-residential property, it is generally

only the element of the gain arising after 5th April 2019 (but see further below).

Disposals of UK residential property by non-UK resident individuals or trusts must be reported to HMRC within 30 days of completion, together with a payment on account (see Section 6.30). There is currently an exemption from payments on account for taxpayers within the UK self-assessment system, but this will cease to apply for disposals taking place after 5th April 2020.

Non-UK residents disposing of an interest in any entity (e.g. a company), where UK property held by that underlying entity accounts for 75% or more of its gross asset value, and the disposing taxpayer has held at least a 25% interest in the underlying entity at any time in the last five years, are subject to UK CGT on the element of their gain arising after 5th April 2019.

While non-UK residents are not generally subject to UK CGT on the element of any gain on non-residential property in the UK arising prior to 6th April 2019, the full gain arising will be chargeable where the owner has used the property in a trade carried on in the UK through a branch, agency or other permanent establishment.

For disposals of UK residential property taking place between 6th April 2015 and 5th April 2019, non-UK resident companies were subject to UK CGT on the element of the gain arising after 5th April 2015. However, while the tax was technically classed as CGT, it was computed at normal Corporation Tax rates (except where ATED was payable on the property: see Section 7.18).

Non-Residents and Overseas Property
Overseas property held by non-UK residents should generally be outside the scope of UK taxation; with three main exceptions:

- UK IHT on property held by a non-UK resident individual who remains UK domiciled,
- UK CGT arising on property disposals made during a period of 'temporary non-residence' (generally less than five years), and
- UK CGT arising on the disposal of an interest in an entity that holds overseas property, but which also holds UK property accounting for 75% or more of its gross asset value

Chapter 3

How to Save Income Tax

3.1 INTRODUCTION TO INCOME TAX

Income Tax was introduced by William Pitt (the Younger) in 1799 as a 'temporary measure' to raise the revenue required to fight the Napoleonic Wars. Bonaparte may have met his Waterloo in 1815, but it seems the British taxpayer is still paying for it!

The tax was initially charged at a single rate of two shillings in the pound (10% in today's terms). The top rate rose to a (previous) all-time high of 95% under Harold Wilson's Labour Government in the 1960s. Rates remained fairly high (with a top rate of 60%) until Nigel Lawson's tax-cutting Budget of 1987 established 40% as the top rate.

This remained the top rate until Alistair Darling introduced the additional rate (now 45%) on income over £150,000 in 2010. At the same time, the withdrawal of personal allowances for those with income over £100,000 created an effective rate of 60% (for 2019/20 and 2020/21 this falls on income between £100,000 and £125,000).

In 2013, George Osborne went even further, with additional tax charges that have created even higher effective tax rates for many parents with income between £50,000 and £60,000: over 100% in some cases!

The long history of Income Tax may go some way towards explaining some of its quirks. Badly needed modernisation is often slow in coming. It was only as recently as 1998 that 'the expense of keeping a horse for the purposes of travel to the taxpayer's place of work' ceased to be allowable.

The roots of how Income Tax affects the property investor lie in the 'schedular' system introduced in the 19th Century. Under this system, each type of income was classified separately and taxed under a different 'schedule'. Rental income and certain other property-based income fell under Schedule A.

The term 'Schedule A' was abolished in 2005 and, under the Income Tax (Trading and Other Income) Act 2005 we now refer simply to 'Property Income'. The act's rather lengthy name is often shortened to 'ITTOIA', which, as a fan of Ms Wilcox, I refer to as 'I Toyah' – sounds like an early 1980s album doesn't it?

Until 1995 the rules governing tax on rental income were somewhat archaic and restrictive. The system then underwent something of an overhaul, which resulted in more sensible rules that applied for over twenty years and, quite rightly, treated property letting as a business.

Generally speaking, property letting is still treated more or less as a business, but the 'sensible' era came to an end in 2017, when outrageous new restrictions on tax relief for landlord's interest and finance costs began to come into force.

We will examine the current property income regime in detail in Chapter 4: including the dreadful new restrictions on interest relief.

Where the taxpayer is deemed to be trading, the income falls under a different set of rules, which we will be looking at in Chapter 5.

Other major changes in recent years have included the introduction of 'separate taxation' for husbands and wives in 1990 (before which a wife's 'unearned' income was treated as her husband's for tax purposes); self-assessment, which came into force in 1996; and recognition of the legal status of registered civil partners in 2005.

Despite recent reforms, Income Tax has passed its bicentenary with some of its greatest peculiarities still intact. Indeed, in recent years, our Governments have seemed determined to add to them!

Perhaps the greatest oddity of all, the UK's peculiar tax year-end date of 5th April, has surprised many of us by surviving well into the 21st Century.

3.2   BASIC PRINCIPLES OF INCOME TAX

The UK tax year runs from 6th April each year to the following 5th April. The year ending 5th April 2020 is referred to as '2019/20' and the tax return for this year is known as the '2020 Return'.

Individuals, partnerships and trusts are subject to the self-assessment system for UK Income Tax. Under this system, the taxpayer must complete and submit a tax return for each tax year. The return is normally due for submission to HMRC by:

a) 31st October if completed on paper, or
b) 31st January following the tax year when filed online.

This system now seems likely to continue until at least the 2021/22 tax year, and possibly longer. However, the Government is considering the possibility of making some significant changes in the years ahead. We will look at these potential changes in more detail in Section 3.21.

The taxpayer must also calculate the amount of tax he or she is due to pay, although most tax return software will do this for you. For the minority who still submit their tax return on paper, HMRC will do the calculation if the return reaches them by the due date. Frankly, however, I would not recommend relying on HMRC's calculations.

The Income Tax due under the self-assessment system is basically the taxpayer's total tax liability for the year less any amounts deducted at source or under PAYE.

All Income Tax due under the self-assessment system, regardless of the source of income or rate of tax applying, is payable as follows:

- A first instalment or 'payment on account' is due on 31st January during the tax year.
- A second payment on account is due on 31st July following the tax year.
- A balancing payment (where appropriate) is due on 31st January following the tax year.

Where the payments on account exceed the final self-assessment tax liability for the year, no balancing payment will be due and the taxpayer will receive a repayment of the excess (or may set it off against the first payment on account due for the next year).

Each payment on account is usually equal to half the previous tax year's self-assessment tax liability. However, payments on account need not be made when the previous year's self-assessment liability was either:

a) No more than £1,000, or
b) Less than 20% of the individual's total tax liability for the year.

Hence, where an individual's self-assessment liability for 2018/19 is no more than £1,000, no payments on account will be due on 31st January or 31st July 2020.

Applications to reduce payments on account may be made when there are reasonable grounds to believe the following year's self-assessment tax liability will be at a lower level.

Individuals in employment, or in receipt of a private pension, may apply to have self-assessment tax liabilities of up to £3,000 collected through their PAYE codes for the following tax year. This produces a considerable cashflow advantage.

The self-assessment system is also used to collect NI on self-employed or partnership trading income and certain student loan repayments.

3.3 INCOME TAX RATES

The current UK Income Tax rates and main allowances are set out in Appendix A. Property income forms part of the 'non-savings' or 'other' element of an individual's income and is currently taxed at three rates, namely 20%, 40% and 45%. These same rates also apply to trading income arising from property development, trading or management.

Individuals with total income in excess of £100,000 lose £1 of their personal allowance for every £2 by which their income exceeds this level. This creates an effective rate of Income Tax of 60% on any property or trading income falling into the band between £100,000 and £125,000 (at rates applying for 2019/20 and 2020/21).

The High Income Child Benefit Charge ('HICBC')

An additional Income Tax charge is levied on the highest earner in any household where:

- Any household member has income in excess of £50,000, and
- Child Benefit is being claimed

The additional tax charge is equivalent to 1% of the Child Benefit claimed in the same tax year for every £100 by which the highest earner's income exceeds £50,000. Once the highest earner's income reaches £60,000, the whole of the Child Benefit will effectively have been withdrawn and the charge will have reached its maximum.

Those affected by the charge for 2019/20 will have an overall effective Income Tax rate on income between £50,000 and £60,000 as follows:

No. of Qualifying Children	Effective Tax Rate
1 Child	50.76%
2 Children	57.89%
3 Children	65.01%
4 Children	72.14%
Each additional child	+7.12%

As an alternative to the Income Tax charge, the claimant can choose not to claim Child Benefit.

The highest earner's total annual income for the purpose of the charge is their 'adjusted net income'. This means taxable income less 'grossed up' gift aid and personal pension contributions, making these reliefs extremely valuable to individuals who are subject to the HICBC.

We will look at some other ways of avoiding, or at least mitigating, the HICBC in Section 8.29. In all other sections of this guide, unless expressly stated to the contrary, it is assumed for the purpose of all examples, tables, and other calculations, that the HICBC does not apply.

Future Tax Rates

In the October 2018 Budget, it was announced that the personal allowance, basic rate band and higher rate threshold for 2020/21 are to remain at the same level as in 2019/20.

3.4   CALCULATING THE INCOME TAX DUE

The best way to explain how Income Tax due under self assessment is calculated is by way of an example. To keep things simple for the time being, we will assume that the restriction on relief for interest and finance costs, which is covered in Section 4.5, does not apply in this case.

Subject to this point, the profits could equally be rental profits or property trading profits for Income Tax purposes. Note that property trading profits would generally also be subject to NI, which is not taken into account in this example, but will be examined later in Chapter 5.

The example will also demonstrate the impact that beginning to receive untaxed income, such as rental or trading profits, may have on the timing of an individual's tax liabilities.

Example

In the tax year 2019/20, Meera receives a gross salary of £45,000. She suffers Income Tax deductions totalling £6,500 under PAYE. If Meera had no other income during 2019/20, she would have no self-assessment tax liability: as the tax deductions made at source would cover all of her Income Tax for the year. Many people are in this situation before commencing a property business.

However, for the first time in 2019/20, in addition to her salary, Meera also has profits of £12,000 from a property business. Her Income Tax calculation for 2019/20 is therefore as follows:

Employment Income:	£45,000
Property Income:	£12,000
Less: Personal Allowance:	(£12,500)
Total Income Taxable:	£44,500
Income Tax @ 20% on £37,500:	£7,500
Income Tax @ 40% on balance (£7,000):	£2,800
Total Tax For The Year:	£10,300
Less: Tax paid under PAYE	£6,500
Tax Due under Self Assessment	**£3,800**

Not only does Meera have a considerable amount of tax to pay for 2019/20, her liability is too great for her to be eligible to pay through her PAYE coding and she must make payments on account in respect of 2020/21. Hence, unless Meera has reasonable grounds for claiming her 2020/21 tax liability will be less than that for 2019/20, she will have to make tax payments as follows:

By 31st January 2021:

Tax due for 2019/20:	£3,800
First Instalment for 2020/21:	£1,900
Total payment due:	£5,700

By 31st July 2021:

Second Instalment for 2020/21:	£1,900

By 31st January 2022:
Balancing payment (or repayment) for 2020/21
First Instalment for 2021/22

And so on, every six months thereafter for as long as her self-assessment tax liability exceeds £1,000 per annum.

The example has also demonstrated another very important fact. When you begin to receive any significant level of income that is not taxed at source, such as property rental or trading profits, the tax liabilities arising in the first year can be quite severe. You will need to find the tax on two years' worth of profits within the space of only six months – most of it on one single day. This is what I call the 'double whammy' effect of self assessment!

Of course, once you are 'in the system' and things settle down a bit, you should just be paying fairly similar levels of tax every six months.

Nevertheless, every time your rental or trading income increases significantly, you will be hit by this 'double whammy' effect again!

Wealth Warning
Where an individual is already paying tax under PAYE and also has property rental income, HMRC often attempts to collect the tax due on the property business through the PAYE system. At best, this vastly accelerates the date of collection of the tax due, at worst it can lead to overpayments. While such overpayments may eventually be reclaimed, there will be no compensatory payment of interest. Fortunately, taxpayers have the right to appeal against PAYE codings that attempt to include their rental income in this way and hence continue to pay the tax on this income via the self-assessment system.

Turn to Section 5.5 to see the example in this section revisited where Meera has a property trade and is thus also subject to NI on her profits.

3.5   TAX RETURNS

Nowadays, most people submit their tax returns online and many use specialised software for the purpose, so you may be less aware of which boxes or pages your entries will actually appear in on the final return. However, the way in which property businesses should be reported on the self assessment return (or returns) is summarised below.

Unless expressly stated to the contrary, references to boxes or pages on the tax return throughout this edition of the guide are to the full 2019 UK Self Assessment Tax Return for individuals (form SA100 and its supplementary pages): the latest version available at the time of writing. Although some minor variations in box or page numbers do occur from time to time, they can generally be expected to remain much the same for the foreseeable future.

UK Rental Income

Rental income from UK land and property should be detailed on pages UKP 1 and UKP 2 of the tax return (the UK property supplement: SA105).

Page UKP 1 begins with a few general questions including the number of rental properties you had during the relevant tax year (Box 1).

This may seem like a pretty trivial, innocent question, but it is important to get it right as HMRC will compare this figure with the details of the properties you hold at the land registry.

When completing Box 1, remember to include:

i)   UK properties only (but see further below regarding furnished holiday lets within the EEA)
ii)   Rental properties you hold jointly with another person
iii)   UK properties let as qualifying furnished holiday lets
iv)   Properties not let on arm's length commercial terms (see Section 4.16)
v)   Any property on which you are claiming 'rent-a-room relief' (see Section 4.11)
vi)   All your UK rental properties (see Section 4.3), including any properties from which you actually received no rental income during the year

If you hold any of these properties jointly with another person you should put an 'X' in Box 3. (We will look at joint lettings and some of their potential benefits in more detail in Section 8.2.)

We will deal with the significance of Boxes 2 and 4 later, in Chapter 4.

The rest of page UKP 1 deals with income from furnished holiday lets (see Section 8.17). Details of all other UK property rental income should be entered on page UKP 2.

Furnished Holiday Lets in the EEA

Although it may seem rather odd, the UK property supplement should also be used to report income from furnished holiday lets elsewhere in the EEA (see Section 1.5).

Where you also have a UK property rental business, you will need to complete two UK property supplements: one for your UK property business and one for your furnished holiday lets in the EEA.

When completing a UK property supplement in respect of a furnished holiday letting business in the EEA, Boxes 1 to 4 should be completed in respect of that business only and an 'X' should be placed in Box 18 on Page UKP 1.

Any foreign tax suffered on income from qualifying furnished holiday lets within the EEA should be detailed on Page F 6 of the foreign supplement (see further below), with a suitable explanation in Box 19 on Page TR 7 of the main tax return form (SA100). Remember also to include the relevant amount in the sum entered in Box 2 on Page F 1 of the foreign supplement.

Other Overseas Rental Income

Income from land and property located overseas is treated as a different source of income. With the exception of income from qualifying furnished holiday lets in the EEA, this income should be detailed on Pages F 4 and F 5 which form part of the foreign supplement (SA106). Any foreign tax suffered on this income should also be detailed on Pages F 4 and F 5.

To claim relief for the foreign tax suffered on all your overseas property income (including furnished holiday lets in the EEA), you should include the total eligible amount in the sum entered at Box 2 on page F 1.

Property Trades

Where your property business is deemed to be a trade for tax purposes, you will need to complete the self-employment supplement. A short, two page version of this supplement (SA103S) can be completed in certain restricted circumstances. In most cases, however, you will need to complete the full six page version (SA103F). This includes cases where gross sales income exceeds the VAT registration threshold for the relevant tax year (currently £85,000; see Section 7.12 for further details), or you are claiming any capital allowances (see Sections 3.14 to 3.19).

Multiple Sources

If you have both investment and trading activities then you will need to complete both the UK property supplement (and/or the foreign supplement, as appropriate) and the self-employment supplement.

Casual Property Income

Income falling into Category 2 of the activities defined in Section 2.9, or of the kind described in Section 2.7, should be entered in Boxes 17 to 19 on Page TR 3 of the main tax return form (SA100), with a suitable description in Box 21.

Joint Owners

Where property is held jointly, but not as a partnership, each joint owner must include their own share of property income and expenses on their tax return each year, as appropriate.

Partnership Income

Where any type of property business is operated by a partnership (see Section 2.14), the partners must report their share of partnership income on the partnership supplement. The full version (SA104F) will be required where there is partnership rental income, but the short version (SA104S) can be used where there is only partnership trading income.

A separate partnership tax return (form SA800 plus appropriate supplements) must also be completed on behalf of the partnership, in addition to each of the partners' own tax returns.

Short Returns

HMRC issues short returns (SA200) to selected taxpayers. These are only four pages long, compared with the usual full tax return of eight pages plus supplements. Some property investors whose tax affairs are very simple may receive a short return.

Wealth Warning

If you receive a short return, it remains your legal obligation to ensure all your income and gains are reported. In some cases you should use the normal full return and it is your responsibility to ascertain whether this is the case. You cannot use a short return if:

- You are in a business partnership,
- You are a paid company director,
- Your gross business income exceeds the VAT registration threshold for the relevant tax year (see Section 7.12),
- You have any income from furnished holiday lettings,
- You are claiming the structures and buildings allowance (see Section 3.19), or
- You are claiming any other capital allowances (see Sections 3.15 to 3.18) against property rental income

Completing a short return (if you are issued with one and remain eligible to use it) will make no difference to your tax liability, or its due date for payment.

3.6 AMENDING PRIOR YEARS' TAX RETURNS

After reading one of our Taxcafe.co.uk guides, many readers realise they have missed out on legitimate claims that they could have made in previous years. However, it is often still possible to make claims in respect of earlier years following one of the procedures detailed below.

The Previous Year
Self-assessment tax returns may be amended at any time up to twelve months after the normal online filing deadline. For example, you may submit an amended tax return for 2017/18 at any time up until 31st January 2020. (It is for this reason that I will generally continue to cover the tax rules for 2017/18 throughout this edition.)

Amending the previous year's tax return is a relatively straightforward matter and may be used to make a number of claims, disclaimers, etc, which might not initially have seemed desirable, or which might simply have been missed, such as:

i)   Claims to set off trading losses against other income (see Section 5.11)
ii) Claims to set the capital allowances element of a rental loss off against other income (see Section 4.12)
iii) Disclaimers of capital allowances (see Section 3.18)
iv) Rent-a-room relief claims (see Section 4.11)

The previous year's tax return may also be amended in order to implement claims for business expenditure which has previously been missed, such as:

v)   'Use of home' (see Section 3.11)
vi) Business mileage (see Section 3.12)
vii) Repairs expenditure initially thought not to be allowable (see Section 4.7)

Amendments to the previous year's tax return under this simple procedure are quite commonplace and can be seen as a normal part of the self-assessment regime.

Wealth Warning
Amending an earlier year's return means it is open for enquiry once again (for a period of twelve months) and HMRC may investigate any aspect of the return. While this should not prevent legitimate claims being made, it is a risk that should be borne in mind.

Earlier Years

Earlier years can only be amended by making a formal 'tax repayment claim'. This facility is only open where errors or mistakes have arisen. Claims must be based on the general understanding of the law at the time the tax return was originally submitted. HMRC will, of course, interpret this as meaning **their** understanding of the law!

The facility cannot be used to make claims based on a change in the general understanding of the law and is only available for a period of four years following the end of the relevant tax year. For example, a tax repayment claim for 2015/16 must be made by 5th April 2020.

Amending earlier years' returns under the 'tax repayment claim' facility is a more formal procedure and can only be used if there are errors in the original return. Generally it cannot be used to make a claim that has simply been missed, such as those detailed at (i) to (iv) above.

It could be used to claim expenditure that has been omitted, such as the items detailed at (v) to (vii) above (although a landlord could not use this facility to claim business mileage prior to 2017/18 – for the reasons explained in Section 3.12).

However, tax repayment claims under this facility are a more exceptional occurrence and should not be undertaken lightly as they are, in effect, a clear admission that you 'got it wrong'. The 'wealth warning' set out above therefore becomes even more important. Hence, while this is a useful facility that I have used several times to obtain tax repayments for new clients, it should generally only be used where there are significant amounts at stake and you are absolutely certain of the grounds for your claim. If in doubt, take professional advice.

Practical Pointer

The items listed at (i) to (vii) above are by no means an exhaustive list and I have encountered many other examples of items that might warrant an amendment to the previous year's tax return, or a more formal tax repayment claim. The key is to be sure your claim is worthwhile, bearing in mind the points made above.

3.7   REGISTERING A NEW PROPERTY BUSINESS

Guidance issued by HMRC suggests anyone starting a new property business should register within three months. In the case of a new property trade, this is quite correct and we will take a closer look at the relevant reporting requirements in Section 5.6.

The guidance also states that landlords should 'contact Revenue and Customs for a self assessment and a land and property form, or register as self-employed'.

Wealth Warning

Landlords starting a property letting business should **not** register as 'self-employed' or as a 'business'. Self-employment income is subject to NI; rental income is not. By registering as self-employed, landlords may incur NI liabilities which, by rights, they should not have to pay.

It is, however, advisable to follow HMRC's first suggestion and notify them of the start of your property business by registering for self-assessment. This can be done online at: www.gov.uk/register-for-self-assessment/overview.

If you are already registered for self-assessment, there is no need to register again, but you will need to ensure your tax return includes details of your new property income and is submitted on time.

When registering for self-assessment, it is important to remember that you are **not** self-employed for tax purposes (unless you have a property trade, for which see Section 5.6). As a landlord with rental income, you should follow the link from 'If you're not self-employed' in order to get to form SA1 to register for self-assessment.

When completing form SA1, in response to the question 'Why do you need to complete a tax return?' you should tick the box for 'I'm getting income from land and property in UK': unless your rental income comes from an overseas property, in which case tick the box for 'I'm getting taxable foreign income of £300 or more'.

The law actually only requires you to register for self-assessment by 5th October following the tax year in which your letting business commences rather than within three months, as suggested by HMRC. Generally, however, it is probably better to get it done sooner rather than later, but:

Practical Pointer

Some taxpayers registering a new business with HMRC within the same tax year as they commenced their business have been issued a notice to deliver a tax return for the previous year. Once a notice has been issued, there is an obligation to complete a tax return, and hence unnecessary extra work has been created.

My advice to new landlords is therefore to register for self-assessment shortly after the end of the tax year in which your business commences (see Section 4.3 regarding the date on which a new letting business is deemed to commence for tax purposes).

But see Section 5.6 regarding new property trades!

HMRC can withdraw a notice to deliver a tax return where it has been issued unnecessarily: but requesting this will also require unnecessary extra work, so it is still best avoided in the first place!

Strictly speaking, a taxpayer is always required to notify HMRC of any new source of income by 5th October following the tax year in which the 'new source' commences.

A 'new source' for this purpose means the commencement of a property business, rather than a new property within an existing business. It is not necessary to advise HMRC every time you rent out a new property!

However, as explained in Section 4.3, when someone with a UK property business rents out their first overseas property, this does amount to a new source. The same is true for anyone renting out their first UK property, including non-UK residents.

Similarly, commencing a property trade when you already have a property investment business, or vice versa, will also constitute a new source of income.

In practice, there are not usually any penalties for a delay in reporting a new property investment business, as long as the tax return includes the new source of income and is completed and submitted on time.

However, for anyone not already within the self-assessment system, it is essential to report the new source of income by the 5th October deadline so that a 'Unique Taxpayer Reference' ('UTR') number can be issued in time for them to complete and file their tax return by the due date.

It is now almost impossible to file a tax return without a UTR and there is a considerable delay in issuing new numbers. If you have not reported your new source of income by the 5th October deadline, you will have no legitimate excuse for filing your tax return late just because you did not receive your UTR in time.

In Summary

In summary, to avoid any unnecessary penalties, additional paperwork, or other aggravations, my advice is to notify HMRC of the commencement of a new property business as follows:

- New property trades: within three months (following the procedure detailed in Section 5.6).
- New property investment businesses where you are **not** already within the self-assessment system: as soon as possible after the end of the tax year in which the business commenced.

- New property investment businesses where you **are** already within the self-assessment system: by 5th October after the end of the tax year in which the business commenced or by simply including the new source of income in your tax return.

3.8   NON-RESIDENTS, ETC

As explained in Section 2.15, non-UK residents remain liable for UK Income Tax on rental income receivable from property situated in the UK and on profits derived from developing, or trading in, UK property. They may also be subject to UK Income Tax on other profits from a property business based in the UK, such as a property management business, or a UK-based property developing or property trading business dealing in overseas property.

Certain classes of non-UK resident individuals with taxable income in the UK are entitled to the same personal allowances as UK residents (see Appendix A), and may set these off against that income. These include British Nationals resident abroad, nationals of states within the EEA (see Section 1.5), Crown servants, residents of the Isle of Man or the Channel Islands and residents of other countries that have a suitable double taxation agreement with the UK.

UK residents who are also UK domiciled are liable for UK Income Tax on all worldwide income as it arises.

UK resident but non-UK domiciled individuals may choose to only pay UK Income Tax on income from property situated abroad as and when they remit it back to the UK. This option, known as the 'remittance basis', often comes at a price, and we will look at the taxation of these individuals in more detail in Section 8.25.

Note, however, that an individual resident in the UK for at least 15 of the previous 20 UK tax years is generally deemed to be UK domiciled for all UK tax purposes.

The tax concepts of residence, domicile, and deemed domicile can sometimes be fairly complex. Residence is examined in detail in Section 8.32 and domicile, including deemed domicile, is exhaustively covered in the Taxcafe.co.uk guide 'How to Save Inheritance Tax'. Broadly though, in most cases, it is safe to say that, if you have British parents and have lived in the UK all your life, you are most probably UK resident and domiciled.

3.9   CLAIMING DEDUCTIONS

Whatever type of property business you have, there will usually be expenses that may be claimed as a deduction from your profits.

Some deductions are very much dependent on the type of business and we will therefore examine some of the specific types of deductible expenditure in the next two chapters.

Firstly, however, it is worth dealing with some of the basic principles that apply to deductions claimed in any type of property business.

Accruals versus Cash

The general rule under UK tax law is that expenses are deductible when they are incurred (known as the 'accruals basis'), rather than when they are paid (known as the 'cash basis').

For example, under the accruals basis, if a landlord has some roof repairs carried out on a rental property in March 2020, they may deduct the cost in their accounts to 5th April 2020, even if the roofer doesn't invoice them until May and they do not pay the bill until July.

The accruals basis must be used unless one of the alternative cash bases applies. The cash basis for small trading businesses is examined in Section 5.12. Qualifying taxpayers must elect to use this basis.

The cash basis for landlords applies automatically when the landlord qualifies, unless the landlord elects to opt out. We will examine this cash basis in Section 4.18.

The Government seems very keen on promoting the use of the cash basis by all small businesses and claims this is all being done in the name of 'simplification'. However, while the alternative cash bases may suit some small business owners, my view is they are generally disadvantageous for property business owners.

Hence, while we will examine the use of the cash bases described above in Sections 4.18 and 5.12, it is assumed throughout the rest of this guide (unless specifically stated to the contrary) that accounts and tax returns are being prepared on an accruals basis.

Wholly and Exclusively

All expenses must be incurred wholly and exclusively for the purposes of the business and, naturally, must actually be borne by the taxpayer.

The term 'wholly and exclusively' is enshrined in tax law but is not always interpreted quite as literally as you might think.

Example
Saleema pays £50 per week for gardening services. This covers the upkeep of her own garden and that of the house next door, which she also owns and rents out. This is what we call 'mixed use'. The gardening costs are partly private

expenditure and partly incurred for Saleema's property business. This does not mean all the gardening expenditure falls foul of the 'wholly and exclusively' rule. The correct interpretation is to say that part of the gardening expenses are incurred wholly and exclusively for business purposes and to claim an appropriate proportion.

Nevertheless, any expenditure incurred for the benefit of the taxpayer or their family will not be allowed as a business deduction. Where there is a 'dual purpose' (i.e. both business and private elements exist), the strict position is that none of the expenditure is allowable.

This contrasts with 'mixed use' expenditure, as in our example above, where a reasonable apportionment between the business and private elements is possible so that the business element may still be claimed.

The distinction between 'dual purpose' and 'mixed use' is a difficult one. The best explanation I can provide is that with 'dual purpose' expenditure, the business and private elements generally take place simultaneously. This is why most business clothing is not allowable, since it performs the personal functions of providing warmth and decency at the same time as giving the wearer the appropriate appearance for their work.

The 'Revenue versus Capital' Issue

As well as being incurred 'wholly and exclusively' for the purposes of the business, expenditure must usually also be 'revenue expenditure' if it is to be claimed for Income Tax purposes.

The term 'revenue expenditure' refers to expenditure incurred on an ongoing basis in order to earn revenue (i.e. income) in the business. Expenditure on the acquisition or enhancement of a long-term asset of the business will generally be 'capital expenditure' (although, as we shall see later, this does not usually extend to interest and finance costs).

In the tax world, all business expenditure will be either 'revenue' or 'capital'. Capital expenditure may not usually be claimed for Income Tax purposes, but will often be deductible in CGT calculations (though not always!) Some Income Tax relief for certain types of capital expenditure is, however, given in the form of 'capital allowances' or 'replacement of domestic items relief'. We will examine these reliefs further in Sections 3.14 to 3.19 and 4.10 respectively.

Whether expenditure is capital or revenue depends not only on the nature of the expenditure but also on the type of business you have.

Capital expenditure is a particularly significant issue in a property investment or property letting business as a great many of your expenses will be deemed to be capital for tax purposes. We will therefore cover some more specific examples relevant to property investment businesses in the next chapter.

Before that, however, let's look at a simple example to illustrate the difference between capital and revenue expenditure.

Example
Willie runs a chain of sweet shops. As part of his expansion programme, he opens two new shops, one in Midchester and one in Normingham. He buys the freehold of the Midchester shop, but rents the premises in Normingham.

The Midchester shop is a long-term capital asset of Willie's business. The cost of buying the freehold is therefore a capital expense, deductible only for CGT purposes if and when Willie decides to sell the property. This treatment also extends to all costs incurred in the purchase, such as legal fees and SDLT. (But see Section 4.4 for the treatment of interest and finance costs.)

The Normingham shop, however, is only rented and Willie does not own any long-term asset. The rent paid is a direct cost of making sales of sweets in Normingham and thus represents a revenue cost that Willie may deduct against his profits for Income Tax purposes.

> **Practical Pointer**
> Many capital expenses that you incur will be deductible in the event of a sale of the underlying property. That sale may take place many years from now. It is important, therefore, to keep the receipts and other documentary evidence of this expenditure in a safe place: as it may save you a significant amount of CGT one day!

Grants & Insurance Claims

Any grants or insurance claims received should be deducted from the underlying expense.

> **Tax Tip**
> If you incur deductible expenditure that is also the subject of an insurance claim, you may claim the expenditure as and when it is incurred and need only credit the insurance claim (as a 'negative expense') back into your accounts when it is received. This could be in a later tax year, giving you a tax cashflow advantage to partly compensate for the cashflow disadvantage you suffer while waiting for your claim to be sorted out.

VAT on Expenses

If you are unable to recover the VAT on any expense then, as long as the underlying expense itself is deductible, you may also include your irrecoverable VAT cost in the deduction claimed. This is a simple reflection of the fact that, in such cases, the business expense incurred is the VAT-inclusive cost. We will return to the question of when VAT may be recoverable in Chapter 7.

Commencement & Pre-Trading Expenditure

You may incur some expenses for the purposes of your property business before it even starts. Such expenses incurred within seven years before the commencement of your business will usually still be allowable if they would otherwise qualify under normal principles. In such cases, the expenses may be claimed as if they were incurred on the first day of the business.

The expenses do, however, need to relate to the same business as the one you eventually start. For property letting businesses, this means they must fall into the same one of the four categories described in Section 4.1.

3.10   ADMINISTRATIVE EXPENSES

One category of expenses common to any type of business is administrative expenses, or business overheads. This heading is very broad and can extend, among other things, to the cost of running an office, motor and travel costs, and support staff's wages.

In Sections 3.11 to 3.13, we will look at the most common types of administrative expenditure in a property business. While the amounts involved may not always be significant, it is well worth claiming the deductions you are rightfully entitled to. Many property business owners overlook some of these expenses and pay more tax as a result but, with a little extra effort, claiming these items can help to reduce your tax bill.

The items covered in Sections 3.11 to 3.13 are not meant to be an exhaustive list. Almost anything that meets the 'wholly and exclusively' rule, and which qualifies as 'revenue expenditure' (see Section 3.9 for explanations of these terms), may be claimed for Income Tax purposes; although, sadly, most entertaining expenditure is specifically excluded.

3.11   USE OF HOME & OTHER PREMISES COSTS

Many people with a property business handle their business administration from a room in their home, just like many other small businesses. In these cases, the taxpayer may claim an appropriate proportion of their household bills as a business expense.

Generally, the proportion to be used is based on the number of rooms in the house, excluding bathrooms, toilets, kitchens, landings and hallways.

The claim should be further restricted where there is also some private use of the part of the house which is used in the business.

Example
Shakira spends about 30 hours per week running her property business from a small room in her house. The house also contains a living room, a kitchen, a bathroom and two bedrooms. Shakira's house therefore has four rooms which count for the purposes of our calculation. The room which Shakira uses for business also has some private use which she estimates to amount to around 10% of the room's total use. Shakira may therefore claim 90% of one quarter, or 22.5%, of her household bills as a business expense.

In practice, where the private use of the part of the house used in the business is negligible, HMRC has not usually sought a further reduction in the proportion of household expenses claimed.

Wealth Warning
Exclusive business use of part of your home can have a detrimental effect on your CGT position, as we shall see in Chapter 6.

The household expenses to be included in the office cost calculation would generally comprise:

- Heating and lighting (electricity, gas, oil, coal, etc.)
- Cleaning (cleaners' wages and/or cleaning materials)
- Council tax
- Water rates or metered water supplies
- General repairs to the fabric of the building
- Insurance
- Mortgage interest or rent

Note that, if part of the taxpayer's mortgage interest on their own home is already being claimed on the basis that part of the mortgage has been used to fund business expenditure (e.g. the deposit on a rental property), that part must be excluded from the household expenses used to calculate the claim for business use of the home (i.e. it cannot be counted twice!)

Sections BIM 47800 to BIM 47825 of HMRC's own Business Income Manual provide instructions to tax inspectors telling them to accept reasonable claims for an appropriate proportion of the above costs. (It may be useful to refer them to these sections if you encounter any resistance to a claim.)

HMRC's instructions acknowledge there are a variety of acceptable methods for apportioning household expenses where there is business use of the home and no method is mandatory.

The instructions do, however, draw a distinction between running costs (heating, lighting, cleaning, and metered water) and fixed costs (all other items listed above). They then go on to suggest running costs should be apportioned according to actual use, whereas fixed costs should be apportioned according to the room's availability: although their own examples do interpret this in different ways.

In practice, the key point is to be reasonable. Where the business use is quite extensive (say 20 hours or more per week) it will generally be reasonable to claim the same proportion of all household costs (as in Shakira's case in the example above). Where there is only moderate business use, however, (say less than 20 hours per week) it will usually be reasonable to restrict the claim for fixed costs to a lower proportion. One potential method for doing this is illustrated in the example below.

Example
Rhodri has five rooms in his house excluding the kitchen, bathrooms and hallway. One of these is his study, which he uses for business just nine hours per week. The study is also used privately for an average of one hour per week.

Rhodri's total household costs for the year are:
Running costs: £2,500
Fixed costs: £8,000

Rhodri uses his study for business purposes for nine hours per week out of total actual usage of ten hours per week on average. He therefore claims the following proportion of his running costs: £2,500 x 1/5 x 9/10 = £450.

Rhodri also considers that his study is available for use 16 hours per day (it has no bed so cannot be used at night). This equates to 112 hours per week. He therefore claims the following proportion of his fixed costs: £8,000 x 1/5 x 9/112 = £129.

This gives him a total claim in respect of his household expenses of £579.

The 'number of rooms' allocation method is not compulsory and any other method that produces a reasonable result may be applied instead. Some consistency in the allocation method used would generally be expected.

Note that any mortgage interest element within a residential landlord's claim for 'use of home' needs to be separated out and treated in accordance with the regime described in Section 4.5. For example, if £6,000 out of the £8,000 of fixed costs incurred by Rhodri represents mortgage interest, and he is a residential landlord, then £96 (£6,000 x 1/5 x 9/112) of his 'use of home' claim will need to be separated out and dealt with as an interest cost subject to restricted relief as shown in Section 4.5.

Minimal Use

HMRC's instructions also suggest that small claims not exceeding £2 per week, or £104 per year, will be acceptable for even the most minimal amounts of business use. This simple claim is available to all property businesses as an alternative to the more complex calculations considered above. For those with minimal business use of their home, it will make sense to simply claim this small deduction.

Note that the claim should be restricted, as appropriate, where the business has not been running for a full year. Some actual business use of the home is also required, even if only very small.

Flat Rate Deductions

A system of flat rate deductions for business use of the taxpayer's home is available for trading businesses. (See below regarding property letting businesses.)

The flat rate deductions are an alternative method available **instead** of the proportionate calculation discussed above.

The amount of the deduction is calculated on a monthly basis according to the number of hours spent wholly and exclusively working on business matters at the home. The rates applying are:

Hours worked in the month	Deduction allowed for the month
25 to 50	£10
51 to 100	£18
101 or more	£26

Strictly speaking, this flat rate deduction regime is only available to trading businesses. Whether, in practice, HMRC will permit landlords with property rental income to use the regime still remains to be seen. However, their own manuals do tell their inspectors that where 'there is only minor business use of the home you may accept a reasonable estimate'. It is hard to see what grounds they could have for not accepting the use of the same flat rate deductions that are available to other businesses as a reasonable estimate.

Having said all that, the flat rate deductions are not exactly generous, so I find it difficult to believe many property business owners working from home at least 25 hours per month will want to use them anyway.

Anyone who feels it is not worthwhile performing complex calculations to arrive at a suitable proportion of household expenses can still claim the simple deduction of £2 per week described above in any case.

Business Premises

If your property business grows to the point where you need to rent premises from which to run it, the rent, business rates and other running costs you incur will generally be an allowable expense.

Expenditure on purchasing or improving your own business premises will always be treated as capital in nature, whatever type of business you have.

If you buy a property to run your business from, you will be able to claim any interest and other finance charges incurred. The same principles that are outlined in Section 4.4 (for rental property purchases) will apply to determine which interest and finance charges qualify for relief. For residential landlords, the restrictions in the rate of relief applying (see Section 4.5) will also apply to interest or finance charges on funds used to buy your own business premises.

The running costs, including business rates, of a property you purchase for use as your business premises may also be claimed as annual overheads.

Having business premises does not prevent you from also making a 'use of home' claim if you continue (as most business owners do) to still carry out some work at home. The principles outlined above remain the same, although, of course, the amount of hours you spend working at home is likely to be reduced.

3.12   MOTOR EXPENSES

The cost of running any vehicles used in your business may be claimed as a business expense. Generally, the vehicle will also have some private non-business use, so an appropriate proportion only is claimed. (Or a proportion is disallowed, depending on how you look at it and how you want to draw up your accounts.) For details on what can be considered to be a business journey, see under 'Travel and Subsistence' in Section 3.13.

The appropriate proportion to claim will vary from one taxpayer to the next. Typically, for a self-employed taxpayer with a property trading business, it will fall in the range 25% to 50%; for landlords with property investment businesses it will tend to be somewhat lower, perhaps 10% to 20%; but these are only rough guides and the appropriate claims may be considerably higher or lower in some cases.

You will need to work out the appropriate proportion applying in your own case based on the specific facts that support your claim. Keeping a mileage log to record your business journeys is the best way to do this and is highly recommended, although not everyone does this. The exact percentage of business use will vary from one year to the next, but a reasonable average rate is usually acceptable unless there is a significant change in your overall pattern of behaviour.

Most vehicles tend to have mixed business and private use but, if you were to buy a van purely for use in your business, then a 100% claim might be justified.

Mileage Rates

Alternatively, you may claim fixed mileage rates instead of the appropriate proportion of actual running costs. (Strictly speaking, this option was not available to landlords from 2013/14 to 2016/17, although many people took the view that the mileage rates represented a reasonable approximation of the business cost and could therefore still properly be claimed.)

For cars and vans, the rate is 45p per mile for the first 10,000 business miles travelled in each tax year, and 25p per mile thereafter. For motorcycles, a single flat rate of 24p per business mile may be claimed.

If claiming fixed mileage rate deductions, it is essential to keep a mileage log (although a mileage log is advisable in any case).

This method has the advantage of simplicity but does have some drawbacks. If claiming business mileage rates, you cannot also claim any running costs or capital allowances (see Section 3.16) for the vehicle; although you can claim a proportion of any finance costs, where relevant (subject to the restrictions discussed in Section 4.5 in the case of residential landlords).

Once you have chosen one method or the other (i.e. either fixed mileage rates, or a proportion of actual running costs and capital allowances), you must normally stick to that method throughout your ownership of the vehicle. However, where a landlord claimed a proportion of actual running costs (plus capital allowances) on a vehicle prior to 2017/18, they may switch to claiming the mileage allowance from 2017/18 onwards if desired.

3.13 OTHER ALLOWABLE COSTS

Some other items of administrative expenditure worth considering are discussed below. However, as explained in Section 3.10, this is not an exhaustive list.

Telephone and Broadband

The cost of business calls and other business use of telephone lines, broadband, etc, may be claimed. Strictly, a detailed analysis of business and private use should be carried out but, in practice, a reasonable estimated allocation will usually be acceptable. A suitable proportion of line rental and other service charges can also be claimed.

Travel and Subsistence

Travel costs incurred for business purposes should generally be allowable. This might include the cost of:

- Visiting existing rental properties or development sites
- Scouting for potential new properties or sites
- Visiting your bank, mortgage broker, solicitor, or accountant
- Visiting hardware stores to purchase goods for use in your business
- Visiting property shows, exhibitions, courses, etc.

Where your trip necessitates an overnight stay, you will additionally be able to claim accommodation costs and subsistence (meals, etc.). Care needs to be taken, however, in the case of any travel with a 'dual purpose'. Travel, subsistence and accommodation costs will only be allowable if your trip was purely for business purposes, or if any other purpose was merely incidental.

If you travel to Brighton for a day to view some properties, for example, the fact that you spent a spare hour at lunchtime sunbathing on the beach will not alter the fact that this was a business trip. If, on the other hand, you take your whole family to Brighton for a week and spend just one afternoon viewing a few properties, then the whole trip will be private and not allowable for tax purposes (except for any additional costs incurred specifically in order to carry out the viewings).

Strictly speaking, subsistence costs may only be claimed where connected with an overnight stay while travelling on business. However, in practice, reasonable expenditure incurred while some distance away from your own home and business base is usually accepted.

Staff Training

Any costs you pay to train your employees should be allowable. Different rules apply to your own training costs, however (see Chapters 4 and 5).

Staff Entertaining

Most entertaining expenditure is not allowable for Income Tax purposes. The only exception, for any business large enough to have employees, is staff entertaining. Please don't take this as carte blanche to have continual parties and meals out 'on the business', as this represents a benefit in kind on which the employees will have to pay Income Tax and you will have to pay 13.8% employer's NI.

There is, however, an exemption for one or more annual staff parties or similar functions costing no more than £150 per head in total. For most businesses, this is sufficient to ensure no-one gets taxed on the annual Xmas party. Naturally, before you can make use of this exemption, you need to have some employees!

And Don't Forget...

Other minor items worth mentioning include:

- Computer and IT costs (although some of these are capital in nature and may be claimed for capital allowances purposes: see Sections 3.14 to 3.18)
- Postage and stationery
- Professional subscriptions (where relevant to your business)

Just remember, if it's 'revenue' and it meets the 'wholly and exclusively' rule (see Section 3.9), it's probably allowable – unless it's business entertaining!

3.14 CAPITAL ALLOWANCES

As explained in Section 3.9, capital expenditure is not usually directly eligible for an Income Tax deduction. Some capital expenditure is, however, eligible for a form of relief known as 'capital allowances'.

The capital allowances available depend on the type of expenditure and sometimes also on the type of property involved. They also depend to a large extent on the type of business, so we will return to look at some specific issues for different types of property business in Chapters 4 and 5.

In this chapter, we will look at the basic principles of the capital allowances regime applying to 'plant and machinery' and motor vehicles used wholly or partly in a property business (Sections 3.15 to 3.18); and to qualifying structures and buildings (Section 3.19). As in the rest of this guide, I will be concentrating on property businesses run by individuals or partnerships. While I will refer to companies occasionally, most of the details relate to other property businesses rather than companies.

Having said that, the capital allowances regime for companies is broadly the same; apart from the rules for cars and other assets with private use (See the Taxcafe.co.uk guide *'Using a Property Company to Save Tax'*.)

The capital allowances regime has undergone several changes in recent years. I will largely ignore capital allowances on expenditure incurred during accounting periods commencing prior to 1st January 2016 throughout this edition. (Except in a few cases where some of the old rules remain relevant.)

3.15 PLANT AND MACHINERY

The term 'plant and machinery' covers qualifying plant, machinery, furniture, fixtures, fittings, computers and other equipment used in a business. What qualifies as 'plant and machinery' for capital allowances purposes depends on the nature of the business, so we will look at this again in Sections 4.9 and 5.9, when the practical application of the rules set out in this section will become more apparent.

The Annual Investment Allowance ('AIA')

The AIA provides 100% tax relief for qualifying expenditure on plant and machinery up to the maximum amount of allowance available for each accounting period. It is available to sole traders, partnerships and companies alike.

The maximum AIA available for each accounting period depends on when the period falls, as follows:

1st January 2016 to 31st December 2018	£200,000
1st January 2019 to 31st December 2020	£1,000,000
1st January 2021 onwards	£200,000

Transitional rules apply to determine the maximum amount of AIA available where an accounting period straddles one of the above dates. The AIA is also restricted where there is an accounting period of less than twelve months' duration. This will often apply to a new business's first accounting period.

Example
Rebecca commences business by letting out her first rental property on 1st February 2020. Her maximum AIA for the period to 5th April 2020 will be: 65/366 x £1m = £177,596.

Transitional Rules

For accounting periods straddling 1st January 2019, the maximum AIA is calculated on a pro rata basis. For example, a landlord with an accounting year ending on 5th April 2019 will be entitled to a maximum AIA for the whole year of:

270/365 x £200,000	£147,945
95/365 x £1m	£260,274
Total	£408,219

But, an additional rule applies to any expenditure incurred before 1st January 2019. The maximum amount that can be claimed in respect of expenditure incurred in the part of the accounting period falling before that date is restricted to £200,000.

For accounting periods straddling 31st December 2020, the maximum AIA will again be calculated on a pro rata basis. For example, a landlord with an accounting year ending on 5th April 2021 will be entitled to a maximum AIA for the whole year of:

270/365 x £1m	£739,726
95/365 x £200,000	£52,055
Total	£791,781

But, an additional rule applies to any expenditure incurred after 31st December 2020. The maximum amount that can be claimed in respect of expenditure incurred in the part of the accounting period falling after that date is restricted to the appropriate proportion of the £200,000 limit. Hence, in the case of the landlord described above, the maximum AIA that could be claimed on expenditure incurred between 1st January and 5th April 2021 would be £52,055.

As explained in Section 4.1, landlords generally use accounting periods ending on 5th April each year. Those with property trades may have different accounting periods. The maximum AIA applying for some other popular accounting periods is as follows:

Year ended	31-Mar	30-Apr	30-Jun	30-Sep	31-Dec
2019					
For the year as a whole	£397,260	£463,014	£596,712	£798,356	£1,000,000
Before 1/1/19	£200,000	£200,000	£200,000	£200,000	n/a
2020					
For the year as a whole	£1,000,000	£1,000,000	£1,000,000	£1,000,000	£1,000,000
2021					
For the year as a whole	£802,740	£736,986	£603,288	£401,644	£200,000
After 31/12/20	£49,315	£65,753	£99,178	£149,589	£200,000

Wealth Warning

As can be seen from the above table, the AIA available on expenditure in the early part of 2021 will, in some cases, be quite restricted. Any excess will attract WDAs at just 18%, or possibly as little as 6% where it falls in the 'special rate pool' (see below). It will therefore be important for businesses with accounting periods spanning 31st December 2020 to plan the timing of their capital expenditure carefully.

Enhanced Capital Allowances

Certain expenditure on new and unused equipment is currently eligible for 'enhanced capital allowances' of 100%. This includes:

- Energy-efficient plant and machinery listed in the official 'Energy Technology List' - see gov.uk/guidance/energy-technology-list
- Environmentally beneficial plant and machinery listed in the official 'Water Technology List' - see watertechnologylist.co.uk

Enhanced capital allowances claims do not use up your AIA and are not generally subject to any monetary limit. These allowances are to be abolished for expenditure incurred after 5th April 2020.

Writing Down Allowances

Expenditure on qualifying plant and machinery, which is neither eligible for the AIA, nor for enhanced capital allowances, is eligible for 'writing down allowances'. The rate of writing down allowances on most plant and machinery is 18%.

Expenditure qualifying for writing down allowances is pooled together with the unrelieved balance of qualifying expenditure brought forward from the previous accounting period. This pool of expenditure is known as the 'main pool'.

The writing down allowance of 18% is calculated on the total balance in the main pool. The remaining balance of expenditure is then carried forward and 18% of that balance may be claimed in the next accounting period. And so on.

However, where the balance in the main pool reduces to less than £1,000, the full balance may then be claimed immediately.

The Special Rate Pool

Certain types of expenditure must be allocated to a 'special rate pool' instead of the main pool. These include:

- Integral features (see Section 4.9 for details)
- Expenditure of £100,000 or more on plant and machinery with an anticipated working life of 25 years or more
- Expenditure on thermal insulation of an existing building used in a qualifying trade

Expenditure in the special rate pool is currently eligible for writing down allowances at just 6%. The rate applying prior to 6th April 2019 was 8%, and transitional rules apply to accounting periods spanning the change.

For example, the rate of writing down allowances applying for a twelve month accounting period ending 31st December 2019 is 8% x 95/365 + 6% x 270/365 = 6.520%.

The special rate pool is particularly relevant to property investors letting out commercial property or qualifying furnished holiday lets and we will therefore return to this issue in Section 4.9. It is worth noting, however, that the AIA may be allocated to any such expenditure in preference to expenditure qualifying for the normal rate of writing down allowance.

Where the balance on the special rate pool reduces to less than £1,000, the full balance may then be claimed immediately in the same way as for the main pool.

3.16 CAPITAL ALLOWANCES ON MOTOR VEHICLES

Capital allowances are generally available on motor vehicles used in a business. Vans and motorcycles are usually eligible for the same allowances as other plant and machinery, as described in Section 3.15 (but see Section 3.17 where there is some private use). Most cars are not eligible for the AIA, but do have their own system of writing down allowances.

There are effectively two different capital allowances regimes for cars. The first regime applies to:

i)   Cars provided to employees,
ii)   Cars owned by a company, and
iii)   Other cars that are wholly used for business purposes

Cars falling under headings (i) and (ii) are referred to as 'company cars'. For full details of the capital allowances regime applying to company cars, see the Taxcafe.co.uk guide *Using a Property Company to Save Tax'*.

Cars falling under heading (iii) are pretty rare as this means the car is owned and used by the owner of the business and there is absolutely no private use of the vehicle. In over thirty years as a tax adviser, I have never encountered such a car.

For the rest of this section, we will therefore concentrate purely on the second regime: i.e. cars owned and used by the business owner themselves, and which have some element of private use.

These cars must each be put in their own individual pool for capital allowances purposes. The rate of writing down allowances available depends on the car's CO emissions and date of purchase, as follows:

- Cars with CO_2 emissions over the 'higher threshold' at the date of purchase attract writing down allowances of just 6% (reduced from 8% with effect from 6th April 2019). The transitional rules for the 'special rate pool' (see Section 3.15) apply in the same way on this expenditure where the accounting period straddles 6th April 2019.

- Cars with CO_2 emissions over the 'lower threshold', but not over the 'higher threshold', at the date of purchase attract writing down allowances of 18%.

The 'higher threshold' is currently 110g/km. For cars purchased between 6th April 2013 and 31st March 2018 it was 130g/km; for cars purchased before 6th April 2013 it was 160g/km.

The 'lower threshold' is currently 50g/km. For cars purchased between 1st April 2015 and 31st March 2018 it was 75g/km; for cars purchased between 1st April 2013 and 31st March 2015 it was 95g/km; for cars purchased before 1st April 2013 it was 110g/km.

The rate of writing down allowances applying is determined when the car is purchased. The same regime continues to apply in later years regardless of subsequent movements in the thresholds. For example, a car purchased in March 2018 with 120g/km of CO_2 emissions will continue to attract writing down allowances of 18% in later years, even though the 'higher threshold' has now been reduced to 110g/km; but a car with the same level of emissions purchased after 31st March 2018 will only attract writing down allowances at 6% (8% prior to 6th April 2019).

The allowances must be restricted to reflect the element of private use. For example, a car purchased in March 2020 for £20,000 that has 115g/km of CO_2 emissions and 80% private use will be eligible for an allowance of £240 (6% x £20,000 = £1,200 less 80%).

A car purchased in March 2020 for £10,000 that has 60g/km of CO_2 emissions and 75% private use will be eligible for an allowance of £450 (18% x £10,000 = £1,800 less 75%).

Note that the unrelieved balance of expenditure to be carried forward to the next period is calculated before the deduction in respect of private use.

'Green' Cars (I'm talking about environmentally friendly cars here, not the colour of the paintwork!)

Cars with CO_2 emissions of no more than the 'lower threshold' (see above) currently attract a 100% first year allowance. The usual restriction for private use still applies and a balancing charge (see below) will continue to apply on disposal of the car.

The 'lower threshold' is expected to remain at 50g/km until 31st March 2021, after which the 100% first year allowance for low emission cars is expected to be abolished.

Balancing Allowances and Charges

When a car with private use is disposed of, a balancing allowance, or charge, will arise, reflecting the difference between the disposal proceeds and the unrelieved balance of expenditure.

A balancing allowance, like any other capital allowance, is a deduction from taxable income. A balancing charge is added to taxable income. Balancing allowances and charges on cars with private use are subject to the same restriction in respect of private use as writing down allowances.

Summary of Capital Allowances on Cars with Private Use

To summarise the position, let's look at an example.

Example
In January 2020, Kenneth buys a car for £25,000 and uses it 40% for his property business and 60% privately. The car has 136g/km of CO_2 emissions.

In his accounts for the year to 5th April 2020, Kenneth claims a writing down allowance of £600 (£25,000 x 6% x 40%). However, the unrelieved balance carried forward to the next year is just £23,500 (£25,000 – 6%).

For the year ending 5th April 2021, Kenneth is able to claim a writing down allowance of £564 (£23,500 x 6% x 40%). The unrelieved balance carried forward this time is £22,090 (£23,500 – 6%).

In February 2022, Kenneth sells the car for £15,000. This gives rise to a balancing allowance of £2,836 (£22,090 - £15,000 = £7,090 x 40%).

Note that, if Kenneth had sold the car for more than £22,090 (the unrelieved balance of expenditure), he would have been subject to a balancing charge. The charge in this case would have been 40% of the excess of the sale price over £22,090.

3.17 ASSETS WITH PRIVATE USE

The capital allowances regime for cars examined in Section 3.16 is echoed to some extent in the case of other assets with both business and private use purchased and used by a business owner.

All such assets must each be placed in their own capital allowances pool, or 'puddle', as I like to call them. The writing down allowances on these 'puddles' will be at either 6% or 18%, as appropriate (see Section 3.15).

A suitable deduction must be made in respect of the private use of the asset. The unrelieved balance on the 'puddle' carried forward to the next period is again calculated before taking account of this deduction.

Balances under £1,000 in 'puddles' cannot be written off like similar small balances in the main or special rate pools (see Section 3.15)

The AIA remains available on assets (other than cars) with an element of private use. The allowance must, however, be restricted to reflect the private use, so the AIA should generally be allocated to other expenditure first, where possible.

The great advantage/disadvantage of the 'puddle' is that a balancing allowance/charge will arise when each asset is disposed of. These balancing allowances or charges are calculated in exactly the same way as for a car with private use, as explained in Section 3.16. Claiming the AIA on assets with private use will naturally mean that a balancing charge arises whenever any proceeds are received on the disposal of those assets.

3.18 FURTHER POINTS ON CAPITAL ALLOWANCES

Before we move on to the structures and buildings allowance, it is worth making a few further points regarding capital allowances on plant and machinery and motor vehicles. Note that the points in this section relate to the allowances covered in Sections 3.15 to 3.17 and do not apply to the structures and buildings allowance or expenditure that qualifies for it.

Both the AIA and all writing down allowances, including allowances on motor cars, are restricted if the business starts part-way through the year or, in the case of a trading business, if accounts are drawn up for a period of less than twelve months.

Writing down allowances may be claimed on used assets the taxpayer introduces into the business, based on their market value at the date of introduction. For example, if a taxpayer has an old computer that they have had for many years and begins using it for business purposes, they may claim writing down allowances on the computer based on its value at that date. The usual deduction for private use continues to apply where appropriate.

Where a car is introduced into the business, the same principles apply, but the date of introduction is used to determine the rate of writing down allowances, rather than the original date of purchase. The 100% first year allowance for low emission cars is not available on a used car.

The AIA is not available on used assets that the taxpayer introduces into the business, or on assets acquired from connected persons (see Appendix B).

None of the usual allowances on plant and machinery or motor vehicles are available in the year that a business ceases. A balancing allowance or charge will apply instead, based on the difference between the unrelieved balance of expenditure and the value of the remaining assets at the date of cessation.

Assets bought on hire purchase continue to be eligible for capital allowances as normal but must be brought into use in the business before the end of the accounting period.

Subject to the above points, the full allowance due is available on any business asset purchased part-way through the year, even on the last day.

Any sale proceeds received for assets used wholly in the business are deducted from the balance on the main pool or special rate pool, as appropriate. Where this gives rise to a negative balance, a balancing charge will arise.

Since the advent of the AIA, most small businesses now have little or no balance of unrelieved expenditure left in their main or special rate pools. Hence, there is a strong chance of a balancing charge arising whenever any asset is sold: unless it is replaced by another qualifying asset of equal or greater value within the same accounting period.

Notwithstanding any of the above, where the disposal proceeds or market value of an asset that ceases to be used in the business exceeds the amount originally claimed for capital allowances purposes (before any private use deduction), the amount of proceeds or market value used in the relevant calculation is restricted to the amount originally claimed.

Capital Allowance Disclaimers

Apart from balancing allowances and charges, capital allowances are not mandatory. The amount of allowance available is effectively a maximum that may be claimed and the taxpayer may claim any amount between zero and that maximum each year.

Why claim less than the maximum?

> **Tax Tip**
> If your total taxable income is less than your personal allowance, any capital allowances you claim may be wasted. Instead, it will generally be better to claim a lower amount of allowances in order to fully utilise your personal allowance against your income (or as much as possible).
>
> The unrelieved balance of expenditure carried forward will then be greater, giving you higher capital allowances next year when, hopefully, they will actually save you some tax!

Some possible exceptions to the above 'tax tip' may arise where your property business is making losses and you are able to obtain tax relief for your capital allowances in a different period. See Sections 4.12 and 5.1.

Note that if a 100% AIA or first year allowance is disclaimed, the expenditure will only attract writing down allowances at the appropriate rate in the following year.

3.19 THE STRUCTURES AND BUILDINGS ALLOWANCE

The structures and buildings allowance ('SBA') applies to expenditure on the construction, renovation, improvement or conversion of qualifying non-residential property after 28th October 2018. It is available to landlords renting out non-residential property, as well as businesses using commercial property in their own trade or profession.

The SBA is given as a straight-line allowance at 2% per annum on the qualifying cost. The main provisos are:

- All contracts for construction works on the relevant project must have been entered into after 28th October 2018
- The structure or building is used in a business chargeable to UK Income Tax or Corporation Tax; including a trade, profession, or 'ordinary' property business (i.e. not a furnished holiday let)
- The cost of land, including rights over land, does not qualify
- Property in residential use does not qualify (see further below)

Where any contract for the construction of a property was entered into before 29th October 2018 then the first point above means the SBA cannot be claimed on the property itself. However, this does not prevent later projects for renovation, conversion or improvement work to the property from qualifying.

SBA is limited to the 'net direct costs relating to physically constructing the asset'. Where relevant, this will include demolition costs, the costs of land alterations or preparations necessary for the construction and other direct costs of bringing the structure or building into existence. However, in addition to excluding the cost of land, SBA does not cover:

- SDLT and other purchase costs
- Costs of obtaining planning permission
- Other land alterations beyond what is necessary for the construction (e.g. landscaping, although landscaping that results in the creation of a separate structure does qualify)
- Land reclamation
- Land remediation (a separate relief is sometimes available for this cost)

The SBA cannot be claimed on expenditure that qualifies for plant and machinery allowances, including 'integral features' and other qualifying fixtures (see Section 4.9).

The SBA claim generally commences on the later of:

a)   The date the expenditure is incurred, and
b)   The date the building/structure is first brought into qualifying use

However, in the case of renovations or improvements to property already in qualifying use, the claim may commence on any of:

i)   The last day works are carried out in relation to the project,
ii)   The first day of the next accounting period commencing after (i), or
iii)   The first day of the next accounting period after the day the expenditure is incurred

For example, a landlord drawing up accounts to 5th April each year, who carries out improvements to a rented commercial property over the period from January to 30th June 2020, may choose to claim the SBA:

- From 30th June 2020 using option (i),
- From 6th April 2021 using option (ii), or
- From 6th April 2020 for expenditure incurred up to 5th April 2020 and from 6th April 2021 for the remainder, using option (iii)

Expenditure incurred prior to the commencement of the owner's business is treated as if it were incurred on the date of commencement. Unlike the pre-trading rules for expenditure that is not capital in nature, there is no limit to how long prior to commencement the expenditure was incurred (subject to the rule that all contracts must have been entered into after 28th October 2018, as stated above).

The SBA is reduced on a time apportionment basis:

- In any period of less than twelve months' duration,
- If the building or structure had not yet been brought into qualifying use at the beginning of the period, or
- Where the SBA claim commences part way through the period (as detailed above)

The current owner may continue to claim the SBA where a property falls into disuse, provided the property was in qualifying use immediately beforehand. However, a new owner must bring the property into qualifying use before they can claim the SBA.

For property investment businesses, a property is in 'qualifying use' when it is being let out at full market rent. The existing owner may continue to claim the SBA during a void that follows a period of 'qualifying use', but a new owner must let the property out (at full market rent) before they may claim the SBA. In all cases, the property must not be in residential use (see below).

The SBA ceases on the fiftieth anniversary of the date the claim first commenced (although this cannot occur until at least 2068, so I strongly suspect we will see changes that render this point obsolete long before then!) The SBA also ceases if a qualifying building or structure is demolished.

When a building or structure is sold, entitlement to the SBA transfers to the new owner. The SBA available for the year of sale is apportioned between the seller and purchaser, with the seller retaining entitlement for the day of transfer. There are no balancing allowances or charges at the point of sale.

Where a qualifying property is purchased from a developer, SBA may be claimed on the purchase price, but with an appropriate exclusion for the cost of the land. The date of purchase is the date the expenditure is incurred in these cases.

Example 1

Emmanuel purchases a new office building from a developer for £2.3m. £450,000 of this cost relates to the land, and £250,000 represents 'integral features' and other fixtures qualifying as 'plant and machinery' (see Section 4.9), so the amount qualifying for SBA is £1.6m. Emmanuel has a 5th April year end and starts to rent out the building on 1st April 2020.

In February 2024, Emmanuel's tenants move out and the building is left empty. On 30th June 2024, he sells it to Beatrice for £2.5m. She finds a tenant and rents the building out from 1st October 2024. In 2028, she has some improvement work carried out. The work is completed on 16th November and costs a total of £1m, of which £150,000 qualifies as 'plant and machinery' for capital allowances purposes, leaving £850,000 qualifying for SBA. Beatrice sells the building to the Modena Relief Foundation for £3m on 31st August 2030. Her accounting year end is also 5th April.

The Modena Relief Foundation is a charity, so it is unable to claim any allowance. It retains the building for many years until eventually selling it to Theresa for £7.5m on 31st December 2067. Theresa uses the building as the headquarters of her property development business for many years. She draws up accounts to 30th June 2068, then to 31st December each year from 2069 onwards.

The annual SBA available on the original building is £32,000 (£1.6m x 2%). The additional annual SBA on the improvements carried out in 2028 is £17,000 (£850,000 x 2%). The following SBA claims may be made:

Emmanuel

2019/20	£32,000 x 5/366 =	£437	(Note 2)
2020/21 to 2023/24		£32,000 per year	(Note 3)
2024/25	£32,000 x 86/365 =	£7,540	(Note 3)

Beatrice

2024/25	£32,000 x 187/365 =	£16,395	(Note 4)
2025/26 to 2027/28		£32,000 per year	
2028/29	£32,000 + £17,000 x 141/365 =	£38,567	(Note 5)
2029/30	£32,000 + £17,000 =	£49,000	(Note 6)
2030/31	£49,000 x 148/365 =	£19,868	(Note 7)

Theresa

Y/e 30/6/2068	£49,000 x 182/366 =	£24,366	(Note 8)
P/e 31/12/2069	£49,000 x 549/365 =	£73,701	(Note 9)
Y/e 31/12/2070	£32,000 x 90/365 + £17,000 =	£24,890	(Note 10)
2071 to 2077		£17,000 per year	(Note 11)
Y/e 31/12/2078	£17,000 x 319/365 =	£14,858	(Note 11)

Notes

1. It is assumed all Emmanuel and Beatrice's tenants pay full market rent
2. Emmanuel's claim starts on 1st April 2020, the day he first rents out the building.
3. Emmanuel's claim continues while the building is unused, up to the date of sale on 30th June 2024.
4. Beatrice's claim cannot commence until she rents out the property for the first time, on 1st October 2024. Her claim is based on Emmanuel's original expenditure and is unaffected by the price she paid to purchase the building.
5. Beatrice can use option (i) above to claim SBA on her improvement expenditure from 16th November 2028 onwards. She needs to be renting the property out on this date for this expenditure to qualify, otherwise her claim on **this** expenditure would not commence until she next rents the property out.
6. The annual claim on both Emmanuel's original cost and Beatrice's improvement expenditure now totals £49,000.
7. Beatrice's claim continues until the date of sale on 31st August 2030.
8. Theresa's claim commences as soon as she brings the property into use in her business; it is based on the original expenditure incurred by Emmanuel and Beatrice and is unaffected by the purchase price paid by Theresa or the Modena Relief Foundation.
9. The claim for the eighteen month period ending 31st December 2069 is increased on a pro rata basis.
10. The claim on the building's original cost comes to an end after fifty years.
11. The claim on the improvement expenditure continues until the day before the fiftieth anniversary of the date that part of the claim commenced, i.e. until 15th November 2078.

The allowances claimed by Emmanuel, Beatrice and Theresa add up to a total of £612,622, but a further £1,837,378 of 'notional allowances' reduced the building's written down value while Beatrice was waiting to rent it out (from 1st June to 30th September 2024) and while it was held by the Modena Relief Foundation. As a result, the written down value of the original cost was reduced to nil on 31st March 2070, fifty years after Emmanuel first brought it into use; and the written down value of the improvement expenditure was reduced to nil on 15th November 2078, fifty years after those works were completed.

Whether, in practice, the information will be available to enable Theresa to make her claims in the 2060s and 2070s is uncertain, but technically she will be eligible (assuming the SBA regime lasts that long).

As noted above, the prices paid for the property on subsequent sales are irrelevant. SBA is based on the original cost of the building and the cost of any subsequent improvements.

Where the person who incurs the qualifying expenditure is not in charge to UK tax, or not using the property in a qualifying business, subsequent owners may still claim the SBA provided the first use of the property after the qualifying expenditure is not residential use. However, the first use of the property will still determine when the fifty year period allowed for the claim comes to an end.

Residential Use

The SBA is not available when a property is in residential use. This includes:

- A dwelling house (i.e. normal residential property including houses, flats, apartments, etc.)
- Residential accommodation for school pupils
- Student accommodation (property that was either purpose built or converted for student use and is available for occupation by students at least 165 days per year)
- Residential accommodation for the armed forces
- Homes providing residential accommodation (but see the exception below)
- Prisons or similar institutions

There is an exception for care homes providing residential accommodation together with personal care for the elderly, disabled, people with mental disorders, or people suffering from alcohol or drugs dependency.

A 'dwelling house' is a building, or part of a building, which has all the facilities required for normal day to day living. Typically, therefore, hotel rooms do not usually constitute dwellings and a hotel would usually qualify for the SBA. A guest house would, however, usually be a dwelling house and would not usually qualify for the SBA.

Any structure on land in residential use, such as the garden or grounds of a house, is itself deemed to be in residential use. Additional facilities provided with serviced apartments (such as a gym or swimming pool) are also deemed to be in residential use and excluded from the SBA.

If the first use of a property following the qualifying expenditure is residential (as defined above), the SBA will never be available on that expenditure. Later expenditure on the same property might qualify, however.

Example 2
Catherine purchases a block of flats from a developer in March 2020 and starts to rent it out. No SBA is available on the cost of the flats as they are in residential use. In 2022, she spends £250,000 converting the bottom two floors of the block into shops and offices. The SBA will be available on the conversion costs giving Catherine a tax deduction of £5,000 (£250,000 x 2%) per year.

Where a building or structure has both qualifying and non-qualifying use, the qualifying costs must be apportioned and the SBA may be claimed on an appropriate proportion. However, no relief is available:

- On workplaces within a dwelling house
- Where the proportion in qualifying use is 'insignificant' (generally taken to mean 10% or less)

Example 3
Sofia purchases a property from the local authority for £800,000. The property was originally constructed in 2020 at a cost of £960,000. The property has six storeys, with shops on the ground floor and flats in the floors above. Sofia may therefore claim an annual SBA of £3,200 (£960,000 x 1/6 x 2%).

Note that Sofia's claim is based on the original cost of the property and is unaffected by the fact the original owner was not in charge to tax. The SBA claim will, however, cease on the fiftieth anniversary of the date the local authority first brought the property into use.

The Allowance Statement

SBA claims require an 'allowance statement'. This is a written statement identifying the relevant building or structure, together with:

a)   The date of the earliest written contract relating to the relevant project
b)   The amount of qualifying expenditure
c)   The date the property was first brought into qualifying use

The owner who incurs the qualifying expenditure makes the allowance statement. Subsequent owners must obtain a copy of the statement.

Further Points

Where the owner grants a lease for thirty-five years or more at a premium then the right to claim the SBA on the property transfers to the tenant if the element of the premium treated as a capital disposal for tax purposes (see Section 4.14) is at least three times greater than the value of the owner's reversionary interest in the property.

A tenant will also be able to claim the SBA on any qualifying expenditure that they incur themselves, regardless of the length of their lease.

The SBA is available on both UK and overseas property (provided the property is used in a business chargeable to UK Income Tax or Corporation Tax).

The claimant must have a relevant legal interest in the land on which the building or structure is located (e.g. a freehold or leasehold interest).

Unclaimed relief is simply lost and cannot be carried forward.

The amount of qualifying expenditure for the purposes of the SBA is subject to a market value 'cap'. In other words, expenditure in excess of market value does not qualify. This rule is only likely to be relevant where work is carried out by a connected party.

Impact on Capital Gains

The amount of SBA claimed by a seller must be added to their sale proceeds for the purposes of calculating the chargeable gain arising on a disposal of the property. Hence, in Example 1 above, when Emmanuel sold the property, the total SBA of £135,977 that he claimed during his ownership would be added to his sale proceeds, increasing them from £2.5m to £2,635,977 and giving him a chargeable gain of £335,977 (£2,635,977 less £2.3m).

The relief provided by the SBA is therefore effectively clawed back on the sale of a property. Nonetheless, SBA claims will nearly always remain worthwhile for individuals or partnerships, since they will generally provide Income Tax relief at much higher rates than the CGT arising on the eventual sale.

Where a property is transferred by way of a 'no gain/no loss' transfer, the transferee will also have to add the SBA claimed by the transferor to any future sale proceeds on the ultimate disposal of the property. The most common incidence of a 'no gain/no loss' transfer is a transfer between spouses (see Section 6.7).

A holdover relief claim on a transfer will have a similar, although slightly different effect, as the SBA claimed by the transferor will effectively be deducted from the cost of the property.

3.20 THE TAX RELIEF 'CAP'

There is an annual limit on the total combined amount of Income Tax relief available under a number of different reliefs. The total amount which any individual may claim under all these reliefs taken together in any tax year is limited to the greater of £50,000 or 25% of their 'adjusted total income' (see below).

The Affected Reliefs

Ten different reliefs are affected. The most important ones for property investors to be aware of are:

- Property loss relief
- Relief for trading losses against other income
- Qualifying loan interest
- Share loss relief

'Property loss relief' refers to your ability to set capital allowances within UK rental losses or overseas rental losses against your other income for the same tax year or the next one (see Sections 4.12 and 4.15).

Individuals with trading losses can set them off against their other income in the same tax year or the previous one. Additional relief applies in the early years of a trade. (See Section 5.11 for further details)

'Qualifying loan interest' is the relief which is given for interest on personal borrowings used to invest funds in a qualifying company (or partnership). This relief will often be claimed by property investors who invest via a company and is covered in detail in the Taxcafe.co.uk guide *'Using a Property Company to Save Tax'*.

'Share loss relief' applies in limited circumstances and allows owners of some private companies to claim Income Tax relief for losses on their shares. Sadly, it is not usually available for losses on property company shares.

Adjusted Total Income

Broadly speaking, 'adjusted total income' means an individual's total taxable income for the year in which relief is being claimed; after deducting gross pension contributions (including tax relief given at source); but before deducting any other reliefs.

3.21 MAKING TAX DIGITAL

The Government is planning to make fundamental changes to the way most UK businesses must keep their business records and report their results to HMRC. This includes landlords with rental income. The proposed new system is called 'making tax digital', or 'MTD' for short.

> **Practical Pointer – The Good News!**
> With the exception of some new requirements for VAT-registered businesses (see Section 7.12) it now seems likely that MTD will not be introduced until at least April 2022, possibly later.

Initially, the Government proposed to make MTD compulsory for most sole trader or partnership businesses (including landlords) with total gross income (before deducting expenses) of £10,000 or more. However, it is now difficult to predict exactly what form MTD will eventually take and who will be required to operate it. Nonetheless, it is still worth taking a brief look at the initial proposals, as it remains possible that many businesses (including landlords) could be required to operate the new system as early as April 2022.

The initial proposals were that all businesses (including landlords) to which MTD applied would be required to:

i) Keep their accounting records in a 'digital' format
ii) Report their results to HMRC on a quarterly basis, four times a year using an online digital reporting system. Results would have to be reported within one month of the end of the quarter

The Government accepts that accounting records kept on spreadsheets are sufficient to meet the digital requirements of MTD: provided that specialised bridging software is linked to those spreadsheets and used to report the results digitally.

The quarterly reports required under MTD were to be simpler than a full set of accounts and would only need to be in summary format. Some accounting adjustments, such as accounting for trading stock and accruing for costs not yet paid would not have been mandatory for quarterly reporting, merely optional. This approach would have simplified the process but also distorted the results.

Instead of completing a tax return, each business owner would have a period of nine months after their accounting period to finalise their accounts, submit adjustments to HMRC, and make a final declaration that the accounts were correct.

While we may see some changes to these proposals if and when MTD is eventually introduced, they currently remain our best guide to what any new system might look like.

Chapter 4

Saving Income Tax on a Property Investment Business

4.1 THE TAXATION OF RENTAL INCOME

In many respects, property letting is treated much like any other business for Income Tax purposes, but it also has many quirks that set it apart. In essence, it is treated as a business, but not as a trade, and this leads to some fundamental differences in tax treatment, as we shall see to both our frustration and our delight.

For tax purposes, property letting needs to be divided into four categories:

- 'Normal' UK property letting
- 'Normal' overseas property letting
- UK furnished holiday letting
- Other furnished holiday letting within the EEA (see Section 1.5)

'Normal' in this context simply means anything other than furnished holiday letting in the UK or the EEA.

Each of these four categories is effectively treated as a separate business. Most of the rules we will examine in this chapter apply equally to each category, but there are a few variations applying to overseas property (see Section 4.15) and furnished holiday lets (see Section 8.17).

Each of the four categories needs to be accounted for and reported on your tax return separately. Hence, you will need to draw up accounts for each category to detail all your income and relevant expenses. However, all the properties within each category are effectively regarded as a single business.

'Normal' UK property letting is generally referred to as a 'UK property business' and 'normal' overseas property letting is generally referred to as an 'overseas property business'. So, for example, if you are letting a number of UK properties on a commercial basis (none of which are furnished holiday lets), this will be treated as a single UK property business and one set of accounts will usually suffice (although many landlords prefer to have a separate set of accounts for each property).

Separate accounts will, however, be required for any non-commercial lettings (see Section 4.16) within any of the four categories.

All rental income must be included within the appropriate category, no matter how modest the source, unless it is fully covered by the 'rent-a-room' scheme (see Section 4.11) or the property income allowance (see Section 4.17).

Technically, landlords may draw up accounts for any period. Unlike other types of business, however, landlords must generally be taxed on the rental profits arising for the tax year running from 6th April to the following 5th April. Hence, while landlords could draw up accounts for a different period and then 'time apportion' the results to produce appropriate figures for the tax year, this would seldom produce any significant advantage and it is far simpler to just produce accounts for the year ending 5th April. This, therefore, is what most landlords do.

Many landlords have the option to choose whether to use traditional 'accruals basis' accounting, or to adopt the 'cash basis'. Indeed, for those who qualify, the cash basis is the default option and those who wish to use the accruals basis need to opt out.

In Section 4.18, we will look at the cash basis for landlords, who qualifies for it, and some of its advantages and disadvantages. On balance, however, my view is that the cash basis will generally be disadvantageous for landlords and for this reason, unless specifically stated to the contrary, it is assumed throughout the rest of this guide that landlords are preparing accounts under the accruals basis.

Nonetheless, for those who qualify for the cash basis, it is worth considering as an option, as it will be advantageous in some cases.

Landlords under the Accruals Basis

Under the accruals basis, income and expenditure is recognised when it arises, or is incurred, rather than when it is received or paid. For example, if you started renting out a property on 12th March 2020, at a monthly rent of £1,000, the income you need to recognise in your accounts for the year ending 5th April 2020 is:

$$£1,000 \times 12 \times 25/366 = £819.67$$

(You are renting it for 25 days in the 2019/20 tax year, which is 366 days in length)

Expenses should also be recognised as they are incurred (see Section 3.9).

4.2   DEDUCTIBLE EXPENDITURE

The rules on what types of expenditure may be claimed as deductions in a property letting business are generally similar to those for other types of business, although there are some important differences. Some of the main deductions include:

- Interest and finance costs (but see Section 4.5)
- Property maintenance and repair costs
- Heating and lighting costs, if borne by the landlord
- Insurance costs
- Letting agent's fees
- Advertising for tenants
- Accountancy fees
- Legal and professional fees
- The cost of cleaners, gardeners, etc, where relevant
- Ground rent, service charges, etc.
- Bad debts
- Pre-trading expenditure
- Landlord's administrative expenditure

If your tenant contributes part of an otherwise allowable expense, you may claim only the net amount that you actually bear yourself.

In the next few sections, we will take a closer look at some of the more common areas of expenditure typically encountered in property letting businesses and examine what determines whether these expenses may be deducted for Income Tax purposes. Please note, however, this is not an exhaustive list, and other types of expenditure that meet the general principles outlined in Section 3.9 will often be allowable. The administrative expenses described in Sections 3.10 to 3.13 should also not be forgotten (in my experience, they often are!)

4.3   WHEN IS A PROPERTY A RENTAL PROPERTY?

You will frequently see me refer to 'rental property'. Whether a property is a 'rental property' at any given time is often crucial in determining whether (or how much of) an item of expenditure is allowable.

Quite obviously, a property is a rental property while it is rented out. For most tax purposes, a property is usually also a 'rental property' when it is:

- Available for letting but currently vacant
- Being prepared for letting
- Being renovated between lettings, with the intention of letting it out again thereafter

In each case, the property's 'rental property' status would be lost if it was actually used for something else (e.g. a family holiday for the owner's spouse and children). Nevertheless, merely sleeping there overnight, while redecorating the property for subsequent rental, should not usually harm the property's status.

Strictly, for Income Tax purposes, a vacant property ceases to be a rental property once a decision is taken to sell it. In practice, however, this rule will not usually be applied where the period between the decision and the sale is relatively brief.

HMRC generally regards the day on which your first rental property within each category (see Section 4.1) is let out for the first time as the first day of your property letting business.

However, any eligible expenditure incurred within the seven year period before your first rental property in the category is first let should remain claimable as 'pre-trading expenditure' (see Section 3.9). This sometimes means the expenditure must be claimed in a later tax year.

Eligible expenses relating to your second, and subsequent, rental properties within each category may generally be claimed as incurred, even if the relevant property is not let by the end of that tax year.

Remember, however, that you have to treat each of the four categories described in Section 4.1 as separate businesses. Hence, a first overseas rental gets treated as a 'first property' even if you already have a portfolio of UK properties. The same goes for your first UK rental when you have a portfolio of overseas properties; your first furnished holiday let; etc.

4.4   INTEREST AND FINANCE COSTS

As most property investors know, there are now restrictions on the **rate** of tax relief available to residential landlords for interest and finance costs. I will look at those restrictions, often known as the wretched 'Section 24', in Section 4.5. Firstly, however, I am going to look at **which** interest and finance costs are eligible to be claimed in the first place.

When Can Interest be Claimed?

Interest is allowable and may be claimed against rental income if it is incurred for the purposes of the property business. There are two ways this can occur:

i)   The interest arises on funds that have been utilised in the business, **or**
ii)   The interest arises on capital introduced into the business

The Capital Introduced Principle

The second heading above provides enormous scope for property investors to claim interest relief for Income Tax purposes.

When a property is rented out for the first time, the value of the property at that date represents capital introduced into the business.

Any other capital expenditure incurred on a rental property also represents capital introduced into the business, including SDLT and legal fees paid on the purchase and the cost of furnishing the property, where relevant. The fact that a deduction cannot generally be claimed for these expenses does not prevent them from being capital introduced into the business.

Hence, subject to 'the catch' explained below, interest relief will generally be available on any borrowings against a rental property up to its original value when first rented out PLUS all the other capital expenditure incurred in purchasing it and preparing it for letting. *It does not matter what the borrowed funds are used for!*

Later, additional, capital expenditure on a rental property, such as capital improvements, counts as further capital introduced (see Section 4.7 regarding the difference between repairs and capital improvements). You cannot double-count the same expenditure, however. For example, if you build an extension on a property before letting it out, its value when first rented out will be increased by this expenditure, so you cannot add it on again as further capital introduced.

For borrowings in excess of the capital introduced in respect of a property, we must rely on the first heading above. In other words, interest relief on these additional borrowings will only be available if the borrowed funds are used for business purposes. (Note that some interest arising under the first heading alone may not be allowable if the landlord is using the cash basis – see Section 4.18 for further details.)

Example 1
Matthew buys an investment property for £100,000 and immediately begins to rent it out unfurnished. He finances his original purchase with a buy-to-let mortgage of £75,000 and pays the remainder in cash. He also pays SDLT of £3,000 and legal fees of £800. Naturally, he is able to claim relief for the interest on his buy-to-let mortgage against his rental income from the property.

A few years later, Matthew re-mortgages the property and borrows an additional £30,000 to bring his total borrowings up to £105,000. He spends the new funds on personal items not related to his property business. Despite having spent the new funds on personal items, Matthew remains entitled to interest relief against his rental income for the first £103,800 of his borrowings: i.e. an amount equal to the property's value when he first rented it out plus the SDLT and legal fees

85

paid on the purchase. The last £1,200 of his borrowings are not eligible for relief, however, as these are in excess of the amount of capital introduced into the business and have not been used for other business purposes either.

After a few more years, Matthew borrows a further £22,000 against the property. This time, he spends £12,000 taking his partner on a luxury cruise but uses £10,000 to improve another rental property. He cannot claim any interest relief on the £12,000 used personally as this does not represent capital introduced into the business. He can claim interest relief on the £10,000 used to improve another rental property as this has been used for business purposes.

Matthew therefore now has a total of £113,800 of eligible borrowings for interest relief purposes out of his overall total of £127,000. (We will look at how investors should calculate their interest relief in this type of situation later.)

Another way to look at the position for interest relief is that:

i)   Borrowings against a rental property up to a sum equal to the original value of that property when first rented out PLUS any other capital expenditure relating to that property are generally allowable (subject to avoiding any 'double-counting' and also 'the catch' described below)

ii)   Other borrowings are allowable when the funds are used for business purposes

Interest will therefore always be allowable if it arises on funds used to purchase or improve rental properties or otherwise expended for the purposes of the property business (subject to the points set out in Section 4.18 where landlords are using the cash basis).

Example 2
Mark takes out a personal loan and spends the funds on improvements to a flat that he subsequently lets out. The interest on his loan is allowable because it has been incurred for the purpose of his property business.

Example 3
Luke has a large property rental business and employs several staff. While the business is generally buoyant, Luke runs into cashflow difficulties in January 2020 and has to borrow an extra £5,000 to pay his staff's wages. Luke's borrowings were used for business purposes and hence the interest he incurs will be allowable for tax purposes.

Example 4
John borrows an extra £50,000 by re-mortgaging his home. He uses these funds for the deposits on two new rental properties. John may claim the interest on the £50,000 of new borrowing as it has been used for business purposes.

Practical Pointer

In a case like John's in our last example, there will usually be the practical difficulty of establishing just how much interest should be claimed. John will already have an outstanding balance on his mortgage, so it would not be right for him to claim all his interest. In practice, we must do an apportionment.

Example 4 Resumed

Prior to re-mortgaging, John had a balance of £120,000 on the mortgage on his home. The extra £50,000 took that balance up to £170,000. John should therefore claim 50/170ths of his mortgage interest for tax purposes.

Repayment Mortgages

Interest calculations are fairly straightforward in the case of an interest-only mortgage, but what about repayment mortgages? The first and most important point to note is that you can only claim relief for the interest element of your loan or mortgage payments. The capital repayment element may not be claimed. Your mortgage provider will usually send you an annual statement detailing the interest charged.

Where you have a repayment mortgage that is only partly allowable for business purposes, an apportionment must be made, as outlined above. However, as you repay capital, the total outstanding balance on the account will reduce, so how do you do your apportionment then? The usual approach is to stick with the apportionment ratio you derived when you first did the re-mortgaging (e.g. 50/170ths in John's case).

Some, more aggressive, accountants might suggest all repayments should be treated as repaying the original 'non-business' element of the loan. This approach may, however, be subject to challenge by HMRC.

Tax Tip

To maximise the business element within your interest payments, arrange for the new funds obtained on re-mortgaging to be allocated to a separate mortgage loan account with the bank. Make the new account interest-only, while leaving the original mortgage account as a repayment account.

In this way, you can put beyond doubt the fact that the capital repayment element belongs exclusively to the 'non-business' part of your mortgage.

'The Catch': What Counts as 'Capital Introduced'?

Our last example raises another important point. John was able to claim interest relief for part of the mortgage on his home because he had spent the funds for business purposes: as deposits on rental properties.

Those deposits, however, also count as part of the capital introduced into the business. In other words, this restricts the investor's ability to obtain further relief for additional borrowings against the rental property.

Let's say John used £25,000 from the mortgage on his home as a deposit on a buy-to-let property purchased for £90,000 and the other £65,000 was made up of £5,000 in cash and £60,000 from a buy-to-let mortgage. Let's also assume John paid a further £3,500 in purchase costs (SDLT, legal fees, etc).

Hence, at this stage, as far as this property is concerned, John has introduced capital of £93,500 into his property business (i.e. the value of the rental property plus his purchase costs), but is already claiming interest relief on borrowings of £85,000 – i.e. the buy-to-let mortgage of £60,000 and £25,000 of the additional mortgage on his home.

John can therefore only automatically claim interest relief on further borrowings against the rental property of just £8,500 – i.e. the same amount he originally funded in cash (£5,000 + £3,500). Any further borrowings will only be eligible for interest relief if the funds are used for business purposes.

What John can do, however, is borrow further funds against his rental properties to repay some or all of the additional £50,000 mortgage on his home. This would mean he was replacing one qualifying loan with another, so he would continue to obtain interest relief on the new borrowings.

HMRC's Changing View on the Capital Introduced Principle

For many years, HMRC was happy to accept the principles outlined above. Then, for a period of a couple of years or so, they began to dispute the 'capital introduced' principle in cases where additional borrowings had been used for non-business purposes (see the previous edition of this guide for details of the potential impact of this change of view).

Thankfully, recent revisions to HMRC's manuals appear to have restored their previous view, and suggest they now accept the 'capital introduced' principle once again. Property investors should therefore be able to claim relief for interest costs under the principles described above without any difficulty. If any problems do arise over this issue, refer HMRC to Example 2 in BIM 45700 in their own manuals.

What Happens When Properties Are Sold Or Cease to Be Used In The Business?

Interest on borrowings used to finance the purchase or improvement of a property will generally cease to be allowable if that property ceases to be used in the rental business (e.g. if it is subsequently adopted as the owner's residence).

However, the eligibility of the interest for tax relief will follow the use of the underlying funds. Consider this example:

Example 5
In 2020, Abel borrows £50,000 secured on his own home, Eden Cottage, and uses the money to buy a rental property, Babel Heights. At this stage, the interest on his £50,000 loan is clearly allowable.

A few years later, in 2023, Abel sells Babel Heights and uses the sale proceeds to buy a new rental property, Ark Villa. Abel's interest payments on the £50,000 loan continue to be allowable as the underlying funds have been reinvested in the business.

In 2025, Abel sells Eden Cottage and moves into a new house in Gomorrah. Abel's mortgage on the new Gomorrah property exceeds the final balance on his Eden Cottage mortgage. The new mortgage therefore includes the original £50,000 borrowing used to acquire a business property and hence the appropriate proportion of Abel's interest payments should still be allowable.

In 2026, Abel sells Ark Villa in order to finance the costs of an extension he is building on his Gomorrah home. At this point, the interest on his £50,000 borrowings ceases to be allowable for Income Tax purposes.

As well as tracking the underlying funds, there is also the possibility that interest relief may sometimes continue to be available under the 'capital introduced' principle (i.e. our second heading at the start of this section).

Example 6
Naamah owns a rental property at 22 Canaan Street that she bought for £100,000 some years ago and which has no mortgage against it. In 2020, she takes out a mortgage of £75,000 on the property and uses this money to buy a second rental property in Judea Gardens. Clearly, at this stage, her mortgage interest is allowable against her rental income.

A few years later, she sells the property in Judea Gardens but the mortgage on her Canaan Street property remains outstanding.

She has sold the property that was purchased with the borrowed funds, but the interest on her Canaan Street mortgage remains allowable because it is also a rental property and the mortgage is less than its value when it was first rented out

Existing Property Introduced into the Business

The interest on a mortgage over a property that is newly introduced into the rental business becomes allowable from that point onwards.

Hence, the interest on the mortgage on your own former home may be claimed from the date on which you make it available for letting.

Furthermore, as the entire value of the property at that date represents capital introduced into your business, you could also re-mortgage the property and the whole amount of interest payable on loans secured on the property, up to its value on the first day you rent it out, will be allowable for tax purposes.

Example 5 Revisited

By 2028, Abel's Gomorrah property is worth £500,000 and his outstanding mortgage is £300,000. Abel re-mortgages the Gomorrah property, realising an additional £150,000, which he uses to buy a new home in neighbouring Sodom.

Abel now starts to rent out his Gomorrah property. The entire interest payable on Abel's £450,000 mortgage will now be allowable against his rental income.

Where an existing property, such as a former home, is introduced into the rental business, the capital introduced will be its value when first rented out. Previous capital expenditure on the property, such as legal fees paid on the purchase, cannot also be counted in this case. The current value of any contents rented out with the property (furniture, etc) can, however, be included.

Loans in Joint Names, etc

Strictly, for interest to be claimed as an allowable cost, it must be a liability of the owner of the business. This generally means the underlying loan must be in the name of the property investor themselves.

By concession, however, HMRC will allow qualifying interest paid by a property investor to be claimed when the underlying loan is:

i)   In joint names with their spouse, or
ii)   In the sole name of their spouse

Under scenario (ii), it is vital that the interest is actually paid by the property investor themselves, even though it is their spouse's liability.

Naturally, the interest is still only allowable if incurred for the purposes of the business, as detailed above.

Other Finance Costs

The treatment of other finance costs, such as loan arrangement fees, will generally follow the same principles as those applying to interest. In other words, these costs will generally be allowable where the borrowed funds either represent capital introduced into the business, or are otherwise used for business purposes.

However, difficulties may occur over the timing of relief for such costs. General accounting principles may sometimes dictate the cost should be spread over the life of the loan. In such cases, the tax treatment will follow the same principles.

Example
Eve has a large rental property portfolio and decides to consolidate her borrowings into one single 20-year loan. The bank charges her an arrangement fee of £20,000 for this new finance. Eve should therefore claim £1,000 each year over the 20-year life of the loan.

After 15 years, however, she decides to re-finance her business again and terminates the 20-year loan agreement. At this stage she may claim the remaining £5,000 of the original fee that she has not yet claimed for tax purposes. She may also claim any early redemption fee she suffers.

In the past, HMRC tended to regard early redemption fees as a personal cost rather than a business cost and did not generally consider them allowable for Income Tax purposes.

However, it is now more generally accepted that refinancing is a normal, commercial, part of a property business and early redemption fees will generally be accepted as an allowable cost for Income Tax purposes, provided there is a good business reason for the early redemption.

As in Eve's case, any unclaimed portion of the original arrangement fees may usually also be claimed in the event of a loan's early termination (as long as they qualified as a business cost in the first place).

The timing of relief for arrangement fees, etc, is unaffected by whether the investor pays them at the outset or adds them to the value of their loan. Furthermore, if fees incurred for business purposes are added to the value of a loan, there is no need to restrict the amount of the subsequent interest charges qualifying for relief.

Accelerating Relief

Spreading relief for loan arrangement fees over the life of the loan is based on generally accepted accounting principles. However, it is important to understand those principles only require the fees to be spread over the useful life of the loan and not necessarily its full legal life.

Hence, for example, if you take out a ten year loan, but fully expect to refinance your property again after five years, then it would be quite reasonable to claim any loan arrangement fees over a five year period rather than a ten year period.

Accelerating tax relief where it is legitimate to do so is usually a good idea in any case, but the changes to the rate of tax relief for interest and finance costs that we will be looking at in the next section mean the savings to be made by accelerating relief for finance costs may currently be absolute ones, rather than mere timing differences.

Where you decide to claim relief over a shorter period than the legal term of your loan, it is important to retain some evidence of your rationale for doing so, such as a business plan that includes your financing policy, for example.

4.5   INTEREST RELIEF RESTRICTIONS

In utter defiance of one of the most important, fundamental principles under which businesses are taxed in the UK, the Government has introduced restrictions on tax relief for interest and finance costs paid by residential landlords.

Before we look at these dreadful restrictions, often known as 'Section 24', it is worth pointing out they do **not** affect:

- Furnished holiday letting businesses (see Section 8.17)
- Landlords renting out non-residential property
- Property investment companies

The restrictions do, however, apply to all individuals renting out 'normal' residential property (i.e. not furnished holiday lets) in the UK or overseas, including those operating:

- As an individual in their own name
- As joint owners
- Through a partnership
- Through a trust

The Restrictions in Detail

Tax relief for interest and finance costs relating to residential property lettings is being restricted to basic rate only. This is being done by phasing out higher rate tax relief for interest and finance costs over a four year period, commencing from 2017/18. The restrictions work as follows:

- 2017/18: 75% deducted as normal, 25% relieved at basic rate
- 2018/19: 50% deducted as normal, 50% relieved at basic rate
- 2019/20: 25% deducted as normal, 75% relieved at basic rate
- 2020/21 onwards: all relieved at basic rate

Any unrelieved excess eligible for relief at basic rate may be carried forward for relief in future years.

Example

Adam has a salary in excess of the higher rate tax threshold each year. He also receives annual rental profits of £40,000 from a residential property portfolio: before deduction of interest and finance costs which amount to £36,000 each year. The annual profit from Adam's rental business is just £4,000, but his tax liabilities on this income are as follows:

	2016/17	2017/18	2018/19	2019/20	2020/21
Profit before interest	40,000	40,000	40,000	40,000	40,000
Less: Deductible interest	36,000	27,000	18,000	9,000	0
	(100%)	(75%)	(50%)	(25%)	Nil
Taxable profit	4,000	13,000	22,000	31,000	40,000
Tax thereon at 40%(A)	1,600	5,200	8,800	12,400	16,000
Basic rate tax relief on					
remaining interest of	0	9,000	18,000	27,000	36,000
Equals (at 20%): (B)	0	1,800	3,600	5,400	7,200
Tax payable (A-B)	£1,600	£3,400	£5,200	£7,000	£8,800

The tax bill on his rental business increases by 450% between 2016/17 and 2020/21. From 2018/19 onwards, his tax bill is actually in excess of his overall profit, and by 2020/21, he will be suffering a tax charge of £8,800 on a profit of just £4,000: an effective tax rate of 220%!

The effect of the restriction on interest relief is to turn a pre-tax profit into a post-tax loss! But the agony does not end there. Adam is a higher rate taxpayer making rental profits. The impact of these restrictions also extends to many landlords who would otherwise be basic rate taxpayers; and even to many who are making rental losses.

Example

Delilah has a salary of £30,000. She also has a portfolio of residential rental properties yielding annual profits (before interest and finance costs) of £33,000. She pays interest of £35,000 each year. Overall, she is making a loss of £2,000, but she is able to fund this from her salary income.

Up to 2018/19, the restrictions on interest relief do not affect Delilah, as the portion of her interest payments she is allowed to deduct is sufficient to keep her total taxable income below the higher rate tax threshold.

But crunch time comes in 2019/20. For this year, she may deduct just 25% of her interest cost (£8,750) leaving her with a taxable 'profit' of £24,250. Adding this to her salary gives her total taxable income of £54,250, pushing her over the 2019/20 higher rate tax threshold of £50,000.

The Income Tax payable at 40% on the top £4,250 of Delilah's taxable income will amount to £1,700. She will be able to claim relief for her interest costs but the rate of relief will be restricted to basic rate: 20%. The tax relief for the interest set against Delilah's top £4,250 of taxable income will thus be just £850, leaving her with a tax liability of £850 to pay (£1,700 – £850).

Delilah will have excess unrelieved interest costs to carry forward, but these will be of no practical help while she continues to make an overall loss.

In 2020/21 things will get even worse for Delilah. She will not be eligible to deduct any of her interest costs from her rental income and will have a taxable 'profit' of £33,000; meaning her total taxable income will exceed the higher rate threshold of £50,000 (see Section 3.3) by £13,000. After deducting basic rate tax relief for her interest costs, she will have a tax liability of £2,600.

To illustrate this in more detail, Delilah's tax calculation for the two years discussed above can be summarised as follows:

	2019/20 £	2020/21 £
Rental profits before interest	33,000	33,000
Deductible interest (25%/Nil)	(8,750)	-
	----------	---------
	24,250	33,000
Salary	30,000	30,000
	----------	---------
Total taxable income	54,250	63,000
Less:		
Personal allowance	(12,500)	(12,500)
	----------	----------
	41,750	50,500
	=====	=====
Income Tax at 20% on basic rate band of £37,500	7,500	7,500
Income Tax at 40% on remaining £4,250/£13,000	1,700	5,200
	----------	---------
	9,200	12,700
Less:		
Tax deducted under PAYE (basic rate tax on salary less personal allowance)	(3,500)	(3,500)
Interest relief against property income at 20%on £24,250/£33,000 (as above)	(4,850)	(6,600)
	----------	---------
Income Tax due	850	2,600
	=====	=====

In summary, by 2020/21, when the Government's vicious attack on landlords has been fully implemented, Delilah will have a tax liability of £2,600 despite making a loss of £2,000 and having thousands of pounds in unrelieved interest costs carried forward. How anyone can call such an outcome 'fair' defies belief!

How Much Interest Attracts Basic Rate Tax Relief?

The amount of interest and finance costs on residential property that attracts basic rate tax relief from 2017/18 onwards is the lowest of the following three amounts:

i) The total qualifying interest and finance costs on residential property for the year (as established under the principles set out in Section 4.4), less (for 2017/18 to 2019/20) the proportion allowed as a direct deduction against rental profits, plus any unrelieved interest brought forward

ii) The taxable residential rental profits for the year

iii) The landlord's total taxable income for the year, excluding interest income, other savings income, and dividends; and after deducting their personal allowance

The unrelieved interest brought forward under (i) means interest that can only be relieved at basic rate; it does not include interest that is fully deductible and is included within rental losses brought forward.

Let's look at these three amounts for Delilah in 2019/20:

Her total qualifying finance costs for the year are £35,000. From this, we deduct the 25% allowed as a direct deduction against rental profits, leaving £26,250. We then add any unrelieved interest brought forward. Let's say this amounts to £6,000, for the sake of illustration, thus giving a total of £32,250 for amount (i).

Amount (ii), Delilah's taxable residential rental profits for the year, is £24,250 (as calculated above). This is after deducting the 25% proportion of her qualifying interest and finance costs for the year that is allowed as a direct deduction in 2019/20.

Delilah's total taxable income for the year is £54,250. Deducting her personal allowance of £12,500 gives us £41,750 for amount (iii).

So, in this case, the three amounts are:

i) £32,250
ii) £24,250
iii) £41,750

Delilah can claim basic rate tax relief on the lowest amount (£24,250).

If we go back to the earlier example of Adam, we can see amount (i) (his total qualifying interest and finance costs, less the proportion allowed as a direct deduction against rental income) was always the lowest amount and was thus the amount on which he claimed basic rate tax relief. This will generally be the case for most profitable rental businesses, but exceptions may arise for landlords with little or no other income.

Example

In 2019/20, Sheba has residential rental profits of £30,000 before deduction of interest and finance costs totalling £24,000. She has no other income.

25% of Sheba's interest costs, or £6,000, is deducted directly from her rental income, leaving her with £24,000 of taxable income. This exceeds the 2019/20 personal allowance of £12,500 by £11,500.

Sheba has a further £18,000 of interest and finance costs eligible for relief at basic rate (75% of her total cost for the year). However, the amount eligible for relief is restricted to £11,500: the amount by which her taxable income exceeds the personal allowance.

Sheba therefore has no tax to pay and unrelieved interest and finance costs of £6,500 to carry forward. These carried forward costs could save her £1,300 in a later year when her rental profits are higher.

This example illustrates the only bit of good news about the interest relief restrictions: landlords like Sheba, whose overall income is quite low, are able to carry forward some of their interest and finance costs rather than set them against income that is covered by their personal allowance.

In other words, such landlords will get effective tax relief for their interest and finance costs (albeit in the future and restricted to basic rate) rather than wasting them as a deduction against income that would not have been taxed anyway.

Further Implications

Changing interest and finance costs from a deduction to a relief (at basic rate) means the landlord's total taxable income increases. We have already seen how this impacts on the use of the personal allowance and basic rate band, but the increase in total taxable income will also affect:

- The High Income Child Benefit Charge (see Section 3.3)
- Withdrawal of personal allowances where taxable income exceeds £100,000 (see Section 3.3)
- The additional rate threshold (see Appendix A)
- CGT rates (see Section 6.4)

Example

Job has residential rental profits of £200,000 before deduction of interest costs totalling £150,000. He has no other income. He and his wife have three small children, so his wife claims child benefit of £2,501. Job's Income Tax calculation for 2016/17 was as follows:

	£
Taxable income (£200,000 - £150,000)	*50,000*
Less: personal allowance	*(11,000)*

	39,000
	======
Income Tax at 20% on £32,000	*6,400*
Income Tax at 40% on £7,000	*2,800*

Total tax due	*9,200*
	=====

From 2017/18 onwards, Job's interest deduction gradually changes into interest relief at basic rate only. This increases his taxable income by £37,500 (25% of his interest deduction) each year. In 2017/18, Job's taxable income was £87,500 and he was subject to the HICBC. In 2018/19, his taxable income was £125,000 and his personal allowance was withdrawn. In 2019/20, his taxable income will be £162,500 and he will be subject to additional rate tax. By 2020/21, his Income Tax calculation will be as follows:

Taxable income	*£200,000*
Income Tax at 20% on £37,500	*7,500*
Income Tax at 40% on £112,500	*45,000*
Income Tax at 45% on £50,000	*22,500*
High Income Child Benefit Charge	*2,501*

	77,501
Less: Basic rate relief on interest	
£150,000 @ 20%	*(30,000)*

Total tax due	*47,501*
	=====

Unlike Adam (our first example in this section), Job has (just about) enough profit to cover his tax bill. Nonetheless, his effective tax rate is still a whopping 95% - and he has no other income to pay it from!

Which Costs are Affected?

The restrictions described in this section apply to interest and finance costs on any amount borrowed for the purposes of generating income from residential lettings. Finance costs include incidental costs of obtaining finance. The restrictions therefore apply to most of the interest and finance costs incurred by a residential landlord, including:

- Buy-to-let mortgages
- Other mortgages and loans used to fund deposits or other business expenditure
- Personal loans or credit cards used to fund furnishings, refurbishment work or other business expenditure
- Hire purchase agreements for the purchase of cars or other assets used in the business
- Business overdrafts

The types of cost affected include:

- Interest
- Charges equivalent to interest (e.g. Sharia compliant mortgages)
- Loan arrangement fees
- Early repayment penalties
- Facility arrangement fees
- Guarantee fees
- Professional fees incurred obtaining loan finance (see Section 4.6)

However, as the restrictions only apply to costs related to borrowings, it would appear some items are not affected: such as bank charges on a business current account.

Costs relating to non-residential property or furnished holiday lets are exempt from the restrictions. Where a landlord has different types of property, some costs will need to be apportioned.

Example
Isaac borrows £1m to refinance his property portfolio. The portfolio consists of furnished holiday lets worth £500,000, commercial property worth £800,000 and residential property worth £700,000: a total of £2m.

The restrictions on tax relief for interest and finance costs will only apply to the element of the loan relating to Isaac's residential property. In this case, it would be reasonable to apply the restrictions to 35% of the costs arising (£700,000/£2m = 35%).

In 2019/20, the total interest and finance costs relating to Isaac's loan amount to £60,000. The amount Isaac can deduct in the normal way, as a direct expense, is as follows:

Residential lettings:	*£60,000 x 35% x 25%*	*£5,250*
Other lettings:	*£60,000 x 65%*	*£39,000*
Total		*£44,250*

Isaac may also claim basic rate tax relief on the remaining costs of £15,750 (£60,000 x 35% x 75%).

The basis for apportioning costs used by Isaac is not the only possible method. He might instead look at the borrowing history prior to the refinancing. Other alternative methods might be available: all that is required is that the apportionment is 'just and reasonable'.

If Isaac had other costs on borrowings wholly related to his residential lettings, these would be wholly subject to the restrictions on relief. Conversely, if he had other costs wholly related to his non-residential property, or his furnished holiday lets, then none of these would be subject to those restrictions.

4.6   LEGAL AND PROFESSIONAL FEES

Legal fees and other professional costs incurred for the purposes of the business may fall into one of four categories for tax purposes:

- i)   Revenue expenditure
- ii)   Capital expenditure
- iii)   Costs of obtaining loan finance
- iv)   Abortive capital expenditure

See Section 3.9 for an explanation of the difference between revenue expenditure and capital expenditure.

Revenue Expenditure

Revenue expenditure may be claimed as a deduction against rental income. These are the costs incurred year in, year out, in earning the rental profits. They will include items such as debt collection expenses, agent's fees and accountancy fees for the preparation of your annual accounts and the business part of your tax return.

Legal and professional costs relating to a tenant's lease of a year or less are also generally allowable (e.g. legal fees for preparing the lease).

However, HMRC regards any expenses connected with the first letting of a property for more than one year as a capital expense that cannot be claimed. Costs relating to subsequent long leases will generally be allowable provided the new lease is on broadly similar terms and for a period of less than 50 years and the property has not been used for some other purpose in the interim.

Capital Expenses

Legal fees and other professional costs incurred for the purchase or sale of properties cannot be claimed for Income Tax purposes within a property letting or investment business. As long as the purchase or sale in question goes through, however, all is not lost, as these items may then be claimed as allowable deductions for CGT purposes when the property is disposed of (see Chapter 6).

This category would include:

- Legal fees
- Estate agent's fees
- SDLT
- Survey fees
- Valuation fees
- Professional costs incurred on a successful planning application

Costs of Obtaining Loan Finance

When purchasing a property, it is only the purchase costs that must be regarded as capital expenditure and which therefore cannot be claimed for Income Tax purposes.

Any costs relating to obtaining finance (typically a mortgage) may be claimed over the useful life of the relevant loan, mortgage, etc, in the same way as loan arrangement fees (see Section 4.4).

Sadly, this means that these costs are also subject to the restrictions described in Section 4.5, but even basic rate Income Tax relief will often be preferable to a CGT deduction at some uncertain time in the future. Furthermore, since HMRC has been known to deny CGT relief for costs that could have been claimed for Income Tax purposes, it will generally be sensible to claim Income Tax relief when you can.

In addition to the loan arrangement fees discussed in Section 4.4, costs of obtaining loan finance will typically also include:

- Mortgage broker's fees
- Lender's survey or valuation fees
- Land registry fees for registering the charge over the property
- A portion of the legal fees for the purchase

Your own survey fees remain a capital expense: it is only additional lender's survey or valuation fees that can be treated as a finance cost.

Land registry fees are typically paid by the purchaser's lawyer and then passed on to the purchaser through the final settlement: so watch out for these in the settlement statement.

While it is perfectly reasonable to claim a portion of the legal fees related to dealing with the lender, registering the security, etc; not everyone does this as it is not always apparent what a suitable proportion might be.

> **Tax Tip**
> Part of the legal fees arising on the purchase of a property will often relate to the raising of finance – i.e. the mortgage. It may therefore be worth arranging to have this element of the fees invoiced separately so they can be claimed for Income Tax purposes, in the same way as loan arrangement fees.
>
> Alternatively, a reasonable estimate of the appropriate proportion may be used instead. This will typically be in the region of a quarter to a third, although it varies from case to case.

Costs such as survey or valuation fees incurred when re-mortgaging a property (for business purposes) should also be treated in the same way as loan arrangement fees.

Abortive Capital Expenditure

As we all know, sometimes a purchase or sale will not go through. In these cases, the investor will often incur costs such as survey or legal fees. Unfortunately, HMRC takes the view that costs related to purchases or sales which do not proceed are not generally allowable for Income Tax and neither will they be allowable for CGT purposes. These are what we sometimes call 'tax nothings'.

There is, however, an argument that any costs incurred before making a decision to purchase or sell a property are part of the regular overhead costs of the property business and are therefore properly claimable as revenue expenditure.

Example
Noah is considering buying an investment property in the Newcastle area. He spots a potential purchase in Gosforth and has a survey done on the property. However, he is unhappy with the result and decides not to pursue this purchase. Noah may claim the cost of the survey as an allowable business expense.

Noah moves his attention to Durham and finds another potential investment property. He has a survey carried out and, happy with the results, this time he decides to proceed with the purchase. Things go well until the owner of the Durham property is made redundant and is forced to take it back off the market. By this time, Noah has incurred substantial legal fees.

Noah's legal fees were incurred after he decided to purchase the Durham property. These fees are therefore abortive capital expenditure that Noah is unable to claim. Noah will, however, still be able to claim the cost of the survey fees for the Durham property as, once again, these were incurred before he made a decision to purchase the property.

To assist claims for 'pre-decision' expenditure of this nature, it is useful to retain documentary evidence that shows the decision to purchase or sell had not yet been taken.

While I believe claims for abortive 'pre-decision' expenditure incurred for the purposes of a property business are perfectly valid, this is a view that HMRC may not necessarily share. Some dispute over claims of this nature may therefore arise.

Professional costs incurred on an unsuccessful application for planning permission are also regarded as 'tax nothings', and generally cannot be claimed for either Income Tax or CGT purposes. However, if you can show that the same costs led to a later, successful, application, they may still be regarded as part of the capital cost of the project for CGT purposes.

Even after accounting for the ability to claim 'pre-decision' expenditure, there are still some property investors incurring substantial costs which end up being classed as 'tax nothings'. This situation is a constant source of frustration to property investors and I would agree it is very unfair.

> **Tax Tip**
> If you are incurring significant costs of this nature, you might sometimes be better off being treated as a property trader. While, as explained in Section 2.3, your tax status is not a matter of choice, if your situation is already pretty borderline, a small shift in your investment strategy may be enough to tip the balance. Having said that, with effective tax rates on trading profits of up to 62%, the instances where investors will be better off as a property trader will be pretty rare!

Abortive capital expenditure is not allowable when the landlord is using the cash basis. See Section 4.18 for further details.

4.7   REPAIRS AND MAINTENANCE

Nowhere in the field of taxation is the question of 'capital or revenue' more difficult than in the area of repairs and maintenance and/or capital improvements. In this section, we will look at some of the general principles applying to this type of expenditure on all rental properties. Other aspects specific to commercial property and to furnished residential lettings are covered in more detail in Sections 4.9 and 4.10 respectively.

Fundamental Principles

There are two fundamental principles which we must consider in order to determine whether any expenditure represents a repair (i.e. revenue expenditure) or a capital improvement (capital expenditure):

i) When a property is first brought into the rental business, any expenditure which is necessary to make it fit for use will be capital expenditure. In most cases, a property will first be brought into use when purchased but the same rule applies when an inherited property or the taxpayer's own former home becomes a rental property.

ii) Subject to (i) above, expenditure which merely restores the property to its previous condition (at a time earlier in the same ownership) will be a repair. Conversely, any expenditure which enhances the property beyond its previous condition within the same ownership will be capital improvement expenditure.

It is always important to bear these fundamental principles in mind: they lie at the heart of the whole 'capital or revenue' question for any expenditure on a property. Fortunately, however, as we shall see later in this section, they are subject to a little more 'leeway' in practice than one might imagine!

The question of what constitutes an 'enhancement' to the property is determined as a question of fact, not opinion. Just because you think a new extension on a building is hideous does not stop it from being classed as an improvement for tax purposes.

Repairs are deductible for Income Tax purposes (as long as the property is a rental property at the time) whereas capital improvements **may** be deductible for CGT purposes (see Chapter 6) or, in the case of non-residential property, an allowance of just 2% per year (see Section 3.19).

The treatment of any incidental expenditure incurred as part of a building project, such as skip hire for example, will follow the treatment of the project itself. This does not extend to interest and finance costs, however, which continue to be treated as set out in Sections 4.4 and 4.5.

Some Illustrative Examples

I could write an entirely separate book covering umpteen different examples of repairs or capital improvements. Here, however, I have tried to set out a few cases which will hopefully serve to illustrate how the principles outlined above apply in practice. Where a new principle emerges in the course of these examples, I have highlighted it for your attention as an 'Emerging Principle'.

Example 1
Melanie buys an old farmhouse intending to rent it out for furnished holiday lettings. However, when she buys the property, it has no mains electricity, no mains sewerage and a large hole in the roof. She spends £75,000 getting the property into a fit state to let it out, including £5,000 on redecoration.

The whole of Melanie's expenditure of £75,000 will be treated as capital expenditure and no Income Tax deduction will be available. The fact that part of the expenditure was for decorating is likely to be regarded as merely incidental to the overall capital nature of the work in this case.

Emerging Principle
Expenditure that might normally be regarded as revenue will be treated as capital where it forms an incidental part of a predominantly capital project. Until 2001 HMRC was prepared to allow some deduction for the 'notional repair' element within capital improvements, but sadly this is no longer the case.

Example 2
Geri has a small townhouse in Kensington which she rents out. She decides to have a conservatory built on the back of the house at a cost of £40,000, including £2,000 to redecorate the room adjoining the new conservatory. Geri's conservatory is a capital improvement and no Income Tax deduction will be available for this expenditure. Once again, the capital nature of this work also extends to the cost of redecorating the adjoining room, as this was necessitated by the major building work.

Example 3
Emma owns a row of shops which she has been renting to a number of sole traders. A massive storm severely damages the roofs of the shops and Emma has these repaired at a cost of £50,000. Emma's expenditure represents an allowable repair cost which she can claim against her rental income.

The same storm also damaged several windows in Emma's shops. The glazier advises her that it will actually be cheaper to replace the original wooden frames with new UPVC double glazing and she agrees to do this. This expenditure remains revenue expenditure despite the fact that the new windows represent an improvement on the old ones.

Emerging Principle
When, due to changes in fashion, or technological advances, it becomes cheaper or more efficient to replace something with the nearest modern equivalent, the fact that this represents an improvement may be disregarded and the expenditure may still be classed as a repair. Replacing single-glazed windows with equivalent double-glazing has been specifically highlighted as meeting this criterion by HMRC.

Example 3 Continued

At the same time, Emma also decides to have bay windows fitted in two of the shops. This element of her expenditure is a capital improvement and will have to be added to the capital value of her shops rather than claimed as a repair.

Emerging Principle

Both capital improvements and repairs may sometimes be carried out simultaneously. In such cases, the expenditure must be apportioned between the two elements on a reasonable basis.

Readers may wonder why this apportionment is allowed here, when it was denied for both Melanie and Geri above. The key difference is that both Melanie and Geri **had to** do the redecoration at the same time as the other work, whereas Emma simply **chose** to install the bay windows. It is the element of choice which makes the difference.

Tax Tip

Where an apportionment of expenditure is necessary, it would be wise to obtain evidence of the allocation made in support of your claim. This can be achieved by asking the builder to separately itemise the repairs and capital improvement elements of the work on their invoices.

Example 4

Victoria has a flat which she has been renting to students for several years. She decides to upgrade the flat to make it more suitable for letting to young professionals. She incurs the following expenditure:

i)   *£16,000 on a new kitchen, including £4,500 on equipment*
ii) *£7,500 redecorating the bathroom, including £2,500 to replace existing fittings and £1,500 to install a shower (there was only a bath before)*
iii) *£5,000 redecorating the rest of the flat*
iv) *£3,000 on rewiring*

New Kitchen

The new kitchen expenditure needs to be examined on a detailed 'item by item' basis. The treatment of each item depends on whether it is:

a)   *An integral part of a fitted kitchen or a free-standing item, and*
b)   *A direct replacement or an improvement*

Any items that represent improvements cannot be claimed as repairs. Hence, for example, installing a new extractor fan within a fitted kitchen, where no such fan had existed before, would be a capital improvement. As the fan is an integral part of a fitted kitchen, this would represent an improvement to the property as a whole and could thus be added to the cost of the property for CGT purposes (subject to the points discussed in Section 6.10).

105

Similarly, buying an additional chest freezer to provide extra capacity for frozen food would also be an improvement, and could not be claimed as a repair. Where the new freezer is a free-standing item, it would represent a separate asset and so could not be added to the cost of the property for CGT purposes.

Fitted Kitchen Units and Integrated Equipment

A fitted kitchen is treated as part of the fabric of the building. The cost of a new fitted kitchen replacing a previous, broadly similar, set of units, work tops, sink, etc, would therefore be accepted as a repair expense. This treatment extends to the replacement of any equipment that is an integral part of a fitted kitchen, such as an integrated cooker or fridge. It does not, however, extend to free-standing items (which are considered below).

Where the replacement of a fitted kitchen can be claimed as a repair, this treatment should also include the necessary additional costs of re-tiling, re-plastering, plumbing, etc.

The usual exemption for 'nearest modern equivalent' continues to apply when considering whether items have been improved or merely replaced. If, however, Victoria's new fitted kitchen incorporates extra storage space or other extra features, then an appropriate proportion of the expenditure will need to be treated as a capital improvement. This would include any new integrated equipment that replaced an old free-standing item.

In an extreme case, where fairly standard units are replaced by expensive customised items using much higher quality materials, then the whole cost of the new kitchen will need to be regarded as a capital improvement.

Free-Standing Items

Free-standing, moveable items are not part of the fabric of the building for tax purposes. This generally includes most free-standing 'white goods' such as fridges, dishwashers, cookers, etc; as well as other moveable items such as tables, chairs, etc.

Victoria will be able to claim the cost of any equipment that is a direct replacement for the old equipment she previously had in the flat. She may also be able to claim part of the cost of any free-standing equipment that represents more than a simple direct replacement. See Section 4.10 for further details.

Anything that is an entirely new item of equipment will be capital expenditure and not allowable for Income Tax purposes. Since free-standing items are separate assets, they will not be added to the cost of the property for CGT purposes either.

Bathroom Fittings

Replacing the existing bathroom fittings should usually be allowable repairs expenditure. Toilets, baths and washbasins are all regarded as part of the fabric of the building, so repairing or replacing them is generally allowable for Income Tax purposes.

Once again, however, replacing the existing fittings with expensive customised items using much higher quality materials would amount to a capital improvement.

*Fitting the new shower will be a capital improvement if this is an extra new item in **addition** to the bath. If the shower **replaces** the existing bath then it should qualify as a repair under the 'nearest modern equivalent' principle.*

Assuming the shower is an additional item, however, the remaining bathroom redecoration costs will need to be apportioned between the repair element and capital improvement element. Any expense arising due to the installation of the shower would have to be treated as part of the capital element.

Redecorating the Flat
Most of the redecoration work, in the absence of any building work in the rooms concerned, should be fairly straightforward repairs expenditure. As usual, we need to be on the lookout for any improvement element, but a great deal of redecorating cost will always fall into the 'nearest modern equivalent' category.

Carpets, curtains and other similar items need to be considered separately. These are classed as 'furnishings' and will be dealt with under the principles set out in Section 4.10. In this context, it makes no difference if you are replacing carpets or curtains that you yourself fitted previously or which you acquired when you purchased the property.

Rewiring
The rewiring will be fully allowable if it is simply 'new for old'. If, on the other hand, Victoria took the opportunity to fit a few new sockets then there would be an improvement element and, as usual, an apportionment would be required. Such an apportionment may also necessitate an apportionment of the redecorating costs, as some of these might also be incurred due to the electrical improvements.

Emerging Principles
The cost of replacing fixtures on a 'like for like' basis, or with their nearest modern equivalents, is regarded as a repair to the property. This includes fitted kitchens and integrated equipment.

Moveable items, such as carpets, curtains and free-standing kitchen equipment, are not regarded as part of the fabric of the building and are therefore subject to different rules (see Section 4.10). (Carpets often cause a lot of confusion as many people see them as a 'fitting'. For tax purposes, however, they are classed as furnishings.)

In complex cases, the question of 'repairs or capital improvements' will need to be examined room by room, or even item by item. The tax treatment of one item may have a knock-on effect on the tax treatment of another item.

Example 5

Mel buys a rather dilapidated house in Sunderland hoping to rent it out to a family or young couple. She gets the house at a very good price owing to its current state of repair but knows that safety regulations would bar her from letting it out to anyone in its current condition.

The house desperately needs rewiring and also some urgent plumbing work, which Mel carries out at a cost of £5,000. This expenditure will have to be treated as part of her capital cost.

At this point the house is basically habitable and will meet all necessary safety regulations, but it could really do with redecorating to make it attractive to the type of tenants Mel is ideally looking for. However, if Mel redecorates at this point then this expenditure is also likely to be regarded as part of the capital cost of the property, especially since part of the redecorating will have been necessitated by the plumbing and rewiring work.

What Mel does instead, therefore, is to first let the house to a group of students for nine months. After that, she is able to redecorate the property and to claim this as a revenue expense deductible for Income Tax purposes.

Tax Tip

Where there is a danger that repairs or maintenance expenditure might be regarded as an incidental part of a capital project, it will be beneficial to delay this element of the work, if possible, until after an intermediate period of letting. In this way, the expenditure becomes an allowable revenue expense. Naturally, any health and safety requirements will have to be observed before undertaking the initial letting period.

Example 6

Danni buys a flat from an elderly couple, intending to rent it out. The elderly couple lived in the flat right up to the date of completion. Although it was a bit 'run down' and the decor was very old-fashioned, it was perfectly habitable and met all applicable safety requirements for a rental property.

Immediately after completion, Danni redecorates the flat in a modern style and then begins to rent it out. Danni's redecoration costs are an allowable maintenance cost for Income Tax purposes, even though she did the work straight away after buying the flat. The flat was already completely habitable and the redecoration work was purely a matter of choice or taste.

Emerging Principle

Normal routine repairs and redecoration work on newly acquired properties is usually considered allowable. Such expenditure will generally be regarded as 'normal' if the property could have been used without it and the price of the property was not significantly affected by its condition.

HMRC's View on Newly Acquired Properties

HMRC's view is that expenditure to rectify 'normal wear and tear' on a newly acquired rental property remains allowable as a deduction from rental income for Income Tax purposes. They take the view that there is only 'normal' wear and tear if the property's condition does not significantly affect its purchase price.

HMRC's manuals also specifically state that any expenditure on a newly acquired rental property which is not allowed for Income Tax purposes on the grounds that it represents capital expenditure should then be allowed for CGT purposes on a disposal of that property.

Accounting Treatment

Where there are no statutory rules to the contrary, HMRC will generally expect the tax treatment of an expense to mirror its treatment in the accounts.

Wealth Warning
It is important to ensure that valid repairs expenditure is not treated as a capital item in your accounts, as this could prevent you from claiming that expenditure for Income Tax purposes.

Repair Cost Provisions

In accounting terms, a 'provision' is a charge made in your accounts in respect of a future cost. Provisions for future costs are not generally allowable until the costs have actually been incurred.

There are a few exceptions to this rule, however, and a provision for repair costs may be allowed for tax purposes if:

i)   There is a legal or contractual obligation to incur the expenditure,

ii)   There is a specific programme of repair work to be undertaken, and

iii)   The accounting provision has been computed with a reasonable degree of accuracy

Example 7
Kylie owns three flats in Donovan Towers, a tenement block in Glasgow. In February 2020, she receives a statutory notice from the council requiring her (and the other owners in the block) to carry out some urgent roof repairs.

The 'Donovan Towers Owners and Residents Association' approaches Jason, a local builder, who provides them with a quotation for carrying out the work. On 4th April 2020, the association formally approves the quotation. Kylie's share of the cost will be £2,000.

Under these circumstances, Kylie may quite properly make a provision for her £2,000 share of the cost in her accounts for the year ending 5th April 2020, even though the work has not even started yet.

Other Repairs

Landlords may generally claim the cost of repairs to any items of equipment, furniture or furnishings in any rental properties.

Repairs to assets classed as 'integral features' within commercial property, furnished holiday lets, or certain communal areas not within any individual dwelling, may sometimes need to be treated as capital improvements. See Section 4.9 for further details.

4.8   TRAINING AND RESEARCH

Many property investors spend a good deal of money on training and research. The first thing to note is the fact that this expenditure is often incurred before the business starts is not, in itself, a barrier to claiming it as a business expense. (Unless it was incurred more than seven years before the business started!)

The cost of books, DVDs, magazines and other information purchased for business purposes is usually allowable. This covers not only industry-specific publications, like trade magazines, but also books and other publications you buy to help you meet your legal and taxation obligations. Books like this one, and many of Taxcafe's other guides, which keep you updated with developments in the field of property taxation, will therefore generally be tax deductible.

The expenditure must be relevant to your business. If you are planning to invest in Spanish property, then the cost of an English-Spanish dictionary might be allowable. A self-help book on diet and yoga, however, would be pushing it too far, even if it does somehow make you a better landlord.

As far as seminars and courses are concerned, the rule is that expenses incurred in updating or expanding existing areas of knowledge may be claimed, but any costs relating to entirely new areas of knowledge are a personal capital expense. This can be a difficult distinction to draw, especially in a field such as property investment, where a great deal of industry knowledge is simply a blend of common sense and experience. It's not like you're training to become a brain surgeon after all!

My personal view is that property investment is a field of knowledge which most adults already have (e.g. from buying their own home) and most such expenses are really only updating or expanding that knowledge and are therefore allowable.

In the end, the decision over any expense claims in this area will inevitably require you to use your own judgement.

4.9 CAPITAL ALLOWANCES FOR LETTING BUSINESSES

As we have seen in previous sections, the most significant amounts of disallowable expenditure in a property investment business derive from capital expenditure on property improvements and on furniture, fixtures and fittings.

As we saw in Chapter 3, however, some capital expenditure is eligible for capital allowances. The rules for capital allowances depend on the type of property being rented.

For some expenditure incurred on non-residential property after 28th October 2018, the structures and buildings allowance ('SBA') provides tax relief at the rate of 2% per year. Full details are set out in Section 3.19.

More generous forms of capital allowances are available on fixtures, fittings, furniture, equipment, and 'integral features' within:

- Commercial property (shops, offices, restaurants, etc.)
- Qualifying furnished holiday lets (see Section 8.17)
- Communal areas in rented residential property not falling within any individual 'dwelling'

The third category would, for example, include equipment in a utility room shared by the occupants of several self-contained flats in a rented building. As this category is fairly rare, I will not repeat it every time we discuss capital allowances in the rest of this section, but it is worth bearing in mind the rules applying to capital allowances in rented commercial property and furnished holiday lets apply equally to communal areas in residential property.

Subject to the exceptions discussed above, residential property does not usually attract any capital allowances at all. (But see Section 4.10 regarding tax relief available in respect of furniture, equipment, etc, in residential rental property.)

Plant & Machinery in Rental Property

Qualifying expenditure within commercial property or qualifying furnished holiday lets may be classed as 'plant and machinery' for capital allowances purposes. Details of the capital allowances regime for 'plant and machinery' are given in Sections 3.14 to 3.18.

The annual investment allowance ('AIA') can be claimed on expenditure on qualifying plant and machinery in commercial rental property or qualifying furnished holiday lets, including 'integral features'.

Wealth Warning

Landlords may lose the right to capital allowances on fixtures and fittings within a commercial property if they grant a lease of two years or more to a tenant and charge a lease premium. As such a premium is wholly or partly regarded as a capital sum for tax purposes (see Section 4.14), the landlord will be treated as having made a partial disposal of the property and may therefore lose the right to claim any capital allowances on assets within it.

A landlord may also lose the right to claim capital allowances on any items not qualifying as 'background' plant and machinery when a property is leased for more than five years. However, this should not generally apply to assets on which the landlord had been able to claim capital allowances previously, before the commencement of the lease.

Finally, landlords may also lose the right to capital allowances on any fixtures or fittings which they lease to the tenant separately under a different agreement to the lease of the property itself. However, this particular problem can often be avoided by making a joint election with the tenant. Furthermore, this can also be a useful method to enable the landlord to retain the right to capital allowances on assets within the property where a lease of two years or more has been granted at a premium as described above.

A landlord can, of course, only claim capital allowances on expenditure they have incurred themselves. Nevertheless, investors with commercial rental property or qualifying furnished holiday lets can obtain immediate tax relief on up to the maximum amount of the AIA each year (see Section 3.15). This will even include expenditure on 'integral features' (see below).

Tax Tip

A couple holding investment property jointly (but not as a partnership) will each be entitled to their own AIA, meaning up to twice as much relief will be available each year!

Qualifying Expenditure on Rental Property

Assets within commercial property and qualifying furnished holiday lets that qualify as plant and machinery for capital allowances purposes include the following:

- Integral features (see below)
- Manufacturing or processing equipment
- Furniture, furnishings, white goods, sinks, baths, showers and sanitary ware
- Sound insulation and gas or sewerage systems provided to meet the special requirements of a qualifying trading activity
- Storage or display equipment, counters and checkouts, cold stores, refrigeration and cooling equipment
- Computer, telecommunication and surveillance systems, including wiring and other links
- Fire and burglar alarms, sprinklers and fire-fighting equipment
- Strong rooms and safes
- Moveable partitioning where intended to be moved in the course of a qualifying trading activity
- Decorative assets provided for public enjoyment in hotels, restaurants and similar trades
- Advertising hoardings, signs and displays

Expenditure on the alteration of a building for the specific purpose of installing qualifying plant and machinery also qualifies for plant and machinery allowances itself.

Qualifying assets within a commercial property or qualifying furnished holiday let are eligible for the same rate of capital allowances whether they are purchased separately or as part of the purchase of the property.

Where a second-hand property is purchased, the purchaser and seller generally have to agree a value for the qualifying fixtures within the property and make a joint election (known as a 'Section 198 Election'), which the purchaser has to submit to HMRC within two years of the date of purchase in support of their capital allowances claim. The agreed value can be anything between £1 and the original cost to the seller of the qualifying items. Sellers generally prefer a low value as this prevents or minimises balancing charges, but this is a matter for negotiation.

For property purchased after 5th April 2014, it is not generally possible to claim capital allowances on any fixtures where the previous owner would have been entitled to make a claim, but failed to do so. Such failures to make legitimate claims are commonplace, so it is vital to check the seller's capital allowances claims history when purchasing second-hand commercial property or furnished holiday lets.

Tax Tip
Sellers can still make retrospective capital allowances claims right up to the time they sell the property, so it will often be possible to ensure that the purchaser's ability to claim capital allowances on fixtures is not diminished or lost – provided appropriate action is taken prior to the date of purchase!

Practical Pointer 1

The requirements for second-hand property detailed above only apply where the property has been in 'qualifying use' at some time after 5th April 2012. For commercial property this will generally be the case but for purchases of residential property the rules are only likely to apply where a previous owner has used the property as a qualifying furnished holiday let at some time since April 2012, or where the property has been rented out since then and has communal areas, as described above.

Practical Pointer 2

The requirements for second-hand property only apply to expenditure on which a previous owner would have qualified for capital allowances. Where no previous owner would have qualified for capital allowances on any particular item, the rules do not apply and the purchaser may claim capital allowances based on a reasonable allocation of the property's purchase price.

Most commonly, this will apply to integral features already in the property prior to 6th April 2008 and which did not qualify for capital allowances at that time. (Provided there is no subsequent owner who purchased the property after that date and had the property in qualifying use any time after 5th April 2012)

Integral Features

Expenditure on assets within a defined list of 'integral features' falls into the special rate pool, attracting writing down allowances at a much lower rate than the usual 18%. This lower rate is currently 6%, having been reduced from 8% in April 2019 (see Section 3.15 for further details).

However, these assets remain eligible for the AIA, so substantial amounts of qualifying expenditure on assets in this category can still attract immediate 100% relief.

The following items are classed as integral features:

- Electrical lighting and power systems
- Cold water systems
- Space or water heating systems, air conditioning, ventilation and air purification systems and floors or ceilings comprised in such systems
- Lifts, escalators and moving walkways
- External solar shading

In a nutshell: All the wiring, lighting, plumbing, heating and air conditioning in any commercial property or qualifying furnished holiday let qualifies for capital allowances, with immediate 100% relief for up to the following amounts spent on these items in each tax year:

2017/18:	£200,000
2018/19:	£408,219
2019/20:	£1,000,000
2020/21:	£791,781
2021/22 onwards:	£200,000

(But see Section 3.15 regarding the transitional rules applying in 2018/19 and 2020/21.)

The integral features regime applies to all expenditure incurred after 5th April 2008, including qualifying items within second-hand buildings purchased after that date (subject to the requirements discussed above).

Any expenditure on integral features that is not covered by the AIA will fall into the special rate pool and attract writing down allowances at just 6% (8% before 2019/20 – see Section 3.15). This includes any items that might otherwise be regarded as falling under one of the other qualifying headings for plant and machinery within rental property given above.

The integral features regime does not apply to expenditure incurred before 6th April 2008 and much of this would not have qualified for capital allowances. The following items of expenditure incurred before 6th April 2008 would, however, qualify for capital allowances:

- Electrical or cold water systems provided specifically to meet the particular requirements of a qualifying trading activity
- Heating, ventilation, air conditioning and air purification systems, including any floor or ceiling which is an integral part of the system
- Lifts, escalators and moving walkways

This remains relevant because it is possible to claim writing down allowances on qualifying expenditure incurred in earlier years, even if no allowances were claimed previously, provided the assets concerned are still used in the business. (Subject to the rules outlined above for fixtures within second-hand properties.)

In the case of a property held by the seller since before 6th April 2008, some integral features will not be subject to the rules for fixtures within second-hand properties (the beneficial implications for the purchaser were explained in 'Practical Pointer 2' above). The relevant features are:

- Electrical lighting and power systems *
- Cold water systems *
- External solar shading

* - Except to the extent that such systems were provided specifically to meet the particular requirements of a qualifying trading activity.

Integral Features Benefits

Combining the integral features regime with the AIA, we can see that many property investors will be able to benefit quite significantly.

Example
In June 2019, Lulach bought an old property and converted it into office units to rent out. The conversion work was completed by September and, although the office units are really just basic 'shells' with the minimum of fixtures and fittings, Lulach's surveyors, Macbeth & Co., nevertheless calculate he has spent £140,000 on 'integral features' and other fixtures qualifying as plant and machinery. Lulach can therefore claim an AIA of £140,000 against his rental income in 2019/20.

(Lulach will also be able to claim the SBA on any conversion costs that do not qualify as plant and machinery – see Section 3.19 for details.)

Furthermore, as we shall see in Section 4.12, property investors may be able to claim any capital allowances in excess of their rental profits against their other income for the same tax year, or the next one (although this relief is subject to certain limitations).

Remember also, that a couple buying property jointly (but not as a partnership) could claim AIAs up to the maximum amounts set out above **each**. Such a couple could potentially benefit from a total tax saving of up to £372,397 in 2019/20 alone: simply by buying the right property! (Based on taxable income of £100,000 each after claiming AIAs)

Replacing Integral Features

Where the assets within a property are eligible for capital allowances, expenditure on replacing part of an integral feature is classed as a capital improvement if such expenditure amounts to more than half the cost of replacing the entire feature within any twelve month period. Capital allowances, including the AIA, remain available on the expenditure. This rule overrides the general principles regarding repairs set out in Section 4.7. Where significant repairs are taking place, it may therefore be worth staggering them over a longer period in order to avoid this problem.

Thermal Insulation of Commercial Property

Expenditure on thermal insulation of an existing commercial building used in a qualifying business also falls into the special rate pool. The AIA is again available on this expenditure.

Landlord's Own Assets

A landlord is unable to claim capital allowances on any assets, such as furniture and equipment, within his or her residential lettings (apart from assets in communal areas not within any individual 'dwelling'). Any landlord may however claim 'plant and machinery' allowances, as detailed in Chapter 3, on equipment purchased for their own business use, such as computers and office furniture.

Capital allowances are available on motor vehicles used in the business, as detailed in Section 3.16. If the landlord acquires their own business premises, they may be eligible for the SBA (see Section 3.19).

4.10 REPLACING FURNITURE, FURNISHINGS & EQUIPMENT

Under 'replacement of domestic items relief' (formerly known as 'replacement furniture relief'), residential landlords may claim the cost of replacing furnishings and other moveable items, including:

- Furniture
- Electrical equipment
- Free-standing 'white goods', such as fridges, dishwashers, etc.
- Carpets and other floor coverings
- Curtains, blinds, etc.
- 'Soft furnishings' (cushions, lampshades, etc.) and bed linen
- Cutlery, crockery and cooking utensils

Any sale proceeds received on the disposal of the old item being replaced must be deducted from the replacement cost being claimed.

The relief does not cover the costs of the original furnishings when the property is first let out, or the cost of additional items.

Landlords may, however, claim part of the cost of a replacement item that performs additional functions compared to the old item it replaces. Hence, for example, where a landlord replaces an old fridge with a fridge-freezer costing £300, but could have purchased a new fridge for £200, they will still be able to claim the £200 direct replacement cost.

Replacement of domestic items relief is not available on items within furnished holiday lets (see Section 8.17), as these are eligible for capital allowances instead.

Items within 'communal areas' lying outside any individual dwelling (e.g. the common parts of a house divided into self-contained flats) are also subject to a different regime and may be eligible for capital allowances (see Section 4.9).

Fixtures, fittings, and anything else that is part of the fabric of the building, are not classed as furnishings for tax purposes and are not eligible for replacement of domestic items relief. However, replacing these items will often be claimable as a repair expense, as discussed in Section 4.7.

4.11 RENT-A-ROOM RELIEF

Rent-a-room relief applies to income from letting out part of your own home as furnished residential accommodation. For this purpose, the property must be your main residence (see Section 6.13) for at least part of the same tax year. The letting itself must also at least partially coincide with a period when the property is your main residence.

The relief covers income from lodgers and even extends to letting a self-contained flat, provided the division of the property is only temporary, and not a permanent conversion.

Complete exemption is automatically provided where the gross annual rent receivable from lettings in the property does not exceed the rent-a-room relief limit of £7,500.

The gross rent receivable for this purpose must include any contributions towards household expenses that you receive from your tenants and any balancing charges arising (see Sections 3.17 and 3.18).

The taxpayer may elect not to claim rent-a-room relief, for example if the letting is actually producing a loss which otherwise could not be claimed. This election must be made within twelve months after the 31st January following the tax year. (E.g. for the tax year 2019/20, the election would need to be made by 31st January 2022.)

Where the gross rent receivable exceeds the rent-a-room limit, the taxpayer may nevertheless elect (within the same time limit as outlined above) for a form of partial exemption. The partial exemption operates by allowing the taxpayer to be assessed only on the amount of gross rents receivable in excess of the rent-a-room limit instead of under the normal basis for rental income.

Example 1
Duncan rents out a room in his house for an annual rent of £8,000. His rental profit for 2019/20, calculated on the normal basis, is £2,800. He therefore elects to use the rent-a-room basis, thus reducing his assessable rental income for 2019/20 to just £500.

The partial exemption available under rent-a-room relief has become attractive to many more landlords renting out a part of their home due to the restrictions in interest relief set out in Section 4.5.

118

Example 2

Linda is a higher rate taxpayer. She rents out a room in her house for an annual rent of £10,000. Computing her rental profits in the normal way would give her allowable interest of £8,000 and other deductible expenses of £400. Back in 2016/17, she was better off paying tax on her actual rental profit of £1,600 rather than claiming partial exemption under rent-a-room relief.

By 2019/20, however, Linda's taxable rental profit has increased to £7,600 due to the restriction in interest relief. She will get basic rate tax relief on a further £6,000 of interest, so her tax bill on an 'actual' basis would be £1,840 (£7,600 x 40% - £6,000 x 20%).

Claiming partial exemption under rent-a-room relief would reduce Linda's taxable rental profit to £2,500 (£10,000 - £7,500) giving her a tax bill, at 40%, of £1,000. Hence, Linda is now better off claiming rent-a-room relief.

Linda's savings under rent-a-room relief will increase next year, in 2020/21; when the claim will save her £1,240.

Other Points on Rent-a-Room Relief

Where the letting income is being shared with another person, the rent-a-room limit must be halved. Oddly, where the income is being shared with more than one other person, there is no further reduction. Hence, three or more joint owners can still all claim half the normal limit.

Where there is any letting income from the same property during the same tax year that does not qualify for the relief, none of the income from the property that year may be exempted.

An election to claim rent-a-room relief is deemed to remain in place for future years unless withdrawn (the same time limit described above applies for a withdrawal).

Rent-a-room relief continues to apply to income from lodgers where additional services are provided, such as cooking, cleaning, etc. Income in excess of the rent-a-room relief limit may, however, be regarded as trading income rather than rental income in these circumstances.

Where you are claiming complete exemption under rent-a-room relief, you should put an 'X' in Box 4 on page UKP 1 of your tax return.

Income eligible for rent-a-room relief is ineligible for the property income allowance (see Section 4.17). Furthermore, where an individual claims actual expenditure against income that would otherwise be eligible for full or partial exemption under rent-a-room relief, they cannot claim the property income allowance that year.

In a few cases, this might mean it is better to claim rent-a-room relief even when allowable expenses exceed £7,500.

Example 3

Bertie rents out a room in his house (his main residence) for an annual rent of £12,000. He has deductible expenses of £7,750 to set against this income, so he would not normally claim rent-a-room relief and would pay Income Tax on his actual profit of £4,250.

However, in 2019/20 he also receives £1,000 from a 'one-off' rental of his holiday home. The allowable expenses deductible from this income under normal principles would only amount to £125.

If Bertie does not claim rent-a-room relief, he cannot claim the property income allowance and would be taxed on total profits of £5,125 (£4,250 + £1,000 - £125).

However, by claiming rent-a-room relief on the income from his main residence, he can exempt the income from his holiday home and be taxed on profits of £4,500 (£12,000 - £7,500), thus reducing his taxable income by £625.

For the sake of illustration, I have assumed Bertie has no allowable interest or finance costs to claim against any of his rental income. If he did, we would also need to factor in the impact of the restrictions to interest relief set out in Section 4.5, in a similar way to Linda in Example 2 above.

4.12 RENTAL LOSSES ON UK PROPERTY

As explained in Section 4.1, all your UK property lettings, apart from furnished holiday lets, are treated as a single UK property business. For loss relief purposes, however, it is necessary to separate UK rental property into three categories:

- Non-commercial lettings (see Section 4.16)
- Furnished holiday lettings (see Section 8.17)
- Other UK rental property (which I will refer to as 'normal' rental property for the sake of illustration)

Losses arising on furnished holiday lettings or non-commercial lettings are subject to special rules, which we will look at in Sections 8.17 and 4.16 respectively.

Losses arising on 'normal' rental property are automatically set off against profits on other 'normal' UK rental property for the same period. Losses on 'normal' UK rental property may also be set off against profits on non-commercial lettings. Any overall net losses from 'normal' rental property remaining after this may be carried forward and set off against future profits from 'normal' UK rental property or non-commercial lettings.

Losses consisting of capital allowances may also be set off against the landlord's other income of the same tax year or the next one (subject to the tax relief 'cap' discussed in Section 3.20).

The treatment of losses from overseas lettings is covered in Section 4.15.

Example
In the tax year 2019/20, Owain has employment income of £70,000, from which he suffers deduction of tax under PAYE totalling £15,500. He also has a portfolio of rented commercial property on which he has made an overall loss of £15,000, including £10,000 of capital allowances. Owain can claim to set his capital allowances off against his employment income, which will produce a tax repayment of £4,000.

How Long Can Rental Losses Be Carried Forward?

Rental losses from 'normal' rental property may be carried forward for as long as you continue to have a 'normal' UK property rental business. There are two major pitfalls to watch out for here.

Firstly, rental losses are personal. They cannot be transferred to another person, not even your spouse, and they do not transfer with the properties. If you die with rental losses, they die with you.

Secondly, if your 'normal' UK property business ceases, you will lose your losses. It may therefore be vital to keep your 'normal' UK property business going. As long as you continue to have at least one 'normal' UK rental property, you still have a 'normal' UK property business.

Example
Fergus has a large UK property portfolio. Despite having made some good profits in the past, by 2019/20 he has rental losses of £1m carried forward. Fergus decides he's had enough and begins to sell off his UK property empire. Before his rental income ceases, however, he buys one small lock-up garage in Preston and starts to rent it out.

Fergus's lock-up garage is enough to ensure he still has a UK property rental business. It doesn't matter that it is tiny by comparison with his previous ventures; this one small garage keeps his rental losses alive, with the possibility of saving him up to £450,000 one day (£1m at 45%).

The only absolutely safe way to ensure you have a continuing 'normal' UK property rental business is to ensure you always have at least one 'normal' UK rental property let out on a commercial basis.

121

However, HMRC will sometimes accept that a total cessation of all 'normal' rental income is not necessarily the same as a cessation of your 'normal' UK rental business, especially where the rental properties are still held.

They will usually accept that the rental business has not ceased:

- Where you can provide evidence that you have been attempting unsuccessfully to let out your property, or
- Where rental has only ceased temporarily whilst repairs or alterations are carried out

They will, however, generally regard the rental business as having ceased if there is a gap of more than three years between lettings and different properties are let before and after the gap.

They may sometimes accept a gap of less than three years as not being a cessation, but not if you have clearly employed all your capital in some other type of business, or spent it for personal purposes, such as buying yourself a new home.

If in doubt though, rent out that garage!

Wealth Warning
An overseas property will not preserve your 'normal' UK property business. A furnished holiday letting or a non-commercial letting (e.g. to your aunt for £1 a year) will not do either.

Another Wealth Warning
On page UKP 1 of the tax return, you are asked to put an 'X' in Box 2 if you do not expect to receive any rental income in the next tax year. Completing this box may be seen as a strong indication that your UK property business has ceased.

I would therefore recommend leaving this box blank where you have rental losses carried forward unless you are absolutely certain you will not have any UK rental income again in the future. (Assuming you are completing your tax return by the normal due date, you cannot yet know that you will not have any rental income in the next tax year anyway.)

The Future of Rental Losses

One of the consequences of the changes to interest relief discussed in Section 4.5 is that landlords with 'normal' residential property are less likely to have allowable rental losses. They will, instead, tend to have excess interest to be carried forward for relief at basic rate. See Section 4.5 for further details.

Even those with existing rental losses are likely to see these effectively 'devalued' and turned into excess interest carried forward for relief at basic rate.

Example

Solomon is a higher rate taxpayer with annual rental profits before interest of £40,000 and interest costs of £50,000. All his rental properties are 'normal' residential property. At the beginning of 2017/18, he had rental losses brought forward of £100,000. Over the next few years, his losses are utilised as follows:

	2017/18	*2018/19*	*2019/20*	*2020/21*	*2021/22*
Profit before interest	40,000	40,000	40,000	40,000	40,000
Deductible interest	(37,500)	(25,000)	(12,500)	0	0
Taxable 'profit'	2,500	15,000	27,500	40,000	40,000
Losses					
Brought forward	100,000	97,500	82,500	55,000	15,000
Set off against profit	(2,500)	(15,000)	(27,500)	(40,000)	(15,000)
Carried forward	97,500	82,500	55,000	15,000	0
Excess Interest					
Brought forward	0	12,500	37,500	75,000	125,000
Arising in year	12,500	25,000	37,500	50,000	50,000
Relieved at basic rate	0	0	0	0	(25,000)
Carried forward	12,500	37,500	75,000	125,000	150,000

As we can see, by the end of this period, all of Solomon's rental losses have effectively been converted into excess interest carried forward for relief at basic rate only.

In 2021/22, he will have taxable income of £25,000 (£40,000 less the final £15,000 of his brought forward losses). This will be taxed at 40%, with interest relief at only 20%, giving him an Income Tax liability of £5,000.

Thereafter, he will have income of £40,000 taxed at 40%, with interest relief at 20%, giving him an Income Tax liability of £8,000 each year.

4.13   OTHER PROPERTY INVESTMENT INCOME

Most forms of income derived from investments in land and property will be subject to Income Tax under the regime outlined in this chapter. This will include tenant's deposits retained at the end of a lease and usually also any dilapidation payments received.

Since 2007, landlords in England and Wales have been required to hold tenant's deposits in escrow. A similar law was introduced in Scotland in 2012. Whatever the legal position, it is important to include deposits retained within your rental income at the end of the lease, but not before. Refunded deposits should never be included in rental income.

Dilapidation payments may sometimes be regarded as a capital receipt instead if the landlord does not rent the property out again (e.g. if the landlord sells it or adopts it as their own home). In a recent case, it was also held that, where the damage to a property is so severe as to lead to a permanent diminution in value, a dilapidation payment might again be regarded as a capital receipt. This is contrary to HMRC's usual view on this issue and it is not yet clear how widely this ruling might be interpreted. Quite possibly, it might only apply in very narrow circumstances similar to the particular case in question. Hence, the general position remains that where the landlord does continue to rent out the property afterwards, dilapidation payments will usually be treated as additional rental income subject to Income Tax.

Where, unusually, a payment is treated as a capital receipt, this will represent a 'part disposal' of the property subject to CGT in a similar way to the premium received on the grant of a long lease (see Section 6.34).

Some items are specifically excluded from property income, including:

- Any amounts taxable as trading income
- Farming and market gardening
- Income from mineral extraction rights

Wayleave (right of access) payments are sometimes included however.

4.14 LEASE PREMIUMS

Premiums received for the granting of short leases of no more than 50 years' duration are subject to Income Tax. The proportion of the premium subject to Income Tax is, however, reduced by 2% for each full year of the lease's duration in excess of one year.

The part of the premium not subject to Income Tax falls within the CGT regime (see Section 6.34) and will be treated as a part disposal of the relevant property.

Example
Alexander owns the freehold to a property and grants a 12-year lease to Kenneth for a premium of £50,000. The lease exceeds one year by eleven years and hence 22% of this sum falls within the CGT regime. Alexander is therefore subject to Income Tax on the sum of £39,000 (i.e. £50,000 less 22%).

If the tenant is running a business from the property (including sub-letting it as a landlord in their own right), the element of the premium which is taxed as income in the hands of the grantor is allowable as a deduction in the tenant's business.

The tenant must, however, claim the allowable element of the premium over the life of the lease. Hence, in Kenneth's case in the example above, he would be able to claim a deduction of £3,250 each year for the twelve years of the lease (£39,000/12 = £3,250).

4.15 OVERSEAS LETTINGS

All of a taxpayer's commercially let overseas properties (with the exception of any furnished holiday lets within the EEA) are treated as a single business in much the same way as, but separate from, a UK property business.

Furnished holiday lets within the EEA (see Section 1.5) are subject to the same special regime as qualifying furnished holiday lets in the UK (see Section 8.17), although, again, these are treated as a separate business.

A UK resident and domiciled taxpayer (see Section 3.8) with overseas lettings is therefore taxed on this income under exactly the same principles as for UK lettings except:

i) Separate accounts will be required for properties in each overseas territory where any double tax relief claims are to be made

ii) Overseas furnished holiday lets outside the EEA are not included within the special regime applying to qualifying furnished holiday accommodation (as detailed in Section 8.17)

Travelling expenses may be claimed when incurred wholly and exclusively for the purposes of the overseas letting business.

The UK tax treatment of losses arising from an overseas letting business is exactly the same as for a UK property business except, of course, that this is treated as a separate business from any UK lettings that the taxpayer has. Hence, again, for loss relief purposes, overseas property must be separated into three categories, as follows:

- Non-commercial overseas lettings (see Section 4.16)
- Furnished holiday lettings within the EEA (see Section 8.17)
- Other overseas rental property (which I will refer to as 'normal' overseas property for the sake of illustration)

As before, the special rules outlined in Sections 8.17 and 4.16 apply to qualifying furnished holiday lets within the EEA and non-commercial overseas lettings respectively.

Losses arising on 'normal' overseas property are automatically set off against profits derived from other 'normal' overseas lettings or non-commercial overseas lettings, with the excess carried forward for set off against future 'normal' overseas rental profits. The same rule as set out in Section 4.12 applies to any capital allowances.

Where there are substantial 'normal' overseas rental losses carried forward, it will be worthwhile ensuring this business continues. The same principles as set out in Section 4.12 will apply here, except that, to continue the business, it is necessary to continue to have 'normal' overseas rental property.

While the property must be let on a commercial basis, and must be outside the UK, it can be in any other part of the world and need not be in the same country as the property that gave rise to the original losses. A loss made in Albania might conceivably be set off against a profit in Zanzibar!

As before, it is essential to remember that a qualifying furnished holiday letting property within the EEA will not suffice to preserve rental losses from 'normal' overseas property.

4.16 NON-COMMERCIAL LETTINGS

Where lettings are not on a commercial or 'arm's length' basis, they cannot be regarded as part of the same UK or overseas property business as any commercial lettings that the taxpayer has. Profits remain taxable, but any losses arising may only be carried forward for set off against future profits from the same letting (i.e. the same property let to the same tenant).

Typically, this type of letting involves the lease of a property to a relative or friend at a nominal rent, considerably less than the full market rent the property could demand on the open market.

Where the tenant of such a non-commercial letting is a previous owner of the property (e.g. a parent of the landlord), the 'Pre-Owned Assets' Income Tax benefit-in-kind charge may apply to the benefit so received by the tenant. In many cases, this will result in the tenant being charged Income Tax on the difference between the nominal rent they pay and full market rent.

4.17 THE PROPERTY INCOME ALLOWANCE

An allowance of £1,000 per year is available to exempt small amounts of property rental income.

Income eligible for rent-a-room relief is ineligible for this allowance. See Section 4.11 for further details of the interaction between these two reliefs and the implications for anyone renting out part of their own home.

Subject to this, the property income allowance applies to an individual's **total** property income for the tax year, both UK and overseas, not to individual properties or leases.

Where the taxpayer's total eligible property income for the tax year exceeds £1,000, they may either deduct expenses as normal, or deduct the allowance from their total income.

The allowance is available to each individual and joint owners may therefore claim up to £1,000 each.

Nonetheless, the allowance is unlikely to be of any use to most landlords with genuine property businesses, but may be useful to anyone who:

- Rents out all or part of their home under circumstances that do not qualify for rent-a-room relief (see Section 4.11);
- Rents out a second home for a short period;
- Starts a property business shortly before the end of the tax year: but bear in mind the ability to deduct 'pre-trading expenditure' when the business starts (see Section 3.9) – this ability would be lost if the property income allowance were used; or
- Has very few allowable costs

As far as the last heading is concerned, any landlord with allowable costs of less than £1,000 would be better off claiming the property income allowance unless computing their results on a normal, actual, basis would lead to a loss which they might be able to utilise in future years. Any capital allowances within such a loss could also be set off against other income in the same tax year or the next.

For higher rate taxpayers with residential lettings who have total allowable costs only a little over £1,000, including some interest and finance costs, it is worth bearing in mind that the property income allowance will be fully deductible whereas their interest and finance costs are not (see Section 4.5).

The property income allowance cannot be claimed if you are receiving **any** rental income from your own company, or a partnership in which you are a partner. These restrictions extend to income from any partnership in which a person 'connected' with you is a partner, and any 'close company' in which you, or a person 'connected' with you, are a 'participator'. See Appendix B for a list of 'connected persons', and see the Taxcafe.co.uk guide *'Using a Property Company to Save Tax'* for an explanation of the other terms used here.

4.18   THE CASH BASIS FOR LANDLORDS

The 'cash basis' of accounting is available to 'unincorporated property businesses', i.e. landlords operating as individuals or partnerships. However, it is **not** available to:

- Businesses with total gross annual rental income exceeding £150,000
- Companies
- Trusts
- LLPs
- Other partnerships with one or more corporate partners

The cash basis is the 'default' option for all eligible landlords. In other words, if you are eligible for the cash basis, it will automatically apply unless you elect to opt out. An election to opt out of the cash basis must be made within one year after the 31st January following the relevant tax year. For example, to elect out of the cash basis for 2019/20, you must make your election by 31st January 2022. The election is made simply by placing an 'X' in Box 5.2 or 20.2, as appropriate, in the UK property supplement of your tax return (see Section 3.5).

Electing out of the cash basis will ensure you are able to continue using the traditional 'accruals basis', which we examined in Sections 3.9 and 4.1, and which it is assumed you are using throughout the rest of this guide.

For the purposes of both the £150,000 threshold and the question of whether you wish to opt out of the 'cash basis', your UK and overseas properties are, as usual, regarded as separate businesses. Hence, you could have £100,000 of gross annual rental income from UK property and £100,000 of gross annual rental income from overseas property and still be eligible for the cash basis for both businesses. Furthermore, you could, if you wish, opt out of the cash basis for one of those businesses but remain in the cash basis for the other.

Where you own any rental property jointly with another person, you must both use the same basis (i.e. either the 'cash basis' or the 'accruals basis') for the relevant property business (UK or overseas). This means many landlords with joint interests in property are unable to use the cash basis.

Example
Samaira owns three UK rental properties, including one that is jointly owned with her brother Tulwar. Tulwar also owns a further nine UK rental properties, including one that is jointly owned with Trinity Properties Limited.

As a company, Trinity Properties Limited is not eligible to use the cash basis. As he owns a property jointly with them, this means Tulwar is also unable to use the cash basis. This, in turn, means Samaira is unable to use the cash basis too, since she owns a property jointly with Tulwar.

The cash basis closely reflects what many landlords actually do in practice and generally means all rent is taxable when received and allowable expenses may be claimed when paid. Subject to the points below, it does not generally alter the question of which expenses are allowable, only the timing of when they may be claimed. There are some important exceptions to this however.

Disadvantages of the Cash Basis

The cash basis is simpler to operate than the normal accruals basis of accounting, but there are a number of reasons why it will not always be beneficial, including:

i)   Rent becomes fully taxable on receipt, even if it relates to a period that extends beyond the end of the tax year

ii)   Expenses that have been incurred but not yet paid at the end of the tax year cannot be claimed

iii)   There is a potential further restriction on interest relief (in addition to the measures set out in Section 4.5) – see further below

iv)   Abortive expenditure relating to potential purchases of new property that are abandoned will not be allowable

v)   Costs of raising loan finance incurred in earlier years and which were being claimed over the useful life of the loan (see Sections 4.4 and 4.6) cannot be claimed

vi)   No deductions will be allowed in respect of lease premiums paid (see Section 4.14)

Further Restriction on Interest Relief

The further restriction on interest relief applies where:

- The total amount borrowed for the purposes of the property letting business (which would otherwise all qualify under the principles set out in Section 4.4), is greater than
- The total value of all the rental properties in the business when first rented out plus other 'capital introduced' (see Section 4.4)

When this restriction applies, the allowable interest under the cash basis is reduced by the appropriate proportion.

Example
Joseph bought a rental property for £100,000 a few years ago. He also paid purchase costs of £2,500 and spent £4,500 on furnishing the property. There were a further £3,000 of initial 'set up' costs, which he was able to claim for Income Tax purposes.

He financed his total costs of £110,000 with a buy-to-let mortgage of £85,000 and a further £25,000 obtained by re-mortgaging his home.

A few years later, he carried out some urgent roof repairs on his rental property at a cost of £5,000. He financed this with a personal loan.

By 2019/20, his total qualifying borrowings (under the principles set out in Section 4.4), are as follows:

Buy-to-let mortgage	*£85,000*
Additional mortgage on home	*£25,000*
Personal loan	*£5,000*
Total	*£115,000*

These give rise to total allowable interest costs of £4,600, which he would be able to claim under the accruals basis (subject to the restrictions in Section 4.5).

However, his total 'capital introduced' (derived on the basis explained in Section 4.4) is as follows:

Value of property when first rented	*£100,000**
Purchase costs	*£2,500*
Furnishings	*£4,500*
Total	*£107,000*

* - As in many cases, where a property is purchased specifically for rental purposes, the value equates to the purchase price

His other 'set up' costs of £3,000 do not count for this purpose as they qualified for Income Tax relief.

If Joseph adopts the cash basis in 2019/20, his allowable interest will be reduced to £107,000/£115,000 x £4,600 = £4,280. He will lose out on £320 of allowable interest. The £4,280 that is allowed will also continue to be restricted as set out in Section 4.5. He will therefore be able to claim a deduction of just £1,070 (25%) and basic rate tax relief on the remaining £3,210 (75%).

An important point to note is that it is only 'capital expenditure' (see Section 3.9) that counts as 'capital introduced' for the purposes of calculating allowable interest. This seldom matters under the accruals basis, as all borrowings used to fund business expenditure qualify for relief. Under the cash basis, however, this distinction is critical.

In the example, I have included the initial cost of furnishing the property as 'capital introduced' (as this is not allowed for Income Tax purposes – see Section 4.10). However, even this is perhaps debatable since the legislation refers to expenditure 'in respect of the property' and one legal interpretation might be that furnishings (see Section 4.10) are not part of the property. Such an interpretation would further reduce Joseph's allowable interest cost under the cash basis to £4,100 – although I would argue my own interpretation is correct.

Further complications arise where the landlord is claiming interest on other borrowings not directly related to any individual rental property.

Example Revisited
Let us now assume that, under the accruals basis, Joseph would also be able to claim part of the hire purchase interest on his car and an element of the original mortgage on his home (before the re-mortgaging referred to above) within his 'use of home' claim (see Section 3.11).

The balance on his hire purchase agreement is £20,000, he uses the car 25% for business purposes and the interest payable during 2019/20 is £4,000.

The balance on his original mortgage (excluding the £25,000 additional re-mortgaging) is £200,000, the interest payable on this balance during 2019/20 is £6,000 and the proportion of fixed costs claimed within his 'use of home' claim is 1.5%. Hence his interest claim under the accruals basis is:

Loans and mortgages (as before)	*£4,600*
Hire purchase (£4,000 x 25%)	*£1,000*
Use of home (£6,000 x 1.5%)	*£90*
Total	*£5,690*

His total qualifying borrowings are now as follows:

Buy-to-let mortgage	*£85,000*
Additional mortgage on home	*£25,000*
Personal loan	*£5,000*
Hire purchase (£20,000 x 25%)	*£5,000*
Original mortgage (£200,000 x 1.5%)	*£3,000*
Total	*£123,000*

His total 'capital introduced' remains £107,000, so his interest claim under the cash basis would now be restricted to £5,690 x £107,000/£123,000 = £4,950.

Joseph is now losing £740 of allowable interest by using the cash basis and can only claim £1,237 (25%) as a deduction; with basic rate relief on the remaining £3,713 (75%).

Interestingly, if Joseph did not include his domestic mortgage interest within his 'use of home' claim, his total allowable claim under the cash basis would increase to £4,993. Landlords using the cash basis and facing this interest relief restriction might therefore do better to exclude claims for balances with low rates of interest.

As usual, these restrictions apply equally to other finance costs paid during the year (but see point (v) above regarding earlier years).

Further Illustration

Let's now look at another example that brings together some of the other disadvantages of the cash basis.

Example

During 2019/20, Safiya receives rent totalling £120,000, pays interest of £70,000 and incurs other expenses of £20,000, including £1,000 for some surveys on properties she later decided not to buy and £5,000 for some roof repairs carried out in March 2020 which she pays in late April.

For interest relief purposes, Safiya has total qualifying borrowings of £1.75m and total 'capital introduced' of £1.65m. £12,000 of Safiya's income was received in the first five days of April 2020 and relates to the rent due for the whole of that month.

Safiya's accountant works out her profit under normal accruals basis principles:

Income due for the year	*£110,000*
(£120,000 - £12,000 x 25/30)	
Less expenses:	
Interest	*£70,000*
Other expenses incurred	*£20,000*
Accrued accountancy fees	*£2,000*
Rental profit	*£18,000*

(£52,500, or 75%, of Safiya's interest expense will be added back to profit for tax purposes and will instead give rise to a tax deduction at basic rate)

If Safiya does not elect to use normal accruals basis accounting, she will fall into the cash basis by default and her profit will then be calculated as follows:

Income received in the year	*£120,000*
Less expenses paid in the year:	
Interest (£70,000 x £1.65m/£1.75m)	*£66,000*
Other	*£14,000*
(£15,000 paid less survey costs not allowed £1,000)	
Net rental income	*£40,000*

(£49,500, or 75%, of Safiya's allowable interest will be added to her income for tax purposes and will instead give rise to a tax deduction at basic rate)

The cash basis would cause a considerable increase in Safiya's tax liability!

It must be admitted that much of the difference arising in Safiya's case is only a question of timing. Nonetheless, she has also permanently lost out on £5,000 worth of allowable expenses (due to the further restriction in interest relief and the denial of relief for her abortive capital expenditure).

And timing is nothing to be sniffed at. Apart from the permanent loss of £5,000 of allowable expenses, a further £17,000 of taxable income has arisen at least a year earlier. For a higher rate taxpayer that means paying £6,800 in tax at least a year earlier, so it's not exactly unimportant.

Advantages of the Cash Basis

In addition to the fact that it is simpler to operate, the cash basis has some other potential advantages. Many of these relate to timing. It is particularly important to note that many landlords who are currently basic rate taxpayers will become higher rate taxpayers in the near future as a result of the restrictions to interest relief covered in Section 4.5. Some will suffer even higher effective tax rates as a result of those restrictions: due to the Child Benefit Charge, the loss of their personal allowance, or being pushed over the additional rate tax threshold.

Hence, the cash basis might sometimes help in the following ways:

i)   The cash basis may sometimes accelerate income into an earlier tax year when the landlord has a lower tax rate

ii)   Expenses incurred during the year but paid after the year end may attract relief at a higher tax rate

iii) Costs of raising loan finance (see Sections 4.4 and 4.6) can be claimed when paid and will not need to be spread over the useful life of the loan. This will not only accelerate relief but may also reduce the impact of the restrictions set out in Section 4.5

As far as point (iii) is concerned, what is not clear is how a loan arrangement fee that is not paid 'up front', but is added to the balance of the loan, should be treated under the cash basis. Arguably, adding the fee to the loan balance might be regarded as paying it, but another view would be that it is only paid as that loan itself is repaid. This would diminish the potential advantage described above.

Capital Expenditure under the Cash Basis

Landlords operating the cash basis may generally claim capital expenditure as it is paid; provided it would otherwise qualify for capital allowances (see Section 4.9) or replacement of domestic items relief (see Section 4.10). Certain expenditure cannot be claimed under the cash basis, however, including cars, land and buildings, 'integral features' (see Section 4.9) and the other excluded items listed in Section 5.12.

With the exception of cars (see below) and expenditure relating to the other excluded items listed in Section 5.12, brought forward balances in capital allowances pools or 'puddles' (see Sections 3.15 and 3.17) are claimed in full in the year the landlord enters the cash basis.

This represents a further advantage of entering the cash basis, but will seldom be of any great benefit as most landlords will already have claimed all their eligible expenditure under the AIA (see Section 3.15).

Landlords using the cash basis should continue to claim capital allowances on cars under the usual principles (see Section 3.16). Landlords using the cash basis cannot claim other capital allowances.

Entering or Leaving the Cash Basis

Transitional rules apply in the year a landlord enters or leaves the cash basis. In effect, these rules ensure that:

- No income escapes tax
- No income is taxed twice
- Expenses cannot be claimed twice

Example Resumed
Safiya opted out of the cash basis in 2019/20, but she decides to use it in 2020/21. This means she will be taxed on the rent she actually receives, with deductions for the allowable expenses she actually pays, but she will also have to make the following adjustments:

i)   *The £10,000 (£12,000 x 25/30) of rent received in the first five days of April 2020 which was excluded from her income in 2019/20 will need to be added to her income for 2020/21*
ii) *The £5,000 she paid for roof repairs in April 2020 cannot be claimed in 2020/21 as she has already claimed this expense*
iii) *The £2,000 accrued for accountancy fees in 2019/20 will have to be deducted from any accountancy fees she actually pays during 2020/21 (if this results in a negative figure, she must report a negative expense)*

Let us also now assume Safiya paid an insurance premium of £1,500 in September 2019 but only claimed half of it in her 2019/20 accounts (under the accruals basis) as it covered the period from October 2019 to September 2020. This would lead to a fourth adjustment under the transitional rules in her 2020/21 accounts, as she would then be able to claim the other half, together with any insurance premiums she actually paid during 2020/21.

Summary

In general, my view is that the cash basis will not usually be beneficial for most landlords for the simple reason that rent is usually received in advance and many expenses are paid in arrears. Hence, the cash basis will generally have the effect of accelerating taxable income into an earlier year. My view is that most landlords will be better off sticking with the accruals basis – BUT it will always be worth considering whether the cash basis might be beneficial when the landlord is eligible.

Chapter 5

How to Save Tax on a Property Trade

5.1 THE TAXATION OF PROPERTY TRADING INCOME

Where your property business is deemed to be a trade, such as property development or property dealing, you will be taxed under a different set of principles to those outlined in Chapter 4. The major points to note are:

i) Properties held for development or sale are treated as trading stock rather than capital assets

ii) Taxpayers with property trades may choose any calendar date as their accounting year end

iii) Profits on property disposals are subject to both Income Tax and NI

iv) There are no restrictions on the rate of tax relief for interest and finance costs incurred in the course of a property trade

v) Most 'abortive' legal and professional fees should be allowed as incurred, as an Income Tax deduction

vi) A broader range of administrative expenditure will be claimable

vii) Capital allowances will usually only be available on your own business's long-term assets

viii) Trading losses may be set off against all your other income and capital gains for the same tax year and the previous one (subject to the restrictions explained in Sections 3.20 and 5.11)

ix) The same trade may involve both UK and overseas properties

x) Non-resident individuals are taxed on trading profits derived from UK land and property and on any trade that is managed in the UK. (For a UK resident but non-UK domiciled individual, a foreign-based property trade deriving profits from overseas properties may be taxed on the remittance basis, with the usual potential drawbacks – see Section 8.25)

xi) Individuals with small trading businesses may elect to use the cash basis outlined in Section 5.12 (which is different to the cash basis for landlords covered in Section 4.18)

5.2 PROPERTIES AS TRADING STOCK

The properties you hold in the business for development and/or sale are not regarded as long-term capital assets. They are, instead, regarded as trading stock.

For tax purposes, all your expenditure in acquiring, furnishing, improving, repairing or converting the properties becomes part of the cost of that trading stock. Many of the issues examined in Chapter 4 regarding the question of whether expenditure is revenue or capital therefore become completely academic. Most professional fees and repairs or improvement expenditure are treated as part of the cost of the trading stock in a property trade. (As explained in Section 3.9, 'revenue expenditure' means expenditure deductible from income; capital expenditure is subject to different rules.)

The way trading stock works for tax purposes can be illustrated by way of an example.

Example Part 1

In November 2019, Camilla buys a property in Cornwall for £265,000. She pays SDLT of £11,200 and legal fees of £1,450. Previously, in October, she also paid a survey fee of £350. Camilla is a property developer and draws up accounts to 31st December each year. In her accounts to 31st December 2019, the property will be included as trading stock with a value of £278,000 made up as follows:

	£
Property purchase	265,000
SDLT	11,200
Legal fees	1,450
Survey fee	350
	278,000

The important point to note here is that, while all of Camilla's expenditure is regarded as revenue expenditure, because she is a property developer, she cannot yet claim any deduction for any of it, because she still holds the property.

Example Part 2

Early in 2020, Camilla incurs further professional fees of £10,000 obtaining planning permission to divide the property into two separate residences. Permission is granted in July and by the end of the year, Camilla has spent a further £40,000 on conversion work. In her accounts to 31st December 2020 the property will still be shown in trading stock, as follows:

	£
Costs brought forward	278,000
Additional professional fees	10,000
Building work	40,000
	328,000

Camilla still doesn't get any tax relief for any of this expenditure.

By March 2021, Camilla has spent another £5,000 on the property and is ready to sell the new houses she has created. One sells quickly for £190,000. Camilla incurs a further £3,500 in estate agent's and legal fees in the process. Camilla's taxable profit on this sale is calculated as follows:

	£	£
Sale proceeds		190,000
Less Cost:		
Total cost brought forward:	328,000	
Additional building costs:	5,000	

Trading Stock prior to sale	333,000	
Allocated to property sold (50%):	166,500	
Add additional costs:	3,500	

		170,000

Profit on sale		20,000

This will form part of Camilla's trading profit for the year ending 31st December 2021.

The additional building spend of £5,000 was allocated to trading stock as this related to the whole property. The legal and estate agent's fees incurred on the sale were specific to the part which was sold and may thus be deducted in full against those sale proceeds.

In the example I have split the cost of trading stock equally between the two new houses. If the new houses are, indeed, identical then this will be correct. Otherwise, the costs should be split between the properties on a reasonable basis – e.g. by total floor area, or in proportion to the market value of the finished properties.

The latter approach would be the required statutory basis if these were capital disposals subject to CGT. Although it is not mandatory here, it might still be a useful yardstick.

The most important point, however, is that, even if Camilla fails to sell the second new house before 31st December 2021, her profit on the first house will still be taxable in full. There is one exception to this, as we shall now examine.

Net Realisable Value

Trading stock is generally shown in the accounts at its cumulative cost to date. On this basis, Camilla's second house, if still unsold at 31st December 2021, would have a carrying value of £166,500 in her accounts.

If, however, for whatever reason, the market value of the property is less than its cumulative cost then, as trading stock, its carrying value in the accounts may be reduced appropriately.

Furthermore, since the act of selling the property itself will lead to further expenses, these may also be deducted from the property's reduced value in this situation. This gives us a value known in accounting terminology as the property's 'net realisable value'.

Practical Pointer
Trading stock should be shown in the accounts at the lower of cost or net realisable value.

Example Part 3
The second new house doesn't sell so quickly, so, in September Camilla decides to take it back off the market and build an extension on the back to make it a more attractive proposition to potential buyers. Unfortunately, however, there are some problems with the foundations for the extension and the costs are more than double what Camilla had expected.

By 31st December, Camilla has spent £30,000 on the extension work and it still isn't finished. Her total costs to date on the second house are now £196,500. Camilla's builder estimates there will be further costs of £12,000 before the extension is complete and the property is ready to sell.

The estate agent reckons the completed property will sell for around £205,000. The agent's own fees will amount to £3,000 and there will also be legal costs of around £750. The net realisable value of the property at 31st December 2021 is thus:

	£	£
Market value of completed property		*205,000*
Less:		
Costs to complete	*12,000*	
Professional costs to sell	*3,750*	

		15,750

Net Realisable Value at 31/12/2021		*189,250*

Since this is less than Camilla's costs to date, this is the value to be shown as trading stock in her accounts. The result of this is that Camilla will show a loss of £7,250 (£196,500 less £189,250) on the second house in her 2021 accounts. This loss will automatically be set off against her £20,000 profit on the first house.

By March 2022, the second house is ready for sale. Fortunately, there is an upturn in the market and Camilla manages to sell the property for £220,000. Her actual additional expenditure on the extension work amounted to £11,800 and the professional fees incurred on the sale were actually £3,900. Camilla's taxable profit on this property in 2022 is thus:

	£	£
Sale proceeds		220,000
Less:		
Value of trading stock brought		
forward, as per accounts:	189,250	
Additional building cost	11,800	
Professional fees on sale	3,900	

		204,950

Taxable profit in year to 31/12/2022		15,050

When Camilla calculates her profit for 2022, she uses actual figures for everything which took place after 31st December 2021, her last accounting date (i.e. the sale price, the final part of the building work and the professional fees on the sale).

However, the property's net realisable value in the accounts at 31st December 2021 is substituted for all the costs which Camilla incurred up until that date. Hence, the apparent loss which Camilla was able to claim in 2021 effectively reverses and becomes part of her profits in 2022.

In this example, some of the actual figures turned out to be different to the estimates previously available. Taxpayers would generally be expected to use the most accurate figures available at the time they are preparing their accounts.

In the case of sale price, however, this should be taken to mean an accurate estimate of the completed property's market value at the accounting date (i.e. 31st December 2021 in this example), rather than its actual eventual sale price.

Potential Changes to Accounting for Trading Stock

As discussed in Section 3.21, the Government may consider allowing businesses to opt out of some accounting adjustments in the future and this could include accounting for trading stock. At present, it is not clear whether this proposal will actually come to fruition and, even if it does, this will probably not be until at least April 2022.

5.3   WORK-IN-PROGRESS & SALES CONTRACTS

Generally, for speculative property developers, their trading stock, as we have seen, is valued at the lower of cumulative cost to date or net realisable value. However, if a contract for the sale of the property exists, the developer has to follow a different set of rules.

This is a complex area of accounting but, broadly speaking, the developer is required to value properties under development, for which a sale contract already exists, at an appropriate percentage of their contractual sale value. This is done by treating the completed proportion of the property as if it had already been sold.

The same proportion of the expected final costs of the development can be deducted from this notional sale. Any remaining balance of development costs is included in the accounts as 'work-in-progress', which is simply a term for trading stock which is only partly completed.

Example

Aayan is building a new house on a plot of land and has already contracted to sell it for £525,000. Aayan draws up accounts to 31st March each year and, at 31st March 2020 the new house is 75% complete. His total costs to date are £320,000, but he expects to incur another £80,000 to complete the house.

Aayan will need to show a sale of £393,750 (75% of £525,000) in his accounts to 31st March 2020. He will, however, be able to deduct costs of £300,000, which equates to 75% of his anticipated final total costs of £400,000 (£320,000 + £80,000). In other words, Aayan will show a profit of £93,750 in his accounts to 31st March 2020, which is equal to 75% of his expected final profit of £125,000. The remaining £20,000 of Aayan's costs to date will be shown in his accounts at 31st March 2020 as work-in-progress.

During the following year, he completes the property at an actual cost of £77,000. His accounts for the year ending 31st March 2021 will show a sale of £131,250, i.e. the remaining 25% of his total sale proceeds of £525,000. From this, Aayan can deduct total costs of £97,000, which is made up of his £20,000 of work-in-progress brought forward and his actual costs in the year of £77,000.

This gives Aayan a development profit of £34,250 for the year ending 31st March 2021.

The effect of this accounting treatment is to accelerate part of the profit on the development. As there is no specific rule to the contrary, the tax position will follow the accounting treatment, so that the developer is taxed on part of their property sale in advance.

It follows that the whole profit on a property for which a sales contract exists will need to be included in the developer's accounts once that property is fully completed. Where this applies, the developer may nevertheless still claim deductions to reflect:

- Any doubt over the purchaser's ability, or willingness, to pay
- Rectification work which is still to be carried out
- Administration and other costs relating to completion of the sale

Practical Pointer

In Section 5.5 we will see that individuals with trading income between £100,000 and £125,000 are subject to an overall effective marginal tax rate of 62% and those with trading income over £150,000 are subject to an overall rate of 47% (at 2019/20 rates). The fact that general accounting principles may require developers to account for part of their profit in an earlier accounting period may not always, therefore, be an entirely bad thing.

Example, continued

Let us assume Aayan has no other sources of income apart from his property development business and he has only one development project in hand during the two year period ending 31st March 2021.

As things stand, his taxable profit of £93,750 for the year ending 31st March 2020 will give rise to an overall combined Income Tax and NI liability of £29,754. His profit of £34,250 for the year ending 31st March 2021 will give rise to a liability of £6,812: a total of £36,566.

If Aayan had not been required to spread his profit and it had all fallen into the year ending 31st March 2021, his total liability would have been £49,139.

Hence, the fact that Aayan is required to account for part of his profit in an earlier year has actually saved him over £12,500.

(2019/20 tax rates have been used throughout this example: see Appendix A. As explained in Section 3.3, 2020/21 rates are expected to be broadly the same)

The outcome will not always be as beneficial as in Aayan's case: especially where the developer has several projects in hand at the same time. However, the example does show that there is a potential benefit to the accounting treatment which some developers are required to follow.

Furthermore, while accounting standards must be adhered to in principle, there is often some leeway regarding the exact amounts to be taken into account in practice. The more profit that falls into an accounting period where the developer has an overall marginal tax rate of 29% or 42%, the less there may be to be taxed in a later period at 47% or 62%. (See Section 5.5 for an explanation of the overall marginal tax rates applying to trading income.)

The proposals outlined in Section 3.21 regarding relaxing the accounting treatment required for trading stock did not extend to situations where a sales contract exists, which we have considered in this section.

5.4   ACCOUNTING DATE

As a property developer or dealer, you may choose any accounting date you like and do not have to stick with a 5th April year end. This provides some useful tax-planning opportunities.

For example, if you feel you are likely to make more sales in the late spring and summer, a 30th April accounting date may be very useful.

Profits made on sales in May or June 2020 would then form part of your accounting profit for the year ending 30th April 2021. For tax purposes, this accounting period falls into the 2021/22 tax year, as it is generally the accounts year end date that determines when profits are taxable.

Under self-assessment, the Income Tax and NI on these profits would not be payable until 31st January 2023, almost ***three years*** after you made the sales!

Early Years

Special rules applying in the first two or three years of a trading business would lead to a different effect: sometimes more beneficial, sometimes less so. Generally, in these early years, if your profit is static, or increasing, you will benefit from an accounting date early in the tax year, such as 30th April.

This usually results in some of your early profits being taxed twice (in two different tax years), but the tax on your later profits is effectively deferred by a year. You will ultimately get a deduction, known as 'overlap relief', for the profits which have been taxed twice, when you cease trading, or sometimes earlier if you change your accounting date.

> **Tax Tip**
> Transferring a trading business to a company counts as ceasing to trade for this purpose and will trigger any overlap relief due (see Section 5.11 for further benefits if this creates a loss).

If you are starting on high profits and expect them to fall thereafter, then a 31st March or 5th April accounting date will generally be preferable.

At present, accounting periods ending during your first three tax years of trading can generally be of almost any duration. Thereafter, you are generally expected to prepare accounts for twelve month periods, unless you change your accounting date.

Under the current rules, you can change your accounting date at any time, although, for the change to be recognised for tax purposes, you cannot generally make a second change within five tax years of a previous change.

Future Rules on Accounting Dates

As part of the proposals for MTD (see Section 3.21), the Government is considering some changes to the rules for accounting periods. The proposals, in brief, are:

- It will be possible to have accounting periods of any length up to twelve months (but never longer)
- The taxable profit for each tax year will be the sum of the taxable profits for all accounting periods ending during that year
- The current 'early years' rules (see above) will be abolished
- Those with an existing entitlement to overlap relief will only be able to claim relief on the cessation of their trade

As with other MTD proposals, these changes are not certain, and are not expected to apply until at least April 2022 at the earliest, in any case.

Tax Tip
Those with an existing entitlement to overlap relief may wish to consider a change of accounting date before April 2022 in order to obtain relief earlier rather than wait until they cease trading. See the Taxcafe.co.uk guide *'Small Business Tax Saving Tactics'* for further details.

5.5   NATIONAL INSURANCE

Unlike a property investment business, the profits of a property trade are regarded as 'earnings' for NI purposes. This means property dealers or developers operating on their own as sole traders, jointly with one or more other people, or in a more formal partnership structure, will be liable for Class 2 and Class 4 NI.

Class 2

Class 2 NI was due to be abolished but, after several stays of execution, it now appears to be sticking around for the foreseeable future. For 2019/20, it is charged at the rate of £3.00 per week. Taxpayers with profits below the 'small earnings exception' limit (£6,365 for 2019/20) are exempt. Class 2 is collected through self-assessment, but is not included within instalments due under that system.

Class 4

Class 4 NI is payable on trading profits at the rates set out in Appendix A. The profits on which it is based are generally the same trading profits as those calculated for Income Tax purposes.

For profits falling to be taxed in 2019/20, this has the result of giving most property traders with no other sources of income the following overall effective tax rates, combining Income Tax and Class 4 NI:

Profits up to £8,632:	Nil
Profits between £8,632 and £12,500:	9%
Profits between £12,500 and £50,000:	29%
Profits between £50,000 and £100,000:	42%
Profits between £100,000 and £125,000:	62%
Profits between £125,000 and £150,000:	42%
Profits over £150,000:	47%

National Insurance for Property Traders in Practice

To see the impact of NI in practice, let's revisit an earlier example.

Example
In Section 3.4, we saw that Meera was paying a total of £3,800 in Income Tax under self-assessment for 2019/20. Let us now assume Meera is a property developer and her £12,000 of property income is a property trading profit. In addition to her Income Tax bill, Meera will also be liable for Class 4 NI of £303 (9% of £12,000 less £8,632) and Class 2 NI of £156, bringing her total self-assessment tax liability up to £4,259.

Taxpayers like Meera with both employment and self-employed trading income may end up paying more NI than the law demands. This can arise where there is more than one source of earned income and the total income from all such sources exceeds the sum of:

    i)   The upper threshold (£50,000 for 2019/20), and
    ii)   The primary threshold (£8,632 for 2019/20)

For the 2019/20 tax year, the relevant sum is £58,632.

In such cases, taxpayers may apply for a refund of the excess NI paid or, if they are able to foresee that this situation is likely to arise, apply for a deferment of their Class 2 or Class 4 contributions.

Tax Tip
If you are already in receipt of other earnings and anticipate that your property trading profits will mean your total earnings for the tax year exceed £58,632, you may wish to consider applying for deferment of NI.

Remember that 'earnings' is generally restricted to employment income and self-employed or partnership trading income. It does not include rental income, pensions, or other investment income.

Age Exemptions

Taxpayers over state pension age on the first day of the relevant tax year are exempt from both Class 2 and Class 4 NI. This includes taxpayers reaching state pension age on 6th April. The state pension age for both genders is currently in the process of being increased from 65 and will reach 66 in October 2020. It is expected to rise again, to age 67, between 2026 and 2028.

Children under 16 on the last day of the tax year are also exempt from both Class 2 and Class 4 NI.

5.6   COMMENCING A PROPERTY TRADE

When you commence a new property trade, you will generally need to register with HMRC as a self-employed trader within three months from the end of the calendar month in which you commence your trade.

Wealth Warning
Failure to register as a self-employed trader within three months of the commencement of trading is subject to a penalty of £100.

In the case of a partnership or joint owners, each individual must register. If any person is already registered due to some other existing source of self-employment trading income, there is no need to register again.

5.7   TRADING DEDUCTIONS: GENERAL

Some individuals or partnerships with small property trades may be able to elect to use the cash basis which we will look at in Section 5.12. Apart from that, the basic principles outlined in Sections 3.9 to 3.12 apply to the deduction of business expenditure from trading profits. Many of the points discussed in Chapter 4 will also remain relevant.

As we already know, under general principles, expenditure must usually be 'revenue expenditure' if it is to be claimed for Income Tax purposes. As we have seen, however, this rule operates quite differently in the context of a property trade. Expenditure on long-term assets for use in the trade will nevertheless continue to be capital in nature, including:

- Office premises from which to run the trade
- Motor vehicles for use in the trade
- Computers
- Building tools and equipment

Capital allowances will be available on much of this expenditure as we shall see in Section 5.9.

Expenses ancillary to the purchase of capital assets continue to be treated as capital expenditure also. Hence, while the legal fees incurred on the purchase of trading stock are a revenue expense, similar fees incurred on the purchase of the business's own trading premises will be capital in nature.

5.8   TRADING DEDUCTIONS: SPECIFIC AREAS

Most forms of business expenditure that meet the criteria outlined in Section 3.9 should be allowable as deductions from trading income. These will include the items we covered in Sections 3.10 to 3.13.

There are a few exceptions that are specifically disallowed, such as business entertaining and gifts. (Even here there can be exceptions to the exceptions.)

In this section, we will quickly look at some of the other main trading deductions to be considered in the specific context of a property trade. As in Chapter 4, however, this is certainly not meant to be an exhaustive list of potential trading expenses.

Interest and Finance Costs

Interest is allowable if it is incurred on funds used for the purposes of the trade. The question of where the borrowings are secured is generally irrelevant (although borrowings secured on the business's own trading premises will follow the same principles as set out in Section 4.4).

The treatment of other finance costs, such as loan arrangement fees, will generally follow the same principles. However, where accounting principles dictate that a cost should be spread over the useful life of the loan, the tax relief will have to be spread over the same period (again following the principles discussed in Section 4.4).

The restrictions on tax relief for interest and finance costs discussed in Section 4.5 do not apply to property trades. Restrictions may, however, apply where properties are temporarily rented out and thus give rise to incidental letting income, as discussed in Sections 2.4 and 2.5.

Legal and Professional Fees

Legal fees and other professional costs incurred on the successful purchase or sale of properties classed as trading stock will be allowed as part of the cost of those properties in the computation of the profits arising on sale. However, costs relating to the purchase or sale of the business's long-term assets remain capital expenses. Other professional costs incurred year in, year out, in earning trading profits may include items such as debt collection expenses and accountancy fees. These costs are deductible as overheads of the business.

Abortive Expenditure

In a property development or dealing trade, abortive costs such as survey fees, advertising or legal fees relating to unsuccessful transactions should be allowed as a trading expense. This should also extend to the costs of any unsuccessful planning applications attempted in the course of the trade. Costs relating to your own business premises are an exception and should be dealt with as discussed in Section 4.6.

Training

Staff training costs are generally allowable. For the business owner themselves, the rule is that expenses incurred in updating or expanding existing areas of knowledge may be claimed, but any costs relating to entirely new areas of knowledge are a personal capital expense. Hence, if you are already a competent plumber but go on a plumbing course to learn the latest techniques in the industry then the cost of this course should be allowable. The cost of the same course would, however, not be allowable if you knew nothing about plumbing.

Health & Safety

Notwithstanding the general rules given in Section 3.9, any expenditure on safety boots, hard hats and other protective clothing or equipment will be allowable. This may sometimes extend to 'all-weather' clothing if the taxpayer spends all or part of their working life outdoors and does not use that clothing for non-business purposes.

5.9   CAPITAL ALLOWANCES FOR PROPERTY TRADES

The basic principles of capital allowances were explained in Sections 3.14 to 3.19. Items typically qualifying as 'plant and machinery' include the following:

- Building equipment and tools
- Computers
- Office furniture, fixtures and fittings
- Vans

Capital allowances cannot generally be claimed on expenditure included within trading stock. Hence, for example, property developers constructing or improving non-residential property cannot claim the SBA (see Section 3.19) on properties held for development, although they may be able to claim it on their own business premises.

Property developers are likely to have greater scope to claim capital allowances than residential property investors but possibly less scope than those with commercial property investments. Property dealers and those with property management businesses will not usually be able to claim quite as many allowances, although the same principles continue to apply.

Capital allowances are available on motor cars used in a property trade, as detailed in Section 3.16.

5.10   PROPERTY MANAGEMENT TRADES

Most of the principles outlined in this chapter apply equally to property management trades. The biggest difference is the fact these trades are unlikely to hold properties as trading stock. Other than their own office premises, any properties held are likely to be investment properties and dealt with in accordance with Chapter 4.

Staff costs are often a significant issue in a property management trade. The NI consequences are examined in Section 7.17.

5.11   TRADING LOSSES

The general rule is you may claim to set trading losses off against your total income for the same tax year and/or the previous one. Where you have claimed to set your losses off against income in one of these years (or you have no such income), you may also claim to set any further losses remaining against capital gains arising in the same year. This gives rise to a number of possible choices (I count eight!)

Any surplus loss remaining is automatically carried forward for set off against future profits from the same trade. This effectively gives rise to a ninth choice: make no claim under the above provisions and carry all your losses forward.

Under a separate provision, losses arising in any of the first four tax years of a new trade may also be carried back against your total income in the three tax years prior to the loss-making year. The loss is relieved against earlier years first.

Under yet another provision, known as 'terminal loss relief', losses arising in the last twelve months of a trade (including 'overlap relief' – see Section 5.4) may be carried back against profits from the same trade arising in the final tax year of the trade and the previous three tax years. In this case, the loss is relieved against the most recent years first.

As we can see, there are many possible ways to relieve trading losses, especially in the early years of a new business. The best choice will depend on the effective tax rates applying in each year and the likelihood of you making profits from the same trade in the future. You generally have until one year after the 31st January following the tax year to decide (the deadline for making claims under most of the above provisions). For example, a claim in respect of a loss arising during 2019/20 must generally be made by 31st January 2022. Whatever choice you make, it is important to remember the same loss can only ever be relieved once.

For the purpose of the above rules, partners are treated as commencing a trade when they join a trading partnership and as ceasing to trade when they leave the partnership.

Sole traders or partnerships transferring a trade to a company (often known as 'incorporation') are treated as ceasing to trade on the date of the transfer. Note, however, that losses which cannot be relieved under any of the above provisions will effectively be lost: they cannot be transferred to the company.

Loss Relief Restrictions

Where trading losses are being set off against income (not capital gains), the relief is subject to the tax relief 'cap' discussed in Section 3.20. This does not apply where the losses are being set against profits from the same trade, or to the extent that the losses include 'overlap relief' (see Section 5.4).

In addition, a 'non-active sole trader' may only claim tax relief against his or her other income and gains for a maximum of just £25,000 of trading losses each year.

Personally, I find the term 'non-active sole trader' to be as much of a contradiction in terms as an 'honest politician', but it is taken to mean someone who spends less than ten hours per week engaged in trading activities. Sadly, this restriction may hit many part-time property developers and other property traders. For those whose business activities average only just over the ten hours per week threshold, it will make sense to keep diaries or other time records to demonstrate hours spent.

Loss relief is also barred for trading losses of a 'non-active sole trader' arising as a result of arrangements made for tax avoidance purposes.

Similar restrictions apply to 'non-active partners' (see Section 8.30).

5.12   THE CASH BASIS FOR TRADING BUSINESSES

Individuals and partnerships with small trading businesses may elect to be taxed under the 'cash basis'. This is generally available to businesses with annual turnover (i.e. total sales) not exceeding £150,000. Those already using the cash basis may continue to do so provided their turnover does not exceed the 'exit threshold' (currently £300,000).

Businesses electing to use the cash basis are taxed simply on the difference between business income received during the year and business expenses paid during the year, instead of under normal accounting principles (the 'accruals basis' – see Section 3.9).

Where the cash basis is being used, there is no distinction between 'revenue expenditure' and 'capital expenditure' (see Section 3.9). Capital expenditure may simply be claimed as it is paid, except for the excluded items listed below.

Excluded Items

Capital expenditure on the following items may not be claimed under the cash basis:

i)   Cars. Motor expenses must continue to be claimed under one of the two alternative methods described in Section 3.12, including capital allowances where appropriate (i.e. where fixed mileage rates are not being claimed).

ii)   Land and buildings. This includes the cost of 'integral features' (see Section 4.9), and other fixtures that might normally qualify for capital allowances, where these are purchased as part of the purchase of business premises. Additional fixtures added to a building later may, however, qualify, and replacements will, of course, usually be correctly classed as repairs and not as capital expenditure.

iii)   Acquisition and disposal costs (the costs of buying or selling the business, or a part of the business).

iv)   Education and training. As explained in Sections 3.13 and 4.8, HMRC regards some of a business owner's own training costs as 'personal capital expenditure' that cannot be claimed for Income Tax purposes.

v)   Non-depreciating assets. Assets that have an expected useful life of 20 years or more, and which will retain at least 10% of their initial value after 20 years, do not qualify.

vi)   Assets not acquired for continuing use in the business.

vii)   Financial assets. This would cover obvious items such as stocks and shares or offshore bonds, as well as other types of financial instrument.

viii)   Intangible assets. The cost of intangible assets cannot be claimed unless they have a fixed life of less than 20 years. This includes any form of intellectual property, such as patents, trademarks or copyright. Note, however, that most expenditure on software is actually just a licence to use the software, so this would not be prevented from qualifying.

Costs incurred in connection with the purchase or sale of any of these items (e.g. legal fees, SDLT, etc) are also prohibited. This exclusion is extended to the costs of any abortive, or unsuccessful, attempts to buy or sell any of these items.

The cost of vans or motor cycles may be claimed under the cash basis, but if the purchase cost is claimed in this way, the mileage allowances explained in Section 3.12 will not be available.

Premiums paid to take out a lease on business premises would be excluded under heading (ii). Under normal accounting rules, part of the premium could usually be claimed for Income Tax purposes (see Section 4.14). Those using the cash basis might therefore be better off negotiating a higher level of rent instead.

It is important to remember the above restrictions only apply to capital expenditure. They do not apply to other valid business expenditure, such as the cost of trading stock, repairs and maintenance, or licence fees.

Prior to 2018/19, any capital expenditure, except cars, that would normally qualify for capital allowances could be claimed under the cash basis.

Further Restrictions

Trading businesses using the cash basis are limited to a maximum claim of £500 per year in respect of interest on cash borrowings. Losses arising under the cash basis can only be carried forward for set off against future profits from the same trade and will not be eligible for the other reliefs described in Section 5.11.

In view of these restrictions, and the turnover limits described above, it seems unlikely that the cash basis will benefit many property developers or dealers. A few property management businesses might perhaps benefit but, again, the restrictions on loss relief and interest relief will often make the cash basis unattractive.

5.13 THE TRADING INCOME ALLOWANCE

An allowance of £1,000 per year is available to exempt small amounts of trading income. Where an individual's total gross trading income for the tax year exceeds £1,000, they may either deduct expenses as normal, or deduct the allowance from the total income.

The taxpayer may also deduct expenses as normal where this gives rise to a trading loss. As we saw in Section 5.11, the relief available for trading losses is quite versatile.

The trading income allowance can be used against casual income, including casual property income (see Section 2.7), following the same principles. However, only a maximum of £1,000 of trading income allowance is available to each individual in each tax year (for example, if £600 is set against casual income, only a maximum of £400 can then be set against trading income).

Where appropriate, a taxpayer can claim both the trading income allowance (against trading income or casual income) and the property income allowance (against rental income or anything else classed as property income – see Chapter 4) in the same tax year.

The trading income allowance is not available on partnership trading income. Furthermore, the allowance is not available at all if you receive any self-employed trading income (as an individual sole trader), or casual income, from your own partnership or company. This restriction extends to income from the same partnerships and companies as for the property income allowance (as detailed in Section 4.17).

Chapter 6

How to Save Capital Gains Tax

6.1 THE IMPORTANCE OF CAPITAL GAINS TAX

Although its impact is not as immediate as Income Tax, CGT is perhaps the most significant tax from a property investor's perspective (though not those who are classed as property developers or property dealers, as we have already seen).

Most property investments will eventually lead to a disposal and every property disposal presents the risk of a CGT liability arising and drastically reducing the investor's after-tax return. Paradoxically, however, CGT is also the tax that presents the greatest number and variety of tax-planning opportunities. We will be examining some of these further in Chapter 8.

In this chapter, we will be examining the current CGT regime and taking a detailed look at how it affects property investors and other people disposing of property. Before we look at the current regime, however, it is worth recalling how CGT developed.

6.2 THE DEVELOPMENT OF CAPITAL GAINS TAX

CGT was introduced by Harold Wilson's first Labour Government in 1965 to combat a growing trend for avoiding Income Tax by realising capital gains, which at that time were mostly tax free.

The high inflation of the 1970s and early 1980s brought about a significant change after March 1982, with the introduction of indexation relief. This was designed to exempt gains that arose purely through the effects of inflation.

In 1987, CGT moved from a flat rate of 30% to a system where gains were taxed at the taxpayer's top rate of Income Tax. In 1997, Gordon Brown introduced taper relief, designed to reward long-term investment by progressively reducing the effective rate of CGT as investments were held over a longer period. Eventually, we reached the point where the effective CGT rate on most commercial property was just 10%.

Then, suddenly, the golden days were over. In 2008, Alistair Darling abolished both taper relief and indexation relief and, after 21 years, took us back to a flat rate system: this time at 18%. Two years later, the Coalition Government created a 'two tier' system by introducing a 'higher rate' of 28%. In 2016 this expanded to a 'four tier' system with the introduction of lower rates of 10% and 20% for capital gains on most assets; but not on residential property.

Finally then, now that every major political party has 'stuck their oar in', we find ourselves lumbered with a CGT system where there is no protection against the effects of inflation, no reward for long-term investment, and a penalty for investing in residential property!

What the current system actually means is, when you hold property as a long-term investment, inflation alone is likely to push you into a higher tax rate. This makes understanding the tax system and the reliefs and planning opportunities available, more important than ever!

6.3   WHO PAYS CAPITAL GAINS TAX?

CGT is payable in the UK by:

i)   UK resident individuals
ii)   UK resident trusts
iii)   Non-UK resident individuals or trusts disposing of direct or indirect holdings of land or buildings in the UK (further details of the UK CGT regime applying to non-UK residents are given in Section 2.15)

Companies pay Corporation Tax on their chargeable gains, rather than CGT. There were a few exceptions to this for disposals made before 6th April 2019: see Sections 2.15 and 7.18 for details. See the Taxcafe.co.uk guide *'Using a Property Company to Save Tax'* for a thorough analysis of the taxation of capital gains made by companies.

For the rest of this guide, I will be concentrating mainly on category (i) above: UK resident individuals investing in property.

Individuals who are UK resident and UK domiciled, or deemed UK domiciled, are liable for CGT on their worldwide capital gains. Individuals who are UK resident, but neither UK domiciled, nor deemed UK domiciled, remain liable for CGT on capital gains arising from the disposal of UK property, but may opt to only be liable for CGT on 'foreign' capital gains if and when they remit their disposal proceeds back to the UK (see Section 8.25).

The tax concepts of residence, domicile, and deemed domicile were briefly examined in Section 3.8. For a more detailed look at the rules on residence, see Section 8.32, and for a thorough examination of domicile (including deemed domicile), see the Taxcafe.co.uk guide *'How to Save Inheritance Tax'*.

6.4   CAPITAL GAINS TAX RATES

CGT is currently paid at five rates:

- 10% where entrepreneurs' relief is available
- 18% on gains on residential property made by basic rate taxpayers
- 28% on gains on residential property made by higher rate taxpayers
- 10% on most other gains made by basic rate taxpayers
- 20% on most other gains made by higher rate taxpayers

The 18% and 28% rates apply to:

- Any interest in land or property that has ever included a residential dwelling at any time during the taxpayer's ownership
- Contracts for off-plan purchases of residential property
- A few other, very limited, cases

Entrepreneurs' relief is seldom available to property investors, except in the case of furnished holiday lets (see Section 8.17). The relief may, however, be highly valuable to property developers, property dealers and those with property management businesses and we will therefore look at it in detail in Section 6.28.

The 'Higher Rates' of CGT

The higher rates of 20% or 28% apply to capital gains made by an individual to the extent that:
i)   Their total taxable income for the tax year (after deducting their personal allowance), plus
ii)   Their total taxable capital gains arising during the tax year,

Exceeds the basic rate band (see Appendix A).

The basic rate band for 2019/20 is normally £37,500, although this can be increased by making pension contributions or gift aid donations. This simple way to save CGT is explored further in Section 8.28.

Individuals who have sufficient income to fully utilise their basic rate band pay CGT at the higher rates on all their taxable capital gains. Basic rate taxpayers pay CGT at 10% or 18% on the first part of their capital gains until their basic rate band is exhausted. Thereafter, any further gains are taxed at the higher rates.

In all cases, the rate applying is reduced to 10% where entrepreneurs' relief is available (see Section 6.28).

Tax Tip

The rate of CGT you pay is linked to the amount of income you have in the tax year. This means you may be able to reduce your CGT bill by ensuring your gains fall into a tax year in which you have a lower level of income. We will take a closer look at the potential savings arising in Section 8.28.

Example

Boudicca is a property investor with several 'buy-to-let' investments. In December 2019, she sells a residential property and realises a gain of £50,000.

Boudicca's taxable income for 2019/20 is £35,000. Deducting her personal allowance of £12,500 (see Appendix A) means £22,500 of her basic rate band has been utilised, leaving £15,000 (£37,500 – £22,500) available for CGT purposes.

Boudicca deducts her annual exemption of £12,000 (see Section 6.29) from the £50,000 gain, leaving a taxable gain of £38,000. The first £15,000 is taxed at 18% and the remainder at 28%, giving her a CGT bill of:

£15,000 x 18%	*£2,700*
£23,000 x 28%	*£6,440*
Total	*£9,140*

Allocating the Annual Exemption and Capital Losses

Taxpayers are generally free to allocate their annual exemption (see Section 6.29), their basic rate band, and any capital losses that they have available (see Section 6.33), between their capital gains in the most beneficial manner.

This will be useful for anyone who has both gains on residential property and other gains arising during the same tax year. In general, it will be preferable to allocate the annual exemption and any available capital losses to the gains on residential property, although the allocation of the basic rate band will usually have no overall effect (there is usually a 10% differential in the tax rate applying in either case).

It will also make sense to allocate the annual exemption and any available capital losses to gains that are **not** eligible for entrepreneurs' relief: although any available basic rate band **must** be utilised against these gains in priority to any others.

Effective Capital Gains Tax Rates

The CGT rates described above apply to the taxable capital gain, not the total gain. The **effective** rates of CGT can vary tremendously, depending on the circumstances.

6.5 WHAT IS A CAPITAL GAIN?

A capital gain is the profit arising on the disposal, in whole or in part, of an asset, or an interest in an asset. Put simply, the gain is the excess obtained on the sale of the asset over the price paid to buy it. (However, as we will see, matters rarely remain that simple.)

Sometimes, however, assets are held in such a way that their disposal gives rise to an Income Tax charge instead. The same amount of gain cannot be subject to both Income Tax and CGT.

Where both taxes might apply, Income Tax takes precedence, so that no CGT arises. (There is little comfort in this, as Income Tax will generally be charged at a higher rate than CGT and is not subject to any of the various CGT reliefs.)

The most common type of asset sale which gives rise to an Income Tax charge, rather than CGT, is a sale in the course of a trade. In other words, where the asset is, or is deemed to be, trading stock.

If a person buys sweets to sell in their sweet shop, those sweets are quite clearly trading stock and the profits on their sale must be subject to Income Tax and not CGT. This is pretty obvious because there are usually only two things you can do with sweets: eat them or sell them.

Properties, however, have a number of possible uses. A property purchaser may intend one or more of several objectives:

a) To keep for personal use, either as a main residence or otherwise
b) To provide a home for the use of family or friends
c) To use the property in a business
d) To let the property out for profit
e) To hold the property as an investment
f) To develop the property for profit
g) To sell the property on at a profit

Objectives (a) to (e) make the property a capital investment subject to CGT.

It has always been the case that, where objectives (f) and/or (g) are the sole or main purpose behind the purchase of the property, then this will render the ultimate gain on the property's sale a trading profit subject to Income Tax. As discussed in Section 2.9, the ultimate gain may now be treated as a trading profit where these objectives are merely **one of the main purposes** behind the purchase.

In the majority of cases, objective (g) is present to some degree. This alone does not necessarily render the gain on the property's sale a trading profit subject to Income Tax. This point is discussed further in Section 2.9.

In practice, there is often more than one objective present when a property is purchased and objectives (f) and (g) may exist to a lesser or greater extent. In many cases, the correct position is obvious but, in borderline situations, each case has to be decided on its own merits.

Some of the key factors to consider are described in Section 2.9. Here though, it is perhaps worth looking at a few more detailed examples.

Example 1
James bought a house in 1990 which he used as his main residence throughout his ownership. In 2005 he built an extension, which substantially increased the value. He continued to live in the house until eventually selling it in 2020.

This is clearly a capital gain because James carried on using the house as his private residence for many years after building the extension. Furthermore, the house will be exempt from CGT, as it was James's main residence throughout his ownership.

Example 2
Charles bought a house in 1990 and used it as his main residence for five years. In 1995, he moved into a new house and converted the first one into a number of flats. Following the conversion, Charles let the flats out until he eventually sold the whole property in 2020.

Charles has also realised a capital gain as the property was initially acquired as his own home, he occupied it for five years, and the conversion work was clearly intended as a long-term investment. (Charles would have a partial exemption under the main residence rules.)

Example 3
William, a wealthy man with three other properties, bought a derelict barn in 2018. He developed it into a luxury home. Immediately after the development work was complete, he put the property on the market and sold it in early 2020.

This would appear to be a trading profit subject to Income Tax. William simply developed the property for profit and never put it to any other use. (But see Section 2.9 regarding the importance of the investor's original intentions.)

Example 4
Anne bought an old farmhouse in 2019. She lived in the property for three months and then moved out while substantial renovation work took place. After the work was completed, she let it out for six months. Halfway through the period of the lease she put the property on the market and sold it with completion taking place the day the lease expired.

This is what one would call 'borderline'. Anne has had some personal use of the property, and has let it out, but she has also developed it and sold it after only a short period of ownership. This case would warrant a much closer look at all of the circumstances. It ***should*** be decided on the basis of Anne's intentions but who, apart from Anne herself, would ever know what these truly were?

Such a case could go either way. The more Anne can do to demonstrate her intention had been to hold the property as a long-term investment, the better her chances of success will be. Her personal and financial circumstances will be crucial. For example, if she had got married around the time of the sale, or had got into unexpected financial difficulties that forced her to make the sale, then she might successfully argue for CGT treatment.

Note that, just because the profit arising on a sale is a capital gain, this does not necessarily mean it is subject to CGT. A number of assets may be exempt from CGT, including motor cars, medals and Government securities. Most importantly for property investors, the taxpayer's only or main residence is also exempt and we will return to this in Section 6.13.

The bad news is no relief is allowed for capital losses derived from exempt assets.

6.6   WHEN DOES A CAPITAL GAIN ARISE?

For CGT purposes, a disposal is treated as taking place as soon as there is an unconditional contract for the sale of an asset. The effective disposal date may therefore be somewhat earlier than the date of completion of the sale. This is an absolutely vital point to remember when undertaking any CGT planning.

Example
Aidan completes the sale of a residential investment property on 8th April 2020. However, the unconditional sale contract was signed on 1st April 2020. Aidan's sale therefore falls into the 2019/20 tax year and any CGT due will be payable by 31st January 2021. As we shall see in Section 6.30, this actually means the due date of payment is delayed in this case, although in previous years it would have meant it was accelerated by a year.

Apart from the due date for payment of CGT, the deemed disposal date can also impact on the applicable rate of CGT (see Section 6.4); the extent of any available reliefs (see Sections 6.13 and 6.14); whether or not the taxpayer is UK resident (see Section 8.32); and many other important factors. So it's always critical, but especially this year, when we need to know whether the disposal is on or before, or after, 5th April 2020!

Where the contract remains conditional on some event beyond the control of the parties to it, then the sale is not yet deemed to have taken place for CGT purposes. The most common scenarios here are for the sale to be conditional on:

- Completion of a satisfactory survey
- Approval of finance arrangements
- The granting of planning permission

Many English investors who have travelled north of the border get caught out by the Scottish system where the conclusion of missives generally creates an unconditional binding contract.

What if there is no sale?

The conclusion of an unconditional contract only determines the **date** of the disposal for CGT purposes. If the sale falls through, then no sale will have taken place and there will be no disposal for CGT purposes.

6.7   SPOUSES AND CIVIL PARTNERS

There are a number of cases where, although an asset is held as a capital investment, there is deemed to be no gain and no loss arising on a disposal. The most important instance of this is that of transfers between spouses or registered civil partners. The effect is that these transfers are *totally exempt* from CGT.

Despite a number of other proposed changes we will see later in this guide (see Section 8.4, in particular), there are no proposals to change *this* exemption and transfers between spouses after 5th April 2020 will remain exempt from CGT, although the consequences of those transfers may change.

The exemption comes into force on the date of marriage or registration and continues to apply for the whole of any tax year during any part of which the couple are living together as spouses or civil partners.

Separated couples remain 'connected persons' (see Section 6.9) after the exemption has been lost. Divorced couples only become unconnected persons for tax purposes after the grant of a decree absolute.

If the couple separate, the exemption ceases to apply at the end of the tax year of separation.

6.8   THE AMOUNT OF THE GAIN

Having established that a gain is subject to CGT, we now need to work out how much the gain is. The essence of this is the gain should be the excess obtained on the sale of the asset over the price paid to buy it. However, in practice, thanks to the many complexities introduced by tax legislation over more than 50 years, there are a large number of other factors to be taken into account.

Hence, one has to slightly amend the definition to the following:

'A capital gain is the excess of the actual or deemed proceeds arising on the disposal of an asset over that same asset's base cost.'

A shorter version of this is: Gain = Proceeds Less Base Cost

The derivation of 'Proceeds' is examined in Section 6.9 below. 'Base Cost' is covered in Sections 6.10 and 6.11.

6.9   PROCEEDS

In most cases, the amount of 'Proceeds' to be used in the calculation of a capital gain will be the actual sum received on the disposal of the asset. However, from this, the taxpayer may deduct incidental disposal costs in order to arrive at 'net proceeds', which is the relevant sum for the purposes of calculating the capital gain.

Incidental disposal costs which may be deducted from sales proceeds include any expenditure incurred wholly and exclusively for the purpose of making the sale, such as legal fees, estate agents' commission, advertising costs and the cost of producing a 'Seller's Pack'.

Professional fees incurred for the preparation of valuations required for CGT purposes may also be included in disposal costs.

Example
In March 2020, George sells a house for £375,000. In order to make this sale, he spent £1,500 advertising the property, paid £3,750 in estate agents' fees and paid £800 in legal fees. His net proceeds are therefore £368,950 (£375,000 LESS £1,500, £3,750 and £800).

Now this sounds very simple, but it is not always this easy.

Exceptions

There are a number of cases where the proceeds we must use in the calculation of a capital gain are not simply the actual cash sum received. Some of the most common exceptions are set out below.

Exception 1 – Connected persons

Where the person disposing of the asset is 'connected' to the person acquiring it, the open market value at the time of the transfer must be used in place of the actual price paid (if any).

Example

Mary sells a property to her son Philip for £500,000, at a time when its market value is £800,000. She pays legal fees of £475. Mary will be deemed to have received net sale proceeds of £800,000 (the market value). The legal fees she has borne are irrelevant, as this was not an 'arm's-length' transaction.

See Appendix B for a list of 'connected persons'. Note, however, that the exemption for transfers between spouses (see Section 6.7) takes precedence over the market value rule for transfers between connected persons.

Exception 2 – Transactions not at 'arms-length'

Where a transaction takes place between 'connected persons', there is an automatic assumption that the transaction is not at 'arm's-length' and market value must be substituted for the actual proceeds.

There are, however, other instances where the transaction may not be at 'arm's-length', such as:

- The transfer of an asset between partners in an unmarried couple
- A sale of an asset to an employee
- A transaction which is part of a larger transaction
- A transaction which is part of a series of transactions

The effect of these is much the same as before – the asset's market value must be used in place of the actual proceeds, if any.

The key difference from Exception 1 is that it's the circumstances involved in the transaction that determine whether or not it's at 'arm's-length', rather than there being an automatic assumption that it is not at 'arm's-length' simply because of the relationship between the parties.

Example

John has a house worth £200,000. If he sold it for this amount, he would have a capital gain of £80,000. Not wishing to incur a CGT liability, John decides to sell the house to his friend Richard for £120,000. However, John only does this on condition that Richard also gives him an interest-free loan of £80,000 for an indefinite period.

The condition imposed by John means this transaction is not at 'arm's-length'. John will be deemed to have sold the house for £200,000 and will still have a capital gain of £80,000.

Wealth Warning

Where a person has disposed of an asset at less than an 'arm's length' value, whether to a connected person or not, there is a danger of Income Tax charges arising if the original owner later derives any benefit from the transferred asset. IHT charges may also arise if the original owner dies within seven years of making the transfer. These charges do not apply to transfers between spouses however.

Exception 3 – Non-cash proceeds

Sometimes all or part of the sale consideration will take a form other than cash. The sale proceeds to be taken into account in these cases will be the market value of the assets or rights received in exchange for the asset sold.

Example

Matilda is an elderly widow with a large house she no longer needs, so she offers it to Stephen, who lives nearby with his wife and young children. Rather than pay the whole amount in cash, Stephen offers £150,000 plus his own house, which is worth £200,000.

Matilda incurs legal fees of £2,400 on the transaction and pays SDLT of £1,500 to acquire Stephen's house. 75% of the legal fees are for the sale of her old house and the rest for the purchase of Stephen's.

Matilda's total sale proceeds are £350,000. This is made up of the cash received plus the market value of the non-cash consideration, i.e. Stephen's house. Matilda may deduct her incidental costs of disposal from her proceeds in her CGT calculation. This is unaltered by the existence of non-cash consideration: the transaction has still taken place on 'arm's-length' terms. However, as far as her legal fees are concerned, it is only the element relating to the disposal of her old house (£1,800) that may be deducted. The element relating to the purchase of Stephen's house will be treated as an acquisition cost for that house, as will the SDLT Matilda paid.

Hence, the net sale proceeds to be used in Matilda's CGT calculation are £348,200 (£350,000 LESS £1,800).

Exception 4 – Structures and Buildings Allowance Claims

As explained in Section 3.19, any SBA claimed by the property owner must be added to their sale proceeds.

6.10 BASE COST

The 'Base Cost' is the amount that may be deducted in the CGT calculation in respect of the cost of the asset being disposed of. The higher the base cost, the less CGT payable!

In most cases, the basic starting point will be the actual amount paid. To this may be added:

- Incidental acquisition costs (e.g. legal fees, SDLT)
- Enhancement expenditure (e.g. the cost of building an extension)
- Expenditure incurred in establishing, preserving or defending title to, or rights over, the asset (e.g. legal fees incurred as a result of a boundary dispute)

Interest payable and any other costs associated with raising finance, i.e. mortgaging or re-mortgaging the property, cannot be included in the base cost. For rental property, these are dealt with as set out in Sections 4.4 and 4.5.

Survey fees will often be part of the cost of raising finance, especially if the survey was only carried out at the lender's request. However, a survey carried out at the purchaser's own instigation prior to their making, or finalising, any offer for the property may be claimed as an acquisition cost for CGT purposes.

Any costs claimed for Income Tax purposes cannot also be claimed for CGT purposes. As explained in Section 4.7, however, any expenditure on newly acquired rental properties that is not allowed for Income Tax purposes on the grounds that it is capital in nature should be allowed for CGT purposes on a disposal of that property.

Example
George (remember him from Section 6.9?) bought a house in July 1984 for £60,000. He paid Stamp Duty of £600, legal fees of £400 and removal expenses of £800.

Shortly after moving into the house, George spent £3,000 on redecorating it. £1,800 of this related to one of the bedrooms, which was in such a bad state of repair that it was unusable. The remainder of the redecorating expenditure merely covered repainting and wallpapering the other rooms in the house.

In March 1985, George's neighbour erected a new fence a foot inside George's back garden, claiming this was the correct boundary. George had to take legal advice to resolve this problem, which cost him £250, but managed eventually to get the fence moved back to its original position.

In October 1987, the house's roof was badly damaged by hurricane-force winds. The repairs cost £20,000, which, unfortunately, George's insurance company refused to pay, claiming he was not covered for an 'Act of God'.

In May 1995, George did a loft conversion at a cost of £15,000, putting in new windows and creating an extra bedroom. Unfortunately, however, he had not obtained planning permission and, when his neighbour filed a complaint with the council, George was forced to restore the loft to its original condition at a further cost of £8,000.

In August 1998, George had the property extended at a cost of £80,000. He also incurred professional fees of £2,000 obtaining planning permission, etc.

When George eventually sold the property in March 2020 for £375,000, his base cost for CGT purposes was made up as follows:

- *Original cost - £60,000*
- *Incidental costs of acquisition - £1,000 (legal fees and Stamp Duty, but not the removal expenses, which were a personal cost and not part of the capital cost of the property)*
- *Enhancement expenditure - £1,800 (restoration of the 'unusable' bedroom; the remaining redecoration costs are not allowable, however, as the other rooms were already in a fit state for habitation and George's expenditure was merely due to personal taste, rather than being a capital improvement)*
- *Expenditure incurred in defending title to the property - £250 (the legal fees relating to his neighbour's new fence)*
- *Further enhancement expenditure - £82,000 (the cost of the new extension, including the professional fees incurred to obtain planning permission)*

Total base cost: £145,050

Notes to the Example

i.   If the house were George's only or main residence throughout his ownership, his gain would, in any case, be exempt from CGT. However, we are assuming that this is not the case here for the purposes of illustration.

ii. The cost of George's roof repairs do not form part of his base cost. This is not a capital improvement, but repairs and maintenance expenditure of a revenue nature.

iii. Neither the cost of George's loft conversion, nor the cost of returning the loft to its original condition, form part of his base cost. This is because enhancement or improvement expenditure can only be allowed in the capital gains calculation if the relevant 'improvements' are reflected in the state of the property at the time of the sale.

iv. Based on net proceeds of £368,950 (Section 6.9), George has a capital gain of £223,900 (£368,950 - £145,050) before any applicable reliefs.

Wealth Warning
An additional point to note under (iii) above is that enhancement or improvement expenditure is only deductible if still reflected in the state of the property at the date of **completion** of the sale.

Practical Pointer
George might be able to argue that part of the cost of the loft conversion was still reflected in the state of the property at the date of sale. It is always worth looking at these things in detail!

6.11 BASE COST – SPECIAL SITUATIONS

As with 'Proceeds', there are a number of special situations where 'Base Cost' is determined by reference to something other than the amount paid for the asset. The major exceptions fall into two main categories:

- The asset was not acquired by way of a 'bargain at arm's length'
- The asset was acquired before 1st April 1982

Inherited Assets
All assets are 'rebased' for CGT purposes on death. Hence, the base cost of any inherited asset is determined by reference to its market value at the date of the previous owner's death. Note that, whilst transfers on death are exempt from CGT, they are, of course, subject to IHT. See the Taxcafe.co.uk guide *'How to Save Inheritance Tax'* for further details.

Example 1
Albert died on 20th January 2001, leaving his holiday home, a cottage on the Isle of Wight, to his son Edward. The property was valued at £150,000 for probate purposes. In August 2002, Edward had a swimming pool built at the cottage at a cost of £40,000. He sold the cottage for £397,000 in March 2020. Edward's base cost is £190,000. His own improvement expenditure (£40,000) is added to the market value of the property when he inherited it. Any expenditure incurred by Albert is, however, completely irrelevant.

Assets acquired from spouses
As explained in Section 6.7, when an asset is transferred between spouses, that transfer is treated as taking place on a no gain/no loss basis. In the case of a subsequent disposal, the transferee spouse effectively takes over the transferor spouse's base cost.

Example 2
Henry bought a house for £350,000 in 1999. He spent £100,000 on capital improvements and then gave the house to his wife Katherine in 2001. Katherine had the house extended in 2003 at a cost of £115,000 and eventually sold it in 2020 for £750,000. Katherine's base cost for the house is £565,000. This includes both her own expenditure and her husband's.

The 'no gain/no loss' rule does not apply in the case of a transfer on death, when the inheritance rules explained above take precedence.

Where the transferor spouse originally acquired the property before April 1998 and transferred it to the transferee spouse before 6th April 2008 (but not on death), the indexation relief that the transferor would have been entitled to at that time (if they had actually sold the property) is added to the transferee spouse's base cost.

Example 3

Andrew bought a house for £100,000 in March 1985. In March 2008, he transferred the house to his wife Sarah. If Andrew had actually sold his house before 6th April 2008, he would have been entitled to indexation relief at 75.2%, i.e. £75,200. Sarah's base cost for the house is therefore £175,200.

Details of indexation relief rates applying to a transfer between spouses any time between 1st April 1998 and 5th April 2008 (inclusive) can be found in the 20th edition of this guide.

Where a part share in a property has been transferred between spouses, the same principles apply to the part transferred.

Assets acquired from connected persons or by way of a transaction not at 'arm's length'

As explained in Section 6.9, the transfer of an asset to a connected person is deemed to take place at market value. The market value rule also applies in other circumstances where an asset has not been acquired by way of a transaction at 'arm's length' ('Exception 2' in Section 6.9 provides further guidance).

In both cases, for the person acquiring an asset by way of such a transfer, the market value at that date becomes their base cost.

Assets with 'held-over gains'

From 6th April 1980 to 13th March 1989, it was possible to hold over the gain arising on the transfer of any asset by way of gift. Since then, it has only been possible to hold over gains arising on transfers by way of gift that are:

- Transfers of qualifying business assets, or
- Chargeable transfers for IHT purposes

Gains may not be held over on transfers into a 'settlor-interested trust' after 9th December 2003. This is a trust that includes the transferor, their spouse or, from 6th April 2006, a dependent minor child of the transferor, as one of its beneficiaries.

The base cost of an asset that was subject to a hold-over election when it was acquired is reduced by the amount of the held over gain.

Example 4

In January 1989, Arthur gave Camelot to his son Lancelot. Camelot's market value at that date was £100,000 and Arthur and Lancelot jointly elected to hold over Arthur's gain of £70,000. In 1990 Lancelot had the property extended for £55,000. Lancelot's base cost is £85,000 (£100,000 LESS £70,000 PLUS £55,000 – his own enhancement expenditure is still added on, as normal).

Where the held over gain arose before 6th April 2008, the amount held over will be the gain arising after indexation relief. Hence, as with transfers between spouses (see above), where the transferor originally acquired the property before April 1998, the transferee's base cost will effectively include the indexation relief that the transferor would have been entitled to if they had actually sold the property.

As explained in Section 3.19, where a gain on non-residential property is held over after October 2018, any structures and buildings allowance claimed by the transferor will effectively be deducted from the transferee's base cost.

Assets acquired for non-cash consideration
Where an asset was acquired for non-cash consideration, its base cost will be determined by reference to the market value of the consideration given.

Assets acquired before 1st April 1982
Where an asset was acquired before 1st April 1982, its market value at 31st March 1982 must be substituted for its original cost. Enhancement or improvement expenditure may only be included where incurred after 31st March 1982.

6.12 CAPITAL GAINS TAX RELIEFS

It is at this point in the CGT calculation, after deducting the base cost, that most reliefs and exemptions may be claimed, where appropriate. These include:

- Principal private residence relief (for taxpayers selling their current or former only or main residence). This is covered in detail from Section 6.13 onwards
- Private letting relief (where a property eligible for principal private residence relief has also been let out as private residential accommodation). See Section 6.14
- Relief for reinvestment of gains in Enterprise Investment Scheme shares or Seed Enterprise Investment Scheme shares (see Sections 8.21 and 8.23 for further details)
- Set off of trading losses arising in the same tax year or the next one (see Section 5.11)
- Holdover relief on gifts of business assets (this is not generally available on investment property apart from furnished holiday lets: see Sections 8.17 and 8.18; see the Taxcafe.co.uk guides

'Using a Property Company to Save Tax' or *'How to Save Inheritance Tax'* for a full analysis of this relief)

- Holdover relief in respect of chargeable transfers for IHT purposes (see Section 8.9)
- Holdover relief on transfer of a business to a limited company (see the guide *'Using a Property Company to Save Tax'*)
- Rollover relief on replacement of business assets (see Section 8.27)

All these reliefs are claimed before entrepreneurs' relief, capital losses and the annual exemption. We will look at these last three items later, but first we must look at the most important relief for the residential property investor: principal private residence relief.

6.13   PRINCIPAL PRIVATE RESIDENCE RELIEF

Most people are aware that the sale of their home is exempt from CGT. In technical terms, this is known as the principal private residence ('PPR') exemption. What is less well known is just how far PPR relief may currently extend, especially when combined with other available exemptions and reliefs.

Each unmarried individual, and each legally married couple, is entitled to the PPR exemption in respect of their only or main residence. The PPR exemption currently covers the period during which the property was their main residence PLUS their last eighteen months of ownership.

Example
Elizabeth bought a flat for £160,000 in July 2012. In July 2018, she married Philip and moved out of her flat. In January 2020, she receives an offer to sell the flat for £195,000, but is concerned about her potential tax liability.

Elizabeth needn't worry. If she makes this sale, her gain on the flat will be exempt under PPR relief. The first six years of her ownership are exempt because it was then her main residence and the last eighteen months because it was a former main residence.

Sadly, in the 2018 Budget, the Chancellor announced proposals to reduce the final period of exemption under PPR relief from eighteen months to just nine months. It is proposed that the reduced period of exemption will apply to disposals taking place after 5th April 2020.

Where the property owner is disabled or resident in a care home, the final period of exemption is three years.

What if the property has been let out?

The final period of exemption under PPR relief is always available on any former main residence, regardless of whether the property is let out during that final period. Hence, letting the property after you have moved out will make no difference to your CGT position during this period. (Income Tax is, of course, due on the rental profits.)

If you retain the property for longer than the final period of exemption allowed under PPR relief after it ceased to be your main residence, you will no longer be fully covered by the PPR exemption alone. However, at this point, another relief may currently come into play: private letting relief. We will examine this in the next section.

Does The Property Have to Become Your Main Residence Immediately on Purchase to Qualify?

To be *fully* exempt from CGT under the PPR exemption alone, the property will generally need to become your only or main residence immediately on purchase; or perhaps shortly afterwards, under the circumstances outlined in Section 6.17.

> **Practical Pointer**
> Technically, a property that was your only or main residence at some point and which you then sold no more than eighteen months after purchase should also currently be fully covered by PPR relief. Disposals after 5th April 2020 will need to take place within nine months of purchase for this to apply.
>
> However, such short periods of ownership could lead to doubts over whether the property was genuinely a capital asset (see Sections 2.9 and 6.5 for further details). Similarly, a very short period of occupation can lead to doubts over whether it is genuinely a private residence (see Section 8.10). Nonetheless, where there are good reasons for the short period of ownership and residential occupation, full relief may be available.

If you don't fit one of the situations above, you won't be fully covered by PPR relief alone. However, you will still get a proportional relief based on your period of occupation of the property as your main residence, plus last eighteen months of ownership (nine months for disposals taking place after 5th April 2020).

Combined with other reliefs, this will often be enough to prevent any CGT arising, but you may have to report the gain on your tax return.

Example
Alexander buys a house in December 2013 as an investment and lets it out for two years. In December 2015, he sells his own home and moves into the new house. Alexander then sells the new house in December 2019. Alexander has used the house as his main residence for four years out of six and hence will be exempt on four sixths of his capital gain by virtue of PPR relief.

Alexander cannot benefit from the additional final period of ownership rule because he was living in the house at the time anyway. The extra eighteen or nine month period is not given in addition to an exemption for actual occupation during the same period. This is why when people ask me, "Do you need to live in the house at the beginning to get PPR relief?" I always answer, "No, but it works best that way."

Tax Tip
Occupying a property as your only or main residence will produce the best result if this is not at the end of your period of ownership.

What If Part Of The Property Is Unused?

The PPR exemption is not restricted merely because part of the property is left vacant and unused. Restrictions may apply, however, where part of the property is used for some purpose other than the owner's private residential occupation.

The position for gardens, grounds and outbuildings is different and is examined in Section 6.16.

6.14   PRIVATE LETTING RELIEF

In the previous section, we saw how the PPR exemption extends to cover the capital gain on a former only or main residence for a further eighteen months after it ceases to be your own home (nine months for disposals after 5th April 2020).

Additionally, any property that qualifies as your only or main residence at any time during your ownership, and which you have, at some time, let out as private residential accommodation, will also currently qualify for private letting relief (but see further below for disposals after 5th April 2020). This relief will also apply where you let out a part of your home.

Private letting relief is given as the lowest of:

    i)   The amount of gain already exempted under PPR relief,
    ii) The gain arising as a consequence of the letting, and
    iii) £40,000

Usually, it is the lower of (i) and (iii), especially if the property has been let out ever since the owner ceased to reside in it.

Example
Margaret purchased her flat for £100,000 in March 2005. It was her main residence until March 2011, when she moved out and began to rent it out. In March 2020, she sells the flat for £180,000.

A total of seven and a half years of her ownership is exempt under PPR relief –
the six years she lived in it and the final eighteen months of her ownership. Her
total gain over 15 years is £80,000. Half of this (7½ out of 15) is covered by
PPR relief, leaving £40,000, which is covered by private letting relief. Hence,
Margaret has no CGT liability on her flat!

Multiple Sales of Former Homes

The £40,000 limit described above applies to every property that has been
your only or main residence at any time during your ownership. Hence,
even if you were to sell two or more former homes during the same tax
year, you could still be entitled to up to £40,000 of private letting relief
on each property.

What if the property was let out <u>before</u> becoming your main residence?

At present (until 5th April 2020), any property that qualifies for partial
exemption under PPR relief, and which has also been let out as private
residential accommodation at <u>any time</u> during the taxpayer's ownership,
is also eligible for private letting relief. Hence, private letting relief
currently applies equally where a property is let out first and then
subsequently becomes the owner's main residence.

If, in the latest example, Margaret had instead rented her flat out from
2005 to 2007, then lived in it as her main residence for six years before
continuing to rent it out again, the result would be exactly the same.

As we have already seen though, there is no additional benefit to be
derived from the extension to the PPR exemption for a former main
residence's final period of ownership if, in fact, it is still your main
residence throughout that time in any case. We left Alexander in just this
sort of situation in Section 6.13. How will private letting relief operate in
his case?

Example
Alexander, as we know, had a rented property from 2013 to 2015, which he
then lived in as his main residence from 2015 to 2019. His total capital gain
was £180,000 and four sixths of this was covered by the PPR exemption. This
leaves him with a gain of £60,000. He will be able to claim private letting relief
of £40,000, leaving a taxable gain of just £20,000.

This may not be the end of the story, as Alexander will probably still have his
annual exemption to reduce his taxable gain further (see Section 6.29). This
would reduce his taxable gain to just £8,000 (£20,000 - £12,000), giving him a
CGT bill somewhere between £1,440 (18%) and £2,240 (28%). Even at the
most, this is still just 1.24% of his total gain of £180,000.

Disposals after 5th April 2020

For disposals taking place after 5th April 2020, the Government is proposing to restrict private letting relief to periods when the owner of the property is in "shared occupancy" with a tenant. In other words, it will be restricted to periods when you are renting out part of your home while it is still your main residence.

The proposed restriction will apply to all letting periods in respect of any property disposed of after 5th April 2020, regardless of when the letting took place. Hence, it will have a significant retrospective effect on property rented out prior to April 2020.

Furthermore, it is also proposed that private letting relief will be denied for any lettings in the course of a trade. This will take the relief away from many live-in guest house or hotel owners (these types of property are considered further in Section 8.19).

At the time of writing, the relevant legislation intended to enact these proposals has not yet been passed by Parliament, so they remain 'proposals' at present. Nonetheless, it seems likely that the Government will probably go ahead with them. Hence, for the remainder of this guide, we will assume the proposals, as they stand, will become law on 6th April 2020.

Readers must, however, remember there remains a chance, albeit slim, that the proposals could be altered, or even abandoned, before then.

Planning for the Proposed Change

The proposed change will mean most landlords are unable to claim private letting relief on property disposals after 5th April 2020. The only time the relief will still be available is where the landlord has had a lodger or other tenant in their own home in circumstances similar to the example in Section 6.26.

This will give rise to substantial increases in CGT liabilities for many people selling a former home. We will look at some potential solutions to this in Sections 8.5, and 8.34 to 8.36.

6.15 PLANNING WITH PRINCIPAL PRIVATE RESIDENCE RELIEF

In our first example in Section 6.14, Margaret managed to make a tax-free capital gain of £80,000 despite living in her flat for only six years out of a total of fifteen and she didn't even need to use her annual exemption. This remarkable result arose due to the powerful combination of reliefs currently available for a former main residence.

Things were not quite so rosy for Alexander and he did end up with a tax bill after only six years of ownership, despite living in the property for four years. To some extent this shows how much better the PPR exemption works if you move into the property as your main residence immediately on purchase.

However, Alexander's effective tax rate of just 1.24% still shows how the combination of reliefs available on a property occupied as your main residence at any time during your ownership may currently operate to eliminate most, if not all, of any taxable capital gain.

Sadly, it looks like things will be quite different for sales taking place after 5th April 2020. If we take the same facts as in Section 6.13, but simply assume everything moves forward in time by one year (and also assume the proposed changes discussed in Sections 6.13 and 6.14 are enacted), then:

- Margaret would benefit from PPR relief for six years and nine months out of her total ownership period of 15 years. This would exempt £36,000 out of her £80,000 gain, but she would not get any private letting relief. Deducting her annual exemption of £12,000 (say) would still leave a taxable gain of £32,000, giving her a tax bill somewhere between £5,760 and £8,960.
- Alexander would continue to benefit from PPR relief of £120,000 but would not get any private letting relief. Deducting his annual exemption of £12,000 (say) would leave a taxable gain of £48,000, giving him a tax bill somewhere between £9,690 and £13,440. His maximum effective tax rate increases from 1.24% to 7.5%.

In Chapter 8 we will look at ways in which the PPR exemption and its associated reliefs can be used to allow a taxpayer to invest in property with little or no exposure to CGT and we will consider the impact of the proposed changes applying to disposals after 5th April 2020.

6.16   GARDENS AND GROUNDS

There have been a large number of cases before the Courts over whether the 'grounds' of a house, including some of the subsidiary outbuildings, are covered by the PPR exemption.

In the usual situation, where a house has a reasonably normal sized garden and perhaps a shed, a garage or other small outbuildings, there is no doubt that the entire property is covered by the PPR exemption.

Naturally, we are talking here only of the situation where there is no use of any of the property other than private residential occupation.

Where the whole property is let out at some point, so that private letting relief currently applies, the garden and 'modest' grounds continue to be covered by the relevant reliefs in the same way as outlined in previous sections.

The general rule for grounds is that these are deemed to form a normal part of the property where they do not exceed half a hectare (1.235 acres) in area (including the area on which the house stands). Beyond this, it is necessary to argue that any additional space is required 'for the reasonable enjoyment of the dwelling-house as a residence'.

What does this mean? Well, unfortunately, this is one of those rather enigmatic answers that judges love to give and which can only be decided on an individual case-by-case basis.

The whole situation changes once any part of the property is used for any other purpose. Here the position differs for buildings or gardens and grounds. Gardens and grounds obtain the same exemptions that are due on the house itself as long as they are part of the 'private residence' at the time of sale.

For subsidiary buildings, it is necessary to apportion any gain arising between the periods of residential occupation and the periods of non-residential use.

Example
Lady Jane has a large house with grounds totalling half a hectare in area. For several years, she leased half her grounds to a neighbouring amusement park for use as a car park. Within this half of her grounds there is a small outbuilding that was used as the parking attendant's hut.

When the amusement park gave up its lease over Lady Jane's grounds, she hired a landscape gardener to restore them. The outbuilding reverted to its previous use as a storage shed for garden equipment.

In 2020, Lady Jane sold the entire property. Apart from the lease of the car park, the whole property had been used as her main residence throughout her ownership.

Lady Jane's main house and her entire grounds will be fully covered by the PPR exemption. However, the element of her gain relating to the outbuilding must be apportioned between the periods of private use and the period of non-residential use. The non-residential element of the gain will be chargeable to CGT.

Tax Tip
Lady Jane may have been better off demolishing the outbuilding prior to the sale of her house. No part of her gain would then have related to this building and her entire gain would have been covered by the PPR exemption. Naturally, it is only worth doing

this if demolishing the building does not impact on the whole property's sale price by more than the amount of the potential tax saving.

Wealth Warning
Unlike the house itself, the PPR exemption does not extend to unused outbuildings or gardens and grounds and ***actual use*** for private residential purposes is required.

6.17 DELAYS IN OCCUPYING A NEW HOME

Many people buy a 'run-down' property and then embark on substantial renovation works before occupying it as their own main residence. In other circumstances, a planned move may be held up by unforeseen delays in selling the existing home.

The tax rules cater for this and the PPR exemption specifically extends to cover any period of up to one year in which the taxpayer cannot occupy a newly acquired property due to either:

i)   An unavoidable delay in selling their old property, or
ii) The need to await the finalisation of renovation or construction work on the new property

During this period, it is possible for both the old and new properties to simultaneously be covered by the PPR exemption. Of course, the scope for claiming this exemption is lost if the new property is being used for some other purpose between purchase and initial occupation as the taxpayer's main residence (although private letting relief might apply to this period in appropriate circumstances and where the property is sold before 6th April 2020).

For disposals taking place after 5th April 2020, it is proposed to increase the one year period allowed under these circumstances to two years (this proposal is part of the same draft legislation I referred to in Section 6.14).

At present, HMRC will only allow the initial one year period to be extended to up to two years under exceptional circumstances. This extension is not granted lightly and is reserved for genuine cases of delay caused by factors beyond the taxpayer's control. You would also be expected to have done everything in your power to facilitate the property being ready for your occupation within the original one year period.

If the delay in occupation extends beyond the permitted period, PPR exemption is lost for the whole period prior to occupation of the property.

The initial period allowed for renovation of property also applies to a new property built on a vacant plot of land.

The property or land must be bought with the intention of adopting it as your main residence and must not be used for any other purpose prior to occupation.

6.18   TEMPORARY ABSENCES

The PPR exemption remains available in full for certain temporary periods of absence, as follows:

i)   Any single period of up to three years, or shorter periods totalling no more than three years, regardless of the reason,

ii) A period of up to four years when the taxpayer or their spouse is required to work elsewhere by reason of their employment or their place of work, and

iii) A period of any length when the taxpayer or their spouse is working in an office or employment whose duties are all performed outside the UK.

These temporary absences are only covered by the PPR exemption if:

a) PPR relief has not been claimed on any other property in respect of the same period (see further below),

b) The taxpayer occupies the property as their main residence for a period before the absence period, *and*

c) Either:

- The taxpayer occupies the property as their main residence for a period after the absence period, or

- In the case of absences under (ii) or (iii) above, the taxpayer or their spouse is prevented from resuming occupation of the property following their absence by reason of their place of work or a condition imposed by their contract of employment that requires them to reside elsewhere (such a condition needs to be a reasonable requirement to secure the effective performance of their duties).

These rules take precedence over the rules on whether a property qualifies as a private residence during the absence period (see Sections 6.20 and 6.21): unless the property undergoes a significant 'change of use' (such as being converted into a shop or office, or into multiple dwellings).

Barring a 'change of use', however, there is nothing to prevent the taxpayer from renting out the property during a qualifying absence period and still obtaining PPR relief for that period.

Benefits and Pitfalls

Only periods for which the owner actually **claims** PPR relief on another property must be excluded. This opens up a whole area of tax planning, especially for individuals who move away from home to take up employment elsewhere.

In some cases, however, the absence rules may actually be disadvantageous. In Section 8.16 we will look at the potential pitfalls and how to avoid them.

6.19 PROPERTIES HELD IN TRUST

A trust is a separate legal entity in its own right for tax purposes. The PPR exemption extends to a property held by a trust when the property is the only or main residence of one or more of the trust's beneficiaries.

However, the PPR exemption is not available on a property held by a trust if a hold-over relief claim was made on the transfer of that property into the trust (see Section 8.9). In some cases this may lead to a difficult decision:

- Decline to make a hold-over relief claim at the outset and pay some CGT immediately, or
- Make the hold-over relief claim and risk paying a great deal more CGT on the eventual sale of the property

In essence, one has to weigh up the prospective current tax bill against the ultimate tax potentially arising in the future.

Properties with held over gains already held in trust before 10th December 2003 are still eligible for PPR relief in respect of periods of occupation by a beneficiary as their main residence prior to that date. The additional period of relief at the end of the trust's ownership does not apply however.

Similar restrictions apply where a hold over relief claim has been made when a property was transferred out of a trust. Once again, PPR relief cannot be claimed on a subsequent disposal of that property by the transferee.

Despite these restrictions, trusts can still be used as a means to obtain PPR relief on properties occupied by adult children or other friends and relatives. We will return to this subject in Section 8.14.

Trusts also have their own annual exemption. This is generally half the amount of an individual's annual exemption (see Section 6.29), but must be further reduced where the same person has transferred assets into more than one trust.

Subject to any available reliefs (including entrepreneurs' relief), trusts pay CGT at the higher rates of 20% and 28%.

6.20   WHAT IS A RESIDENCE?

Before we go any further, it is worth pausing to consider what we mean when we refer to a property as a taxpayer's residence.

As we will see in Section 6.22, we are sometimes concerned with situations where a taxpayer has more than one residence. One of these will be their main residence and will qualify for PPR relief.

But no property can be a **_main_** residence until it is **_a_** private residence of that individual taxpayer or married couple.

The question of whether a property qualifies as the owner's private residence at any given time is generally decided purely as a question of fact: based on the principles which I shall outline throughout the rest of this section. In some cases, however, those principles are subject to the additional rules set out in Section 6.21.

Having said that, it is worth pointing out that the additional rules in Section 6.21 can never apply to a disposal of UK property by an individual who has been UK resident throughout their ownership of that property. Hence, most UK residents selling UK property will only need to be concerned with the basic principles covered below.

Residence Principles

A residence is a dwelling in which the owner habitually lives. While it needs to be habitual, however, their occupation of the property might still be occasional and short.

Example
Constantine owns a small cottage in Pembrokeshire but lives and works in London. Constantine bought the Pembrokeshire cottage as a holiday home, but only manages to visit it about two or three times each year, when he will typically stay for the weekend. Despite the rarity of Constantine's visits to his cottage, it nevertheless qualifies as his private residence.

Some actual physical occupation of the property (including overnight stays) is necessary before it can be a residence. Constantine's situation is probably just about the minimum level of occupation that will qualify.

'Dwelling' means a property suitable for occupation as your home and can include a caravan or a houseboat. It will not, however, include a plainly unsuitable property such as an office, shop or factory. (Although there are flats over shops and offices that are dwellings!)

To 'live' in a property means to adopt it as the place where you are based and where you sleep, shelter and have your home. In principle, these guidelines apply equally to both UK and overseas property, so a foreign property could also be classed as the owner's residence: although this is now subject to the additional rules set out in Section 6.21.

Some other use of a property at other times, when not occupied as the taxpayer's private residence, does not necessarily prevent it from qualifying as a residence. If such a property were treated as your main residence though, there would be a proportionate reduction in the amount of PPR relief.

Example

On 1st April 2010, Bonnie bought a small cottage on Skye for £100,000. For the next ten years, she rented the cottage out as furnished holiday accommodation for 48 weeks each year and occupied it herself for the remaining four weeks. Bonnie's regular occupation of the cottage is enough to make it a residence. In this example we are also going to assume it is her main residence throughout her ownership.

On 1st April 2020, Bonnie sells the cottage for £204,000, realising a total capital gain of £104,000. For the eight and a half years from April 2010 to September 2018, Bonnie is only entitled to PPR relief on 4/52nds of her capital gain, reflecting her private use of the property. As usual, Bonnie is entitled to full relief for the last eighteen months of ownership (this would be nine months if her disposal took place after 5th April 2020).

Bonnie's capital gain amounts to £10,400 per year (£104,000/10), so her total PPR relief is therefore as follows:

£10,400 x 8½ x 4/52 =	*£6,800*
£10,400 x 1½ =	*£15,600*
Total:	*£22,400*

Bonnie will also be entitled to private letting relief of £22,400 (under current Government proposals, this relief will not be available on a disposal taking place after 5th April 2020: see Section 6.14). Assuming her annual exemption of £12,000 is available in full her taxable capital gain will be just £47,200. (Bonnie may also be entitled to other reliefs. We will therefore return to this example in Section 8.17.)

Bonnie is still able to treat the cottage as her private residence, even though she is renting it out as holiday accommodation. However, where a property is rented out for longer periods under a lease, it cannot be regarded as the owner's residence during the period of the let.

A residence for CGT purposes must also be a property in which the taxpayer has a legal or equitable interest. A legal interest means any form of ownership, sole or joint, including freehold, leasehold, commonhold, or the tenancy of a property rented under a lease.

An equitable interest is less easy to define. Generally it must mean some sort of right over the property itself and not merely an ability to reside in it. Hence, for example, if an individual stays rent free with family or friends, they are occupying the property under gratuitous licence and clearly have no equitable interest.

Occupation of property may also be under contractual licence, such as staying in a hotel, hostel, guest house or private club. This again does not give the guest any equitable interest in the property.

An unmarried partner in a co-habiting couple may perhaps have an 'equitable interest' in the couple's home when it is owned wholly by the other partner, although this point has not yet been tested in court in connection with CGT.

For married couples, the principles regarding residences and main residences must be applied to the couple as a single unit. Hence, for example, if William owns a property in Brixham which he has never visited, but his wife Mary stays there regularly, then that property must be counted as a private residence of the couple.

If an individual or married couple has only one property that qualifies as a private residence, then that property must be their main residence for CGT purposes. Indeed, HMRC's own Capital Gains manual sets out the principle that where an individual's main home is occupied under licence, but they also own another residence, the residence which that individual owns must be regarded as their main residence for CGT purposes.

Once an individual or married couple has more than one eligible private residence, we need to work out which is their main residence. We will look at this issue in Sections 6.22 to 6.24.

6.21   PRIVATE RESIDENCE RESTRICTIONS

In some cases, the principles set out in Section 6.20, which determine whether a property qualifies as the owner's private residence, are subject to an additional rule.

For taxpayers who are non-UK resident at the time of the disposal, the additional rule applies to any period throughout their ownership of the property.

For taxpayers who are UK resident at the time of the disposal, the additional rule only applies to determine whether a property qualifies as their private residence during periods after 5th April 2015.

The Rule for UK Residents

For taxpayers who are UK resident at the time of the disposal, a property cannot be their private residence for any part of any tax year from 2015/16 onwards unless the owner is either:

a)   Resident for tax purposes (for at least half of that tax year) in the country in which the property is located, or
b)   Physically present in the property at midnight on at least 90 days during that tax year

For the second test, 'days' spent in the property by the owner's spouse may also be counted, as well as 'days' spent (by either of them) in another residential property which the taxpayer owns in the same country (but the same 'day' cannot be counted twice).

For the years in which the property is purchased or sold, the 90 day requirement is proportionately reduced, as appropriate. For example, where a property was purchased on 1st May 2019, the test for 2019/20 under (b) above becomes 84 days (90 x 341/366 – rounded up).

The Cinderella Syndrome

For the purpose of the '90 day test' you need to be present in your home at midnight in order for a day to be counted. This could mean that, like Cinderella, you may need to leave the ball (or party, dinner, friend's house, bar, restaurant, etc) early in order to get back home by midnight.

This may seem like a really petty point (indeed it is), but I would not put it past HMRC to make use of it when your day count is exactly 90 or only just over.

Who Is Affected?

The additional restrictions affect three types of taxpayer:

i)   Non-UK residents disposing of UK property
ii)   UK residents disposing of overseas property, and
iii)   UK residents disposing of UK property after having been non-UK resident at some earlier point in their ownership of the property after 5th April 2015

I will take a closer look at the impact on UK residents disposing of overseas property in Section 6.23.

Those falling in the third category will often benefit from the 'periods of absence' rules in Section 6.18, which take precedence over the rules outlined in this section.

6.22 SECOND HOMES

The detailed rules on what constitutes a private residence are set out in Sections 6.20 and 6.21. Any reference to a 'residence' or 'private residence' in this section is based on the assumption that the property in question qualifies as a private residence under those rules.

For CGT purposes, each unmarried individual and each legally married couple can generally only have one main residence at any given time. Many people, however, have more than one private residence.

When someone acquires a second (or subsequent) private residence they may, at any time within two years of the date they first occupy the new property as a private residence, elect which of their properties is to be regarded as their main residence for the purpose of the PPR exemption.

The election must be made in writing and sent to the taxpayer's tax office. An unmarried individual must sign the election personally in order for it to be effective. A married couple must both sign the election.

There is no particular prescribed form for the election, although the following example wording would be suitable for inclusion:

> 'In accordance with section 222(5) Taxation of Chargeable Gains Act 1992, [I/We] hereby nominate [Property] as [my/our] main residence with effect from [Date*].'

* - The first such election that an individual or married couple makes in respect of any new combination of private residences will automatically be treated as coming into effect from the beginning of the period to which it relates – i.e. from the date on which they first occupied that new combination of residences. It is this first election for the new combination of residences to which the two-year time limit applies.

Tax Tip
If the two year period for making an election has expired, a new one can be opened up in a number of ways, such as:
- Acquiring an additional private residence
- Selling the main home and moving elsewhere
- Renting out one of the properties for a short period and then re-occupying it as a private residence thereafter

Once an election is in place, it may be changed, by a further written notice given to HMRC under the same procedure, at any time. A new election may be given retrospective effect, if desired, by up to two years. We will take a closer look at the benefits of this in Chapter 8.

Example

Alfred lives in a small flat in Southampton where he works. In September 2015 he also bought a house on the Isle of Wight and started spending his weekends there. In August 2017, he realised his island house had appreciated in value significantly since he bought it. His small mainland flat had not increased in value quite so significantly. He therefore elected, before the expiry of the two-year time limit, that his island house was his main residence.

In March 2020 Alfred sells the Isle of Wight house at a substantial gain, which is fully exempted by PPR relief. Alfred's flat will not be counted as his main residence from September 2015 until the time of sale of his island house. However, should he sell the flat, his final eighteen months of ownership will be covered by the PPR exemption (nine months if the sale takes place after 5th April 2020).

> #### Tax Tip
> As soon as Alfred sold his Isle of Wight house, he should have submitted a new main residence election nominating the Southampton flat as his main residence once more: with effect from a date eighteen months previously. This would give an extra eighteen months of PPR relief on the flat, while still leaving the Isle of Wight house fully exempt. In fact, where the annual exemption or other reliefs are available, it might be worth backdating the new main residence election a little further (up to two years).
>
> If Alfred sold his Isle of Wight house after 5th April 2020, this would alter the position but it would still be worth backdating the new main residence election by at least nine months.

Regardless of any election, a property may only be a main residence for PPR relief purposes if it is, in fact, the taxpayer's private residence. Hence, a property cannot be covered by the PPR exemption while being let (subject to the exceptions covered in Sections 6.18 and 6.24; and the final period of ownership exemption applying to a former main residence: see Section 6.13). It could nevertheless still attract private letting relief if it were the taxpayer's main residence at some other time and were sold before 6th April 2020.

If one of a taxpayer's residences ceases to be occupied by them as a private residence (e.g. because it is let out or sold), any main residence election that has been made will cease to apply, even an election in favour of a different property!

Wealth Warning

A new election is required every time the taxpayer, or married couple, has a new combination of two or more private residences. Where a third residence is acquired, for example, a new election must be made. Remember a property may qualify as a residence whenever the taxpayer or their spouse has *any* legal or equitable interest in it, no matter how small.

Where the number of private residences reduces to one, no election is required as the sole remaining residence must now be the main residence.

In the absence of a valid election, the question of which property is the taxpayer's main residence has to be determined on the facts of the case. Often the answer to this will be obvious but, in borderline cases, HMRC may determine the position to the taxpayer's detriment. Clearly then, it is *always* wise to make the election!

The factors to be considered when determining which property was a taxpayer's main residence for any given period not covered by an election, include:

- The address given on the taxpayer's tax return
- The address shown on other correspondence, utility bills, bank statements, etc.
- Where a mortgage was obtained over a property before April 2000, whether mortgage interest relief (MIRAS) was claimed
- Whether the mortgage over a property was obtained on the basis that it was the taxpayer's main home
- The security of tenure (leasehold, freehold, etc) held over each residence
- How each residence is furnished
- Where the taxpayer's family spend the majority of their time
- Where the taxpayer is registered to vote
- The location of the taxpayer's place of work
- The location of the medical practices with which the taxpayer is registered (doctor, dentist, etc)
- The registered address for the taxpayer's car

As always, a married couple have to be considered as a single unit.

Each factor above is not conclusive in its own right but will contribute to the overall picture of which property may be regarded as the main residence.

In Section 6.20 we considered the issue of whether a property was occupied under licence or whether an equitable interest existed. Where a taxpayer has only one residence in which they have a legal or equitable interest, a main residence election will not be valid.

My advice, however, is that whenever there is any possibility that a taxpayer may have two or more eligible private residences they should make a main residence election. If this election proves to be invalid, no harm is done and the property in which the taxpayer has a legal or equitable interest will automatically be treated as their main residence.

6.23 HOMES ABROAD

It is important to remember the PPR exemption applies to a taxpayer's main residence, not, as some people have mistakenly thought to their cost, their main <u>UK</u> residence.

Subject to the rules set out in Section 6.21, it is possible for a UK resident individual or married couple to have a private residence overseas.

For periods prior to 6th April 2015, this will continue to be determined purely under the principles set out in Section 6.20.

Where this means the individual or married couple had two or more private residences at some time in the past, and there was no main residence election in place at the time, the position will have to be determined under the principles set out in Section 6.22. Generally, one would expect this to lead to the conclusion that the UK home was the main residence, although there will be exceptions. Naturally, where there was a main residence election in place, this will determine the position.

Where an overseas property was an individual or married couple's main residence for any period of time (whether by way of a main residence election or otherwise), the PPR exemption will apply in the same way as for a main residence in the UK. Private letting relief will also be available in exactly the same way, where applicable. As we have already seen, these reliefs can be extremely valuable!

It is fairly unusual for an overseas property to qualify as a UK resident's main residence as a question of fact: although it can happen (perhaps where the overseas property is the only property in which the owner has any legal or equitable interest, as discussed in Section 6.22). Furthermore, some overseas properties will have been a UK resident owner's main residence at some time in the past when they were resident overseas.

But, apart from these exceptions, in the vast majority of cases, the only way for a UK resident to achieve main residence status on an overseas property is to make a main residence election in favour of that property. As we shall see in Chapter 8, such an election will almost always be beneficial, even if it is only for a short period.

Sadly, it is no longer possible to make a main residence election in favour of an overseas property unless it qualifies as a private residence under the rules set out in Section 6.21. For a UK resident, this will generally mean needing to spend at least 90 days during one or more UK tax years in the foreign holiday home: and that could have foreign tax consequences.

Example

Abdul and Vicky, a UK resident married couple, own a holiday home in Spain. In June 2019, Vicky spends 25 nights in the Spanish property. Abdul spends 25 nights there in August. In January 2020, Vicky returns and spends another 23 nights in the property and Abdul makes a return visit of 20 nights in March.

Between them, the couple have spent 93 nights in the property during 2019/20. They therefore pass the '90 day test', the property qualifies as their private residence and they can make a main residence election in favour of it covering all or part of the 2019/20 UK tax year.

Furthermore, as (like most countries) Spain uses a calendar year for its tax year, neither of them has spent more than 25 days in Spain in any Spanish tax year (assuming the nights in their holiday home were the only nights they spent in Spain). Hence, although it always remains essential to take local advice on such matters, neither Abdul nor Vicky is likely to be treated as resident in Spain for tax purposes.

Assuming the Spanish property did not qualify as Abdul and Vicky's private residence in 2018/19, the time limit for their main residence election will be 6th April 2021. This would appear to remain the case even if the property qualified as their private residence at some earlier time.

Tax Tip

Failing to meet the '90 day test' in one year and then meeting it in the next would appear to be another way to create a new combination of private residences and thus open up a new two year period for making a main residence election – even one in favour of an entirely different property.

Wealth Warning 1

Where an overseas property qualifies as a private residence in one year, having not qualified in the previous year, this will have exactly the same implications for any existing main residence elections as detailed in the previous section.

Wealth Warning 2

Disposals of overseas property may also have foreign tax implications: even when the owner remains UK resident.

It is worth remembering that the '90 day test' is proportionately reduced in the year of acquisition or disposal of the property. Hence, for example, where a foreign holiday home was purchased on 1st February, it would only be necessary to occupy it for 16 nights between then and 5th April for it to qualify as a private residence and thus be eligible for a main residence election covering that period.

Where an overseas property has qualified as a private residence for more than two years, it remains possible to make a main residence election in favour of that property where there is an earlier existing election in favour of another property within the same combination of two or more residences (see Section 6.22).

6.24   JOB-RELATED ACCOMMODATION

In many occupations, it is sometimes necessary, or desirable, for the taxpayer to live in accommodation specifically provided for the purpose. Examples include:

- Caretakers
- Police officers (in some rural areas)
- Pub landlords
- Members of the clergy
- Members of the armed services
- Teachers at boarding schools
- The Prime Minister and the Chancellor of the Exchequer

For people in this type of situation, the PPR exemption may be extended to a property that they own and which they eventually intend to adopt as their main residence.

In these circumstances, the PPR exemption will cover their own property during the period they are living in 'job-related accommodation', despite the fact that their own property is not their residence at that time and even while they are letting it out.

This provides an exception to the general rule that there must be some actual physical occupation of a property for it to be eligible for PPR relief.

This treatment can also be extended to a property owned by the spouse of a person living in job-related accommodation, which the couple eventually intend to adopt as their main residence.

If a taxpayer in job-related accommodation has a property that might qualify as a main residence under these rules but also has another residence, such as a holiday home, they can use a main residence election to determine which property is given the PPR exemption.

The election will also be appropriate where the taxpayer has some legal or equitable interest in the job-related accommodation itself.

6.25   WHAT IF PART OF YOUR HOME IS NOT PRIVATE?

Whenever any part of your home is put to some use other than your own private residential occupation, you are inevitably putting your PPR exemption at risk. In the next two sections, we will look at the most common types of 'other use' and their tax implications.

One fundamental principle to note is that if any part of your home is used exclusively for purposes other than your own private residential occupation throughout the period when that property qualifies as your main residence, then that part will not be eligible for any PPR relief at all.

Hence, in order to maximise your PPR relief, I would generally recommend making some private use of every part of the property at some time while it is your main residence.

Private letting relief does extend to a part of a main residence that has never been used privately by the owner, where appropriate; provided that it remains part of the same 'dwelling' (e.g. bedrooms within a flat that the owner shares with other flatmates). There is sometimes some resistance on this point from HMRC in the case of guest houses and hotels with live-in owners, and the proposed changes discussed in Section 6.14 will mean the relief is definitely no longer available in these cases for disposals taking place after 5th April 2020.

6.26   LETTING OUT PART OF YOUR HOME

Taking a Lodger

HMRC generally accepts that taking in one individual lodger does not necessitate any restriction to the PPR exemption. In this context, a 'lodger' is someone who, while having their own bedroom, will otherwise live as a member of the taxpayer's household.

Other lettings within the same 'dwelling'

Where part of the property is let out under other circumstances, the PPR exemption will be restricted. However, private letting relief is available to cover this restriction and, in this case, will continue to be available after 5th April 2020 (except in the case of guest houses, hotels and other lettings in the course of a trade: see Sections 6.14 and 8.19).

Example
Robert bought his five-storey house for £300,000 in May 2004. From August 2015 to December 2019 he let the top two floors out as a flat. He then resumed occupation of the whole house, before selling it in May 2020 for £750,000. Robert's total gain of £450,000 is covered by the PPR exemption as follows:

Lower three floors: The gain of £270,000 (three fifths) is fully covered by the PPR exemption.

Upper two floors: The gain of £180,000 is covered by the PPR exemption from May 2004 to August 2015 AND for the last nine months of Robert's ownership, a total of 12 years out of 16. Hence, £135,000 of this gain is exempt, leaving £45,000 chargeable.

Robert can then claim private letting relief equal to the lowest of:
    i)   *The amount of PPR relief on the <u>whole</u> property: £405,000 (£270,000 + £135,000),*
    ii)   *The gain arising by reason of the qualifying letting: £45,000, or*
    iii) *£40,000*

The relief is thus £40,000, leaving Robert with a gain of only £5,000. Assuming he has not used his 2020/21 annual exemption elsewhere, this will exempt the remaining part of his gain, leaving him with no CGT to pay at all!

Now, all that Robert probably did was to fit a few locks in order to separate the flat from his home. As a result, re-occupying the whole property was a simple matter and when he came to sell it, it remained a single 'dwelling' for tax purposes.

Property Conversions

The situation is quite different where a property owner has carried out extensive conversion work in order to create two or more separate dwellings. We will examine the position arising in those circumstances in Section 8.12.

Adult Placement Carers

Any occupation of part of your home by another person under an adult placement scheme is disregarded for PPR relief purposes.

6.27   USING PART OF YOUR HOME FOR BUSINESS PURPOSES

Where part of the property is used **exclusively** for business purposes, the PPR exemption is not available for that part of the property for the relevant period.

Where the exclusive business use covers the entire period that the property is the taxpayer's main residence, the exemption for the final period of ownership will also be withdrawn for this part of the property.

The effect on the PPR exemption is the same whether part of the property is being used exclusively in the taxpayer's own business or is being rented out for use in someone else's. However, where it is the taxpayer's own trading business that is concerned, then this part of the property becomes 'business property' for the purposes of a number of tax reliefs, including entrepreneurs' relief (see Section 6.28), rollover relief and holdover relief for gifts.

Where the 'business use' of part of the property requires extensive conversion work, that part will no longer be part of the original 'dwelling' and hence the PPR exemption will not be available for the final period of ownership.

Non-Exclusive Business Use (The 'Home Office')

Where part of the home is used non-exclusively for business purposes, there is no restriction on the PPR exemption. This is a fairly common situation among self-employed people who work from an office or study within their home.

To safeguard the PPR exemption, it is wise to restrict your Income Tax claim in respect of the office's running costs to a maximum of, say, 99%, in order to reflect the room's occasional private use. Hence, for example, if the office is one of four rooms in the house (excluding hallways, kitchen and bathrooms), one would claim 99% of one quarter of the household running costs.

Just about any kind of private use will suffice, such as:

- A guest bedroom
- Additional storage space for personal belongings
- A music room
- A library

Naturally, it makes sense to adopt some form of private use that will only lead to a small reduction in the Income Tax claim.

Tax Tip
While restricting one room to, say, 99% business use, you may also be able to argue for 1% business use in another room, thus effectively reversing the effect of the restriction without affecting your CGT position on the house.

Section 3.11 provides further details of how to claim an expense deduction for Income Tax purposes when using part of your home as an office from which to run your business. Claiming the flat rate allowances should not affect your home's CGT exemption, although it remains important to avoid exclusive business use of any part of the property.

6.28 ENTREPRENEURS' RELIEF

Entrepreneurs' relief provides a reduced CGT rate of 10%. Gains on which entrepreneurs' relief are claimed are taken to use up the individual's basic rate tax band first, in priority to any other gains.

Sadly, entrepreneurs' relief is not generally available to property investors, except in the case of qualifying furnished holiday lets (see Section 8.17).

Nevertheless, entrepreneurs' relief will sometimes be available to property developers and other taxpayers with property trades (see Chapter 2) on the disposal of their own trading premises and other business assets.

Broadly speaking, entrepreneurs' relief is available on the disposal of:

i)   The whole or part of a qualifying business
ii) Assets previously used in a qualifying business that has ceased
iii) Shares or securities in a 'personal company' (see below)

A qualifying business for this purpose is generally a trade, although, as already stated, furnished holiday letting businesses also qualify. We will return to look in more detail at the application of entrepreneurs' relief to qualifying furnished holiday lets in Section 8.17.

A 'part' of a business can only be counted for these purposes if it is capable of operating as a going concern in its own right, but an 'interest' in a business, such as a partnership share, may qualify.

A disposal of assets previously used in a qualifying business must take place within three years after the business ceases.

The individual making the disposal must have owned the business for at least the 'qualifying period' (see below) prior to its disposal or cessation.

The Qualifying Period

The 'qualifying period' for a number of the tests referred to throughout this section is generally two years. However, it is one year where the disposal took place before 6th April 2019 or the business ceased before 29th October 2018.

Associated Disposals

Entrepreneurs' relief may extend to property owned personally but used in the trade of a 'personal company', or a partnership in which the owner is a partner. A number of restrictions apply, however.

The relief is only available where the owner is also disposing of shares in the company, or an interest in the partnership. The stake being disposed of must generally be either:

a) At least a 5% stake, or
b) Their entire remaining stake out of an earlier stake of at least 5%

The property must have been used in the company or partnership's business for at least the qualifying period immediately prior to the sale of the business stake or, if earlier, cessation of the business. In the latter case, the disposal must again take place within three years after cessation.

Assets purchased after 12th June 2016 need to have been owned for at least three years at the date of disposal.

Entrepreneurs' relief is restricted where any payment has been received for the use of the property after 5th April 2008. Where the property was acquired after that date and a full market rent was received throughout the period of use in the company or partnership's trade, no entrepreneurs' relief will be available. Where the property was acquired earlier, or rent was charged at a lower rate, there will be a partial restriction in entrepreneurs' relief.

The definition of a 'personal company' for the purposes of entrepreneurs' relief is broadly as follows:

i)   The individual holds at least 5% of the ordinary share capital
ii)   The holding under (i) provides at least 5% of the voting rights
iii) The company is a trading company
iv)   The individual is an officer or employee of the company (an 'officer' includes a non-executive director or company secretary)
v)   For disposals after 28th October 2018, the individual must either:
      a) Have at least a 5% interest in the both the distributable profits and net assets of the company by virtue of their holding under (i), or
      b) Be entitled to at least 5% of the sale proceeds arising on a disposal of the company's entire ordinary share capital (this option is not available for disposals before 21st December 2018)

Each of these rules must generally be satisfied for at least the qualifying period prior to the disposal in question or, if earlier, the cessation of the business. See the Taxcafe.co.uk guide *Using a Property Company to Save Tax*' for further details.

A disposal of property or other assets used in a trade carried on by the owner's 'personal company', or a partnership in which the owner is a partner, is referred to as an 'associated disposal'. The entrepreneurs' relief available on an associated disposal is also restricted to reflect any periods when the asset was not being used in a qualifying business carried on by the company or partnership.

Planning with Entrepreneurs' Relief

There is no similar restriction on other entrepreneurs' relief claims and a property used in the owner's own qualifying business will be eligible for full relief as long as it was used in that business immediately prior to the disposal or cessation of the business.

Each individual may claim entrepreneurs' relief on a maximum cumulative lifetime total of £10m of capital gains. This maximum applies to all claims made on gains arising after 5th April 2008. Thereafter, the CGT rate on all further business asset disposals will revert to the normal rates set out in Section 6.4.

Example

Arkwright began trading as a property developer in the late 1980s. After over 30 years he decides to retire and ceases trading in September 2019. For just over a year before cessation, Arkwright ran the business from Granville House: a building that he initially purchased as an investment property for £5m and rented out for over 25 years.

In July 2018, Arkwright adopted Granville House as his trading premises and remained there until he ceased trading. After his property development business ceased, Arkwright put Granville House up for sale and sold it for £16m in March 2020, realising a capital gain of £11m.

As Arkwright owned his business for more than two years and sold Granville House within three years of cessation, he is eligible for entrepreneurs' relief. The fact that Granville House was an investment property for over 25 years makes absolutely no difference!

His £11m gain does exceed the £10m lifetime limit, however, so Arkwright's CGT bill is calculated as follows:

	£
Total gain	*11,000,000*
Less:	
Annual exemption	*(12,000)*
Taxable gain	*10,988,000*
CGT due:	
£10m @ 10%	*1,000,000*
£988,000 @ 20%	*197,600*
Total	*1,197,600*

Arkwright is a higher rate taxpayer so, if he had not adopted Granville House as his trading premises, his CGT bill would have been £2,197,600. That's £1m more!

As we can see from the example, adopting an investment property as your own trading premises prior to sale could save you up to £1m.

Not everyone already has a handy trading business like Arkwright, but we will look at how other property investors might benefit from entrepreneurs' relief in Section 8.20.

Note that entrepreneurs' relief is not mandatory and taxpayers may choose whether to claim it. This avoids the need to waste any of the cumulative lifetime maximum on claims that would be covered by the annual exemption or capital losses (see Section 6.33).

Wealth Warning

To qualify for entrepreneurs' relief, the individual making the disposal must have owned the business for at least the qualifying period prior to cessation. A pre-sale transfer of property to a spouse might result in the loss of relief if the spouse did not also own a share of the business for at least the qualifying period.

Tax Tip

On the other hand, it is also worth noting that the £10m cumulative lifetime maximum applies on a 'per person' basis. Hence, if a share in the business were transferred to a spouse for at least the qualifying period prior to cessation, entrepreneurs' relief would be available on total gains of up to £20m.

Another Tax Tip

From a tax point of view, it will almost always be worth transferring a property to a spouse when they are using it in their own trading business. In addition to the possibility of obtaining entrepreneurs' relief, the spouse using the property in their trade would be eligible for several other reliefs, including rollover relief on replacement of business assets (see Section 8.27). The property would also generally be exempt from IHT if held by the partner using it in their own trade.

Against this one must bear the commercial risks in mind. If the trade fails, a property held by the trader's spouse may be safe from creditors. A property held by the trader could be lost.

6.29   THE ANNUAL EXEMPTION

Each individual is entitled to an annual exemption for each tax year. It is available to exempt from CGT an amount of capital gains after all other reliefs have been claimed, including the compulsory set-off of capital losses arising in the same tax year.

Where capital losses are brought forward from a previous tax year, the set-off is limited to an amount which reduces the taxpayer's capital gains in the current year to the level of the annual exemption.

Individuals with more than one capital gain arising in the same tax year may allocate their annual exemption in the most beneficial way.

Any unused annual exemption is simply lost.

> **Tax Tip**
> To make the most of your available annual exemptions, try to time your capital gains so that each disposal falls into a different tax year whenever possible.

The annual exemption for capital gains arising during the year ending 5th April 2020 is £12,000.

Example
Harry has a capital gain of £12,500 in 2019/20, after claiming all relevant reliefs. After setting off his annual exemption of £12,000, he will be left with a taxable gain of just £500.

In this example, as well as many others in this guide, I have assumed the annual exemption is fully available. This will not always be the case and it should be remembered only one annual exemption is available each tax year.

6.30   WHEN IS CAPITAL GAINS TAX PAYABLE?

At present, the total CGT payable for each tax year is due by the following 31st January. Any CGT liability for 2019/20 is due by 31st January 2021.

CGT liabilities are excluded from the instalment system under self assessment (see Section 3.4).

For disposals of UK residential property after 5th April 2020, a payment on account will be required within 30 days after the date of completion. (This rule already applies to some non-residents – see Section 2.15)

Payments on account under the new system will effectively be the full CGT due on the disposal. The payment will be calculated after taking account of the taxpayer's annual exemption and any available capital losses. The calculation may also include reasonable estimates for:

- Any valuations or apportionments required to compute the gain (where the information is not yet available)
- The taxpayer's taxable income for the relevant tax year

6.31   WHAT MUST I REPORT TO HMRC?

Where all of a taxpayer's disposals in a tax year, taken together, give rise to total proceeds exceeding four times the annual exemption, or where any of them give rise to an actual CGT liability, they will all need to be reported on the individual's tax return using the capital gains summary (SA108).

It is also wise to report all disposals in any tax year where an overall net capital loss arises: so that the loss can be recorded and carried forward for relief in the future.

Disposals that are fully covered by PPR relief and private letting relief are exempted from reporting requirements. For the purposes of the tax return, this does not include cases where the taxpayer is additionally relying on the annual exemption or any other relief to ensure full relief from CGT.

At present, if you have any reportable property disposal, you will need to complete a tax return, including the capital gains summary, and attach a copy of your capital gains computation. The return is due for submission by 31st January following the end of the relevant tax year if filed online (i.e. by the same date that any CGT liability is due), or by 31st October if a paper return is used.

If you are not yet in the self-assessment system, it is sensible to advise HMRC that you have a reportable capital gain as soon as possible after the end of the relevant tax year and definitely by 5th October at the latest. This is so that HMRC can issue you with a Unique Taxpayer Reference ('UTR') to enable you to submit your tax return on time. It is almost impossible to submit a tax return without a UTR and, if you have not advised HMRC that you need to do so by 5th October after the end of the tax year, the fact that you do not receive it in time will not be a valid excuse for filing late.

Disposals of UK Residential Property after 5th April 2020

Disposals of UK residential property after 5th April 2020 will need to be reported to HMRC within 30 days of completion, together with the payment on account described in Section 6.30.

Where the individual making the disposal is not in the self-assessment system and has no other reportable gains, it will not be necessary to register for self-assessment (unless there is another reason why they must do so – see Sections 3.7 and 5.6).

Where none of the gain arising is chargeable to CGT, the disposal will not need to be reported under this new system. This will include cases where the gains are wholly covered by PPR relief, private letting relief, the annual exemption, capital losses, or any combination of these reliefs.

Where the individual making the disposal is in the self-assessment system, the rules set out above will continue to apply to determine whether disposals must be reported on their tax return. In some cases, this will mean the disposal must be reported twice: within 30 days of completion and then again on the tax return.

6.32   JOINTLY HELD PROPERTY

Where two or more taxpayers hold assets jointly they must calculate CGT based on their own share of the net proceeds less their own base cost.

Example
George and Charlotte are equal joint owners of a residential buy-to-let property which they bought together for £100,000. In November 2019 they sell it for £200,000. Each person's taxable capital gain is calculated as follows:

	£
Net proceeds (£200,000 x ½)	*100,000*
Less: Base cost (£100,000 x ½)	*(50,000)*
	50,000
Less: Annual exemption	*(12,000)*
Taxable capital gain	*38,000*

George is a higher rate taxpayer, so his CGT bill, at 28%, amounts to £10,640. Charlotte's total income for 2019/20 is less than her personal allowance, so she pays CGT at 18% on the first £37,500 of her gain (the basic rate band) and 28% on the remainder:

£37,500 @ 18%	*£6,750*
£500 @ 28%	*£140*
Total	*£6,890*

The couple's total CGT bill therefore amounts to £17,530 (£10,640 + £6,890)

Had the property been owned by George alone, his CGT liability would have been £24,640 (£100,000 - £12,000 = £88,000 x 28%). The couple have therefore saved £7,110 (£24,640 - £17,530) by owning the property jointly. This is the value of an additional annual exemption

(£12,000 x 28%) plus the saving generated by using Charlotte's basic rate band (£37,500 x 10%: the difference between 18% and 28%).

It can readily be seen there will often be significant CGT savings to be had by owning property jointly. There may also be other good reasons for holding property jointly, including significant Income Tax savings, as we shall see in Section 8.2.

Another point to note when looking at jointly held property is the £40,000 limit for private letting relief (see Section 6.14) applies to each individual. Hence, a total of up to £80,000 may be exempted when property is held jointly. We will examine the potential effect of this in more detail in Chapter 8.

6.33 CAPITAL LOSSES

Capital losses are generally computed in the same way as capital gains. In the first instance, capital losses are automatically set off against any capital gains arising in the same tax year.

Where a taxpayer has an overall net capital loss for the year, it is carried forward and set off against gains in later years BUT only to the extent necessary to reduce future gains down to the annual exemption applying for that later year.

As explained in Section 6.4, individual taxpayers with more than one capital gain arising in the same tax year may generally allocate any available capital losses in the most beneficial way.

Where a taxpayer is claiming entrepreneurs' relief on business assets, however, any capital losses arising on those disposals must be set off against capital gains on assets used in the same business. Entrepreneurs' relief is then claimed on the overall net gain.

Any other capital losses set off against gains subject to entrepreneurs' relief are set off after the relief has been claimed, meaning the relief for those losses is given at an effective rate of only 10% and more of the taxpayer's lifetime maximum will have been used.

Capital losses arising on any transactions with 'connected persons' (see Appendix B) may only be set off against gains arising on transactions between the same parties.

Relief is denied for 'artificial' capital losses arising as a result of transactions carried out with a main purpose of creating a tax advantage.

6.34   LEASES

Granting a long lease of more than 50 years' duration

This is a capital disposal chargeable to CGT. The base cost has to be restricted under the 'part disposal' rules. This means the base cost is divided between the part disposed of (i.e. the lease) and the part retained (the 'reversionary interest') in proportion to their relative values.

Example
Llewellyn owns the freehold of a commercial property in Cardiff. He grants a 60-year lease to Brian, a Belfast businessman moving to the area. Brian pays a premium of £90,000 for the lease. The value of Llewellyn's reversionary interest is established as £10,000. The base cost used to calculate Llewellyn's capital gain is 90% of his base cost for the property as a whole.

Granting a short lease of no more than 50 years' duration
As we saw in Section 4.14, part of any lease premium obtained will be taxable as income. The rest is a capital disposal and is dealt with in the same way as the grant of a long lease, as outlined above.

Assigning a lease
This is treated entirely as a capital disposal and any applicable reliefs may be claimed in the usual way. However, leases with less than 50 years remaining at the time of disposal are treated as 'wasting assets'. The base cost is reduced in accordance with the schedule set out in Appendix C. For example, for a lease with 20 years remaining, and which had more than 50 years remaining when first acquired, the base cost must be reduced to 72.77% of the original amount.

Where the lease had less than 50 years remaining when originally acquired, the necessary reduction in base cost is achieved by multiplying the original cost by the factor applying at the time of sale and dividing by the factor applying at the time of purchase.

Example
John acquires a ten year lease over a building and pays a premium of £10,000. Five years later, John assigns his lease to Asha at a premium of £6,000. When calculating his capital gain, the amount John may claim as his base cost is £10,000 x 26.722/46.695 = £5,723.

Any part of a lease premium that was treated as income in the hands of the grantor under the rules outlined in Section 4.14 will not form part of the grantee's base cost for the lease. The grantee may, instead, be able to claim an Income Tax deduction for this part of the premium, spread over the period of the lease (if the grantee is using the property for business purposes). In the example above, I have assumed for the sake of illustration that this did not apply in John's case.

Chapter 7

Other Taxes to Watch Out For

7.1   STAMP DUTY LAND TAX – INTRODUCTION

Stamp Duty is the oldest tax on the statute books. It was more than a century old already when Pitt the Younger introduced Income Tax in 1799. In 2003, however, for transfers of real property (i.e. land and buildings, or any form of legal interest in them), Stamp Duty was replaced by SDLT.

The rates of SDLT are generally the same regardless of what type of property business the purchaser has. The rates are also mostly unaffected by whether the purchaser is an individual, a trust, a partnership or a company. The rates are, however, different for residential and non-residential property: as we shall see over the next few sections.

SDLT no longer applies to property in Scotland or Wales. We will look at its replacements in Sections 7.19 and 7.22 respectively.

7.2   STAMP DUTY LAND TAX ON RESIDENTIAL PROPERTY

The basic underlying rates of SDLT on residential property are:

Up to £125,000	Nil
£125,000 to £250,000	2%
£250,000 to £925,000	5%
£925,000 to £1.5m	10%
Over £1.5m	12%

Since 2014, these rates have applied on a 'progressive' basis, which represents a major reform compared to the old 'slab' system that applied previously.

It is, however, important to note these rates will seldom actually apply to purchases of property by landlords and other property business owners. Generally speaking, these basic underlying rates will only apply in the case of:

- A purchase by an unmarried individual or married couple who have no other interest in any residential property (subject to the exemption for 'first time buyers' detailed below),
- An unmarried individual or married couple buying a new main residence to replace a former main residence sold within the previous three years, or
- A sale or transfer of a property, or an interest in a property, from one spouse to another (see Section 7.3)

In most other cases, an additional 3% charge will apply to all residential property purchases. We will look at this dreadful charge and the pitiful few exemptions available, in the next section.

Before that, let us look at a brief example of the SDLT arising where the higher charges do not apply.

Example
The SDLT arising on a purchase price of £550,000 where an individual is buying their first, or only, residential property, or replacing a main residence sold within the previous three years, is:

First £125,000 @ 0%:	*£0*
Next £125,000 @ 2%:	*£2,500*
Next £300,000 @ 5%:	*£15,000*
Total:	*£17,500*

First Time Buyers

The exemption for first time buyers applies as follows:

- The first £300,000 is fully exempt
- Purchases over £300,000 but not exceeding £500,000 are subject to a charge of 5% on the amount in excess of £300,000
- Purchases over £500,000 are subject to normal rates (as above)

A 'first time buyer' is someone who has never previously purchased a 'major interest' in a residential property anywhere in the world. A lease with less than 21 years left to run is not a 'major interest'. Joint purchasers must both (or all) qualify as first-time buyers to be eligible for the exemption. Purchases under a qualifying shared ownership scheme may qualify however.

7.3 HIGHER CHARGES ON RESIDENTIAL PROPERTY

Higher SDLT charges apply to most purchases of residential property by landlords, other property business owners and companies. The basic rule is that the higher charges apply to any purchase:

- By an individual who has any interest in more than one residential property at the end of the day of purchase
- By two or more persons jointly where any of them has any interest in more than one residential property at the end of the day of purchase, or
- By a company or other 'non-natural' person

The higher charges are as follows:

Up to £125,000	3%
£125,000 to £250,000	5%
£250,000 to £925,000	8%
£925,000 to £1.5m	13%
Over £1.5m	15%

Purchases under £40,000 are exempt from SDLT but, apart from this, the charges apply on a progressive basis:

Examples
The SDLT arising on a residential property purchased for £100,000 where the higher charges apply is £100,000 @ 3% = £3,000

The SDLT arising on a residential property purchased for £400,000 where the higher charges apply is:

First £125,000 @ 3%:	*£3,750*
Next £125,000 @ 5%:	*£6,250*
Next £150,000 @ 8%:	*£12,000*
Total:	*£22,000*

Replacement of Main Residence

There is an exemption from the higher charges where the purchaser is buying a property that they intend to adopt as their main residence and is replacing a former main residence sold within the previous three years. The entire interest in the former main residence must have been sold, and no part of it can have been sold to a spouse.

The exemption also applies where the entire interest in the purchaser's former main residence is sold within three years **after** the new main residence is purchased. However, in this case, the higher charges will apply in the first place and a refund will have to be claimed later, on the sale of the former main residence.

Where all of two or more joint purchasers are either eligible for this exemption, or will not have any interest in any other residential property at the end of the day of purchase, then the higher charges will not apply (or can be refunded later, as the case may be).

In any other cases involving joint purchasers, the higher charges will apply. This includes cases where one of the joint purchasers lived in the former main residence but did not own any share of it (and has an interest in another residential property).

Example
Prior to their marriage in 2010, Jack and Rose each had their own main residence. After the wedding, Jack moved in with Rose and rented out his old flat. Rose kept her flat in her own name until selling it in January 2020. The couple then bought a new property jointly together for £600,000 and adopted it as their new main residence.

The higher SDLT charges are payable on the new property because Jack is not replacing a former main residence that he owned and he still owns another residential property. This costs the couple an additional £18,000.

There are a few ways of avoiding this problem, but they all have other potential implications, especially where mortgages are involved:

- Rose could buy the new property in her name alone (this may lead to difficulties in obtaining a mortgage). She might also subsequently transfer the property into joint names with Jack (but see Section 7.7 for problems arising if there is a mortgage outstanding at that time)
- They could put their existing main residence into joint names before selling it. Again, this might cause problems if there is an outstanding mortgage (see Section 7.7)
- Jack could sell his old flat before they buy the new property (this may give rise to a CGT liability – see Chapter 6 for details)

If Jack and Rose were not married, the position might be even more difficult as any transfers of property into joint names could give rise to a CGT liability if the property concerned had not always been the existing owner's main residence.

See Chapter 6 for a detailed examination of what is a 'main residence'. Note, however, that it will not be possible to elect which property is, or was, your main residence for the purposes of the higher SDLT charges: it will need to be determined as a question of fact (see Section 6.22 for guidance on this issue).

Other Exemptions

Exemptions from the higher charges apply to:

- Transfers of property, or an interest in property, between spouses
- A purchaser adding to their existing interest in their main residence (e.g. buying the freehold of a property where they already own the leasehold)
- Properties bought for a child subject to the Court of Protection

The reliefs described in Section 7.8 are also available to reduce the charge applying on a simultaneous purchase of multiple properties, or dwellings.

Interests in Residential Property

Subject to the exceptions outlined below, any interest in any residential property anywhere in the world is counted for the purpose of the higher charges. Each individual must include any interests held by their spouse, civil partner or minor children (e.g. property held in trust on their behalf). An 'interest' means any form of legal right to a share in the property for any period of time.

There are a few exceptions, as follows:

- Interests in property worth less than £40,000
- Caravans, mobile homes and houseboats
- Shares of 50% or less in property inherited within the last three years
- Leasehold interests for a period of less than seven years at commencement
- Superior interests where there is a leasehold interest in the property with more than 21 years left to run
- Former main residences that cannot be sold under the terms of a divorce-related court order

7.4 RESIDENTIAL PROPERTY PURCHASES BY 'NON-NATURAL' PERSONS

A special SDLT rate of 15% applies to the entire purchase price on purchases of residential properties in excess of £500,000 by companies and other 'non-natural' persons, such as collective investment schemes, unit trusts, and partnerships in which any 'non-natural' person is a partner.

The rate only applies where a single dwelling is purchased for a price in excess of £500,000, or where one or more separate dwellings included in the purchase of a larger portfolio are worth more than £500,000 each.

Properties are exempt from this special rate when acquired for use in a business. This exemption covers both trading businesses and property investment businesses, so property investment companies should not generally have to pay this punitive rate.

The special 15% rate should not generally apply to most trusts or partnerships made up entirely of individuals as, from a technical standpoint, the purchase is usually still being made by one or more individuals. In case of doubt, however, legal advice is essential!

Where this special rate applies, neither multiple dwellings relief nor the alternative treatment outlined in Section 7.8 is available.

7.5   STAMP DUTY LAND TAX ON NON-RESIDENTIAL PROPERTY

The rates of SDLT on non-residential property are:

Up to £150,000	0%
£150,000 to £250,000	2%
Over £250,000	5%

These rates also apply on a 'progressive' basis. For example, the SDLT payable on the purchase of a non-residential property for £300,000 is:

First £150,000 @ 0%:	£0
Next £100,000 @ 2%:	£2,000
Next £50,000 @ 5%:	£2,500
Total:	£4,500

7.6   APPLICATION OF STAMP DUTY LAND TAX

The thresholds given in the tables in Sections 7.2, 7.3 and 7.5 generally refer to the actual consideration paid for the purchase, whether in cash or by any other means (but see Section 7.7 for potential exceptions).

SDLT is payable on all transfers of property located in England or Northern Ireland; regardless of where the vendor and purchaser are resident, and regardless of where the transfer documentation is drawn up. SDLT has ceased to apply to property in Scotland or Wales (see Sections 7.19 and 7.22 for further details).

SDLT is the legal responsibility of the purchaser or transferee, although the vendor/transferor will sometimes arrange to pay.

Substantial Performance

Liability for SDLT is triggered when a purchase is 'substantially performed'. Generally, this occurs on the earliest of:

a)   Completion of the purchase contract,
b)   Payment of at least 90% of the purchase consideration,
c)   Occupation of the property (including occupation under licence after the date of the contract or lease agreement),
d)   Payment of the first rent (in the case of a lease), or
e)   Subletting of the property (in the case of a lease)

In most cases completion of the purchase contract triggers the liability.

7.7   MARKET VALUE AND MORTGAGES

Generally speaking, there is no 'market value' rule for SDLT and the tax is only payable on actual consideration.

Where property is transferred to a connected company, however, SDLT is payable on the market value. The implications of this are examined in the Taxcafe.co.uk guide *Using a Property Company to Save Tax*.

Market value must also be used for transactions between business partners and their partnership, even changes in partnership shares. See Section 8.30 for further details.

Although transfers between spouses are exempt from the higher charges examined in Section 7.3, there is no general exemption from SDLT at 'normal' rates. Many such transfers are gifts with no consideration, but where a property is transferred subject to a mortgage, the balance outstanding will be treated as consideration for SDLT purposes.

Hence if a woman transfers a house with an outstanding mortgage of £200,000 to her husband, he will have a SDLT liability of £1,500.

In such a case, where possible, it might be worth repaying the mortgage prior to the transfer, or at least reducing it to £125,000: thus avoiding any SDLT charge.

Where property is being put into joint names, SDLT is payable on whatever share of the mortgage the transferee is taking on. Hence, where putting a property into equal joint names with a spouse, a mortgage of no more than £250,000 should not give rise to any SDLT.

The exemption from the higher charges detailed in Section 7.3 only applies to transfers between spouses, so transfers of property, or a share in property, to anyone else will give rise to SDLT charges whenever the mortgage, or share of mortgage, taken over by the transferee is £40,000 or more. (Such transfers also give rise to potential CGT liabilities, as we saw in Chapter 6.)

One way to avoid SDLT charges on transfers of a share of a property subject to a mortgage, to your spouse, or other close relatives, is to use a partnership (see Section 8.30). You must be one of the partners though.

Naturally, all transfers of property subject to a mortgage will need the lender's permission, or the lender will certainly at least need to be advised. Legal advice is strongly recommended!

7.8   LINKED TRANSACTIONS

SDLT is calculated after taking account of any 'linked transactions'. 'Linked transactions' can arise in a number of ways, including a simultaneous purchase of several properties from the same vendor, or connected vendors (see Appendix B for details of 'connected persons').

The effect of the 'linked transactions' depends on whether 'multiple dwellings relief' is claimed. This relief is only available for multiple purchases of residential property.

Basic Rule without Multiple Dwellings Relief

The basic rule that applies where multiple dwellings relief is not claimed is that the 'linked transactions' are treated as if they were a single purchase for SDLT purposes. In practice, this will mainly apply to multiple purchases of non-residential property, although it will also apply to any other 'linked transactions' where multiple dwellings relief is not available.

For example, if a property investor were to buy three commercial properties from the same developer at the same time for £250,000 each, this would be treated for SDLT purposes as if it were one single purchase for £750,000. The SDLT charge would therefore be:

£100,000 @ 2%:	£2,000
£500,000 @ 5%:	£25,000
Total:	£27,000

Multiple Dwellings Relief

Multiple dwellings relief is available where multiple **residential** properties are purchased from the same vendor at the same time.

Where multiple dwellings relief is claimed, the rate of SDLT is based on the **average** consideration paid for each 'dwelling'. The relief is not automatic and must be claimed by the purchaser.

The higher charges detailed in Section 7.3 continue to apply to the average price, where applicable. It is, in fact, hard to envisage a scenario where they will not apply, so I am going to assume they do in the examples that follow.

A minimum charge of 1% applies under multiple dwellings relief, although this will seldom arise in practice.

Example 1

Jat buys five houses from a developer for a total consideration of £1.2m. Without multiple dwellings relief, his SDLT bill would be:

First £125,000 @ 3%:	*£3,750*
Next £125,000 @ 5%:	*£6,250*
Next £675,000 @ 8%:	*£54,000*
Next £275,000 @ 13%:	*£35,750*
Total:	*£99,750*

However, as the average price for each property is just £240,000, Jat claims multiple dwellings relief. The SDLT calculation is then as follows:

First £125,000 @ 3%:	*£3,750*
Next £115,000 @ 5%:	*£5,750*
Total per property:	*£9,500*
x 5 =	*£47,500*

Multiple dwellings relief could also be used to reduce the SDLT charge on a single large property.

Example 2

Pippa is planning to buy a house in Middleton at a cost of £1.25m. Her SDLT bill will currently amount to:

First £125,000 @ 3%:	*£3,750*
Next £125,000 @ 5%:	*£6,250*
Next £675,000 @ 8%:	*£54,000*
Next £325,000 @ 13%:	*£42,250*
Total:	*£106,250*

In order to reduce her SDLT cost, Pippa arranges to buy two small flats from the same developer at the same time as the house. The flats cost £89,000 each, bringing her total consideration to £1.428m, but the average consideration is now just £476,000. Pippa can claim multiple dwellings relief to give her a reduction in her SDLT charge as follows:

First £125,000 @ 3%:	*£3,750*
Next £125,000 @ 5%:	*£6,250*
Next £226,000 @ 8%:	*£18,080*
Total per property:	*£28,080*
x 3 =	*£84,240*

By buying the flats at the same time, Pippa has saved £22,010 in SDLT. That's equivalent to getting a discount of almost 12.5% on the flats!

I assumed here that the higher charges in Section 7.3 would have applied to Pippa's original planned purchase of the house alone. If that were not the case, this strategy would not be worthwhile.

Extra Benefits for Property Investors

Self-contained flats within a single property each constitute a separate 'dwelling' for the purposes of multiple dwellings relief. This provides a major benefit for property investors buying larger properties. If, for example, an investor buys a property that has been divided into four flats, this would constitute four dwellings, so that multiple dwellings relief can be claimed and significantly reduce the SDLT due.

Alternative Treatment

A simultaneous purchase of six or more residential dwellings (from the same vendor, or connected vendors) can alternatively be treated as a non-residential property purchase for SDLT purposes. This may sometimes produce a better outcome than claiming multiple dwellings relief. For example, a purchase of six dwellings for a total of £1.8m would attract SDLT of £84,000: even with multiple dwellings relief. The charge at non-residential rates would be £79,500.

7.9   STAMP DUTY LAND TAX ON LEASES

On the granting of a lease, SDLT is payable on the 'Net Present Value' of all the rent payable under the lease over its entire term.

Where the net present value does not exceed £125,000 (for residential property), or £150,000 (for non-residential property), no SDLT will be payable.

For new leases with a net present value exceeding these limits, SDLT is payable at a rate of 1% on the excess. The rate increases to 2% on any amounts in excess of £5m.

VAT is excluded from the rent payable under the lease for the purposes of SDLT calculations <u>unless</u> the landlord has already exercised the option to tax (this applies to commercial property only).

Example

In January 2020, Clive takes on a ten year lease over a house in Kent at an annual rent of £18,000.

The SDLT legislation provides that the net present value of a sum of money due within the next 12 months is equal to the sum due divided by a 'discount factor'. The applicable discount factor is currently 103.5%. Hence, the 'Present Value' of Clive's first year's rent of £18,000 is £17,391 (i.e. £18,000 divided by 103.5%).

Similarly, the second year's rent, which is due a further 12 months later, must be 'discounted' again by the same amount, i.e. £17,391/103.5% = £16,803.

This process is continued for the entire ten year life of the lease and the net present values of all the rental payments are added together to give the total net present value for the lease. In this case, this works out at £149,699. The SDLT payable by Clive is therefore just £247 (£149,699 less £125,000 = £24,699 x 1% = £247).

It does not matter whether the rent is payable monthly, quarterly or annually, or whether it is payable in advance or in arrears. Net present value is always calculated by reference to the total annual rental payable for each year of the lease.

The current 'discount factor' (103.5%) may be changed in the future, depending on a number of factors, including the prevailing rates of inflation and interest.

Lease **premiums** also attract SDLT at the rates shown in Sections 7.2 to 7.5.

> **Tax Tip**
> It is possible to grant a lease over a non-residential property with a premium of up to £150,000 **and** annual rental with a net present value of up to £150,000 with no SDLT cost whatsoever.
>
> For residential property, there will be an SDLT cost if either amount exceeds £125,000, or if the higher charges shown in Section 7.3 apply to the premium.

7.10   FIXTURES AND FITTINGS

There is a great deal of misunderstanding over the issue of SDLT on fixtures and fittings.

Firstly, it must be understood that 'fixtures' are part of the fabric of the building and are therefore subject to SDLT. This includes items such as fitted kitchens, baths, toilets, sinks, etc, and is unaffected by whether these items qualify for capital allowances (see Section 4.9).

Moveable fittings, however, are **not** part of the fabric of the building and therefore not subject to SDLT. This includes furniture, carpets, curtains and free-standing 'white goods' such as fridges, freezers and washing machines.

It is therefore often possible to allocate a small part of a property's purchase price to the moveable fittings in the property and thus reduce the SDLT cost. For residential property purchases by landlords and other property business owners this will generally save 3%, 5% or 8% of the amount allocated to the fittings and will often be worthwhile. For non-residential property purchases over £250,000, the saving will be 5%.

Remember, however, it is only the moveable fittings that escape SDLT and there will often be very few of these in a non-residential property.

Generally, it is sensible to purchase moveable fittings by way of a side agreement (which may be no more than a handshake). The informality of such an agreement does not, however, prevent it from having to be included as part of the property's purchase price if the amount allocated to the fittings is excessive.

In summary, a small allocation of the purchase price to moveable fittings is a sensible way to reduce your SDLT bill; but be reasonable!

7.11   STAMP DUTY ON SHARES

Before we leave the subject of Stamp Taxes, it is worth mentioning that the rate of Stamp Duty on purchases of shares and securities in excess of £1,000 is just 0.5%.

Purchases not exceeding £1,000 are exempt (although where quoted shares are purchased through a broker, they will usually pass on the Stamp Duty that arises owing to the fact they have purchased a larger block of shares in a single transaction).

This lower rate of Duty led to many tax planning strategies designed to avoid the excessive rates applied to property by making use of this more palatable rate. Sadly, anti-avoidance legislation has now effectively blocked most of the more popular methods.

Nevertheless, for those investing in property through a company, there remains the possibility of selling shares in that company at a much lower rate of Duty than would apply to the sale of individual properties. (But see Sections 7.4 and 7.18 regarding additional or higher tax charges on companies owning any individual residential property worth over £500,000 that is not used for business purposes.)

7.12 VAT – INTRODUCTION

VAT, or Value Added Tax, to give it its proper name, arrived on our shores from Europe in 1973. Despite its comparative youth, VAT is one of the UK's most hated taxes and there are some nasty pitfalls for the unwary property investor.

VAT is currently charged at three different rates in the UK: a standard rate of 20%, a reduced rate of 5% and a zero rate. All these rates may be encountered by property businesses.

For VAT purposes, a sale of a property is a supply of 'goods' and rent on a property is a supply of 'services'. Not all supplies of 'goods and services' are subject to VAT, some are exempt.

The VAT treatment of 'goods and services' in a property business depends on a number of things, including the type of property. Where a supply of 'goods or services' is subject to VAT at any of the three rates given above (including the 'zero rate') it is referred to as a 'taxable supply'.

Goods and services subject to VAT at the standard rate of 20% are often referred to as 'standard-rated'.

VAT Registration

VAT is charged by VAT-registered businesses. Sadly, they do not keep it, but must pay it over to HMRC. They are, however, able to claim back the VAT on their purchases of the goods and services used to make their own taxable supplies.

Where a business is making annual taxable supplies of goods or services in excess of the VAT registration threshold, registration is compulsory. The threshold has been frozen at £85,000 for the five year period from 1st April 2017 to 31st March 2022 pending a detailed review following a recommendation from the Office of Tax Simplification that it should be drastically reduced.

Businesses making taxable supplies of goods or services but whose annual sales are less than the VAT registration threshold may register for VAT voluntarily. This is particularly beneficial for those making 'zero rated' supplies, as we shall see later.

Making VAT Digital

Businesses that are registered for VAT **and** making annual sales in excess of the VAT registration threshold are required to keep their records in digital format, using software compatible with HMRC's systems, and submit their VAT returns using an online digital reporting system. Records may be kept on spreadsheets provided linking software is used to interface with the digital reporting system. The overriding requirement is that there should be no manual re-typing of entries once these have been entered in the business's original digital records.

The Flat Rate Scheme

VAT-registered businesses with annual sales not exceeding £150,000 may join the VAT flat rate scheme. This does not alter the amount of VAT they must charge customers or the amount of VAT they pay on their purchases. What it does alter is the amount of VAT paid over to HMRC.

Under the flat rate scheme, a special reduced rate is applied to calculate the VAT payable to HMRC on the business's sales. However, the downside is the business is unable to recover the VAT paid on most of its purchases.

> ### Wealth Warning
> Any individual, partnership, company, or other entity, registering for the flat rate scheme must apply the reduced VAT rate to **all** their business income, including any rental income that would normally be exempt from VAT.

The flat rate scheme is seldom beneficial to property businesses, with the potential exception of property management businesses and property investors renting out commercial property. Even in these cases, there are 'pros' and 'cons' to be considered.

Furthermore, the introduction of a special rate for 'Low Cost Traders' means many of those who might have benefited in the past will no longer do so. Broadly speaking, this rate applies where a business's VAT-inclusive expenditure on goods amounts to less than 2% of its VAT-inclusive sales income. Capital expenditure and certain other items are excluded for the purpose of this test.

At 16.5% of the business's gross VAT-inclusive sales income, the 'Low Cost Trader' rate provides little benefit. (The VAT within gross standard-rated sales income only amounts to 16.67% in any case!)

Reverse Charges in the Construction Sector

A new 'reverse charge' procedure is to apply to certain types of 'construction services' from 1st October 2020 (postponed from the original planned implementation date of 1st October 2019). Under the reverse charge procedure, the customer must account for VAT on the relevant supplies rather than the supplier. The overall VAT position will be unaltered; it is simply a question of who pays the VAT over to HMRC.

The procedure will only apply where the customer is making relevant taxable supplies of construction services themselves. Hence, the vast majority of property investors will be unaffected by this change, although it may apply to a few property developers.

7.13 VAT ON RESIDENTIAL PROPERTY

Residential Property Letting

Generally speaking, a property investment business engaged primarily in residential property letting does not need to be VAT-registered because the letting of residential property is an exempt supply for VAT purposes.

VAT is therefore not chargeable on rent, although, of course, VAT cannot be recovered on expenses and the landlord should therefore claim VAT-inclusive costs for Income Tax and CGT purposes.

The letting of holiday accommodation is, however, standard-rated for VAT purposes, whether or not it qualifies for the special treatment outlined in Section 8.17.

Beware also that the provision of ancillary services (e.g. cleaning or gardening) may sometimes be standard-rated, and hence subject to VAT at 20%, if the value of annual supplies of these services exceeds the VAT registration threshold.

Some landlords making ancillary supplies of this nature prefer to register for VAT even if they have not reached the registration threshold, as this means they are able to recover part of the VAT on their expenses.

Residential Property Development

Sales of newly constructed residential property are zero-rated for VAT purposes. This means the developer can recover the VAT on their construction costs without having to charge VAT on the sale of the property. (In theory, VAT is charged, but at a rate of zero.)

This treatment is extended to the sale of a property that has just been converted from a non-residential property into a residential property (*e.g. converting a barn into a house*). It is also extended to 'substantially reconstructed protected buildings'. In essence, this means the sale of a listed building following the carrying out of major alterations. Such alterations do, of course, require approval from the authorities.

Property developers carrying out construction work under any of these headings are therefore able to register for VAT and then recover the VAT on the vast majority of their business expenses.

Other Residential Property Sales

Other sales of residential property are generally an exempt supply meaning, once again, that the taxpayer making the sale is unable to recover any of the VAT on his or her expenses. This means VAT cannot be recovered by most residential property investors and dealers.

Property developers who merely renovate or alter existing residential property prior to onward sale are also generally unable to recover VAT on their costs. But where the work qualifies as a 'conversion', as described below, they may at least be able to reduce the amount of VAT payable.

Conversions

A reduced VAT rate of 5% is available for building work carried out on a residential property where the work results in a change to the number of dwellings in the property. This would apply to the conversion of:

- One house into several flats
- Two or more flats into a single house
- Two semi-detached houses into a single detached house

The reduced rate also applies to conversions of commercial property into residential use.

Property investors or developers carrying out projects of this nature should try to ensure they only pay the lower VAT rate from the outset, as it is difficult to recover any excess paid in error.

Renovations of Vacant Property

The 5% rate also applies to renovation work on residential property that had been vacant for two years or more before work commenced.

7.14   VAT ON COMMERCIAL PROPERTY

Commercial Property Letting

For commercial property, there is an 'option to tax'. In other words, the landlord may choose, for each property and on a property-by-property basis, whether or not the rent should be a VAT exempt supply.

If the 'option to tax' is exercised, the rent becomes standard-rated for VAT purposes. The landlord may then recover VAT on the expenses relating to that property. Ancillary services are again likely to be standard-rated, regardless of whether you have opted to tax the rent itself.

Tax Tip
If the potential tenants of a commercial property are all, or mostly, likely to be VAT-registered businesses themselves, it will generally make sense to exercise the 'option to tax' on the property in order to recover the VAT on expenses incurred.

If your tenants themselves have a VAT-registered and fully taxable business (for VAT purposes), then everyone's happy. The problem comes when your tenants cannot recover some or all of the VAT you are charging. And remember that (after a short 'cooling off' period) you cannot change your option on a property for a minimum of 20 years once it has been exercised. Hence, if you opt to charge VAT to a fully taxable tenant, you will probably still need to charge VAT to the next tenant in the same property, even if they cannot recover it.

Sometimes, though, with non-taxable (for VAT) tenants, where you have not yet exercised your option to tax, you can refrain from doing so and negotiate a higher rent to compensate you for your loss of VAT recovery on your own costs.

Example
Norman owns an office building and hasn't yet opted to tax the rents. He has monthly costs of £500 plus VAT (i.e. £600 gross) and expects a monthly rent of £2,500. If Norman opts to tax he will recover £100 a month from HMRC and make a monthly profit of £2,000.

However, Lenny, the prospective tenant, is not registered for VAT. If Norman opts to tax the property, Lenny's rent will effectively be 20% higher, i.e. £3,000 per month. So, as a better alternative, Norman and Lenny agree that Norman will not opt to tax the building but will, instead, charge Lenny £2,750 a month rent. Now Norman is making a monthly profit of £2,150 (£2,750 minus £600) and Lenny's rent is effectively £250 less than it would have been. Norman and Lenny both win and HMRC loses.

Commercial Property Sales & Purchases

Where the 'option to tax' has been exercised by the owner of a commercial property, their sale of that property will be standard-rated and this has major implications for such transactions. Sales of new commercial property are also standard-rated.

Wealth Warning
Where VAT must be charged on a commercial property sale, the SDLT must be calculated on the basis of the gross, VAT-inclusive price. This can lead to combined tax rates of up to 26%! This represents a pretty hefty cost if the purchaser is not

VAT-registered, possibly enough to prevent the sale from taking place in some cases. Imagine a large insurance company buying a new office block in central London – the combined VAT and SDLT cost would be astronomical!

Furthermore, even when the purchaser is able to recover the VAT on their purchase, the extra SDLT paid on that VAT cannot be recovered.

Where a property investor incurs VAT on the purchase of a commercial property, the only way to recover that VAT will be for the investor to exercise the 'option to tax' on the property. In this way, the Government generally forces everyone to maintain the taxable status of the building.

If a VAT-registered property developer incurs VAT on the purchase of a commercial property, they can recover the VAT in the same way as on any other purchase of goods or services for use in the business. This initial recovery is not dependent on exercising the 'option to tax', as the developer has a taxable business for VAT purposes, but ...

Wealth Warning
If VAT has been recovered on the purchase of a commercial property, a sale of that property without first exercising the option to tax would be an exempt supply. If that property were trading stock, this would result in the loss of all the VAT initially reclaimed on its purchase and on any development, renovation or conversion work carried out. Some of the VAT recovered on general overhead costs would probably also become repayable.

Furthermore, when more than £250,000 has been spent on the purchase or improvement of a property for use as the business's own trading premises, a sale of that property within ten years without first exercising the option to tax would also trigger VAT.

7.15   VAT ON PROPERTY MANAGEMENT

Property management services are standard-rated for VAT and hence a property management business will need to be registered if its annual turnover exceeds the £85,000 registration threshold. The taxpayer may still register voluntarily even if the level of sales is below the threshold.

Whether the properties under management are residential or commercial makes no difference for this purpose.

A VAT-registered property management business can recover the VAT on most of its business expenses. There are, however, a few exceptions, as we shall see in the next section.

7.16   INTERACTION OF VAT WITH OTHER TAXES

A VAT-registered business should generally include only the net (excluding VAT) amounts of income and expenditure in its accounts for Income Tax purposes. Where VAT recovery is barred or restricted, the additional cost should be treated as part of the relevant expense.

Expenses subject to restrictions on the recovery of VAT include:

- Business entertaining
- Purchases of motor cars
- Leasing/contract hire of motor cars
- Provision of private fuel for proprietors or staff

As we can see, many of the expenses subject to a VAT recovery restriction are also subject to some form of Income Tax restriction.

A non VAT-registered business should always include the VAT in its business expenditure for Income Tax purposes. Similar principles apply for CGT and Corporation Tax purposes.

7.17   NATIONAL INSURANCE

See Section 5.5 and Appendix A for details of NI rates. The NI treatment of property trading income is also covered in Section 5.5.

Any incidental trading income arising as part of a property investment business may be subject to NI. Subject to this, NI should never be due on property rental income, as it is not usually classed as 'earnings'. Despite this, some HMRC offices have sought to collect Class 2 NI from landlords. Part of the reason for this relates to the way in which landlords have registered for self-assessment (see Section 3.7). Landlords with income from furnished holiday lets have also sometimes been charged Class 2 NI. This is incorrect: property income is not 'business income' for NI purposes and the vast majority of landlords should not, therefore, be subject to Class 2 NI.

Non-trading taxpayers can pay voluntary Class 3 NI in order to secure state retirement benefits, etc, if they so wish. The rate of Class 3 contributions for 2019/20 is £15.00 per week.

Naturally, if you should employ anyone to help you in your property business, their salary will be subject to both employee's and employer's Class 1 NI (at 12% and 13.8% respectively). However, employers are not required to pay employer's NI on earnings up to the upper earnings limit paid to any employee under the age of 21, or qualifying apprentices under the age of 25. Each employer is also currently eligible to claim exemption from the first £3,000 of employer's NI arising in the year (except for a company where the employer's NI relates to one single director/shareholder only).

If you provide an employee with any taxable benefits-in-kind, you will additionally be liable for Class 1A NI (again at 13.8%).

Capital Gains

NI is never payable on capital gains. However, if you are classed as a property developer or a property trader, your profit on property sales will be taxed as trading income and hence will be subject to NI.

7.18   THE ANNUAL TAX ON ENVELOPED DWELLINGS

Additional tax charges apply to UK residential property owned by 'non-natural persons'. The definition of 'non-natural persons' includes companies, partnerships where a company is a partner, and collective investment schemes. Most commonly, the charges apply to companies. They do not apply to property investors operating purely as individuals.

Three charges are involved, only two of which are still current:

- The Annual Tax on Enveloped Dwellings ('ATED')
- CGT at 28% on disposals of property before 6th April 2019
- The 15% rate of SDLT (see Section 7.4)

The charges only apply to single dwellings worth in excess of £500,000. They do not apply by reference to the total value of the property portfolio.

Business Exemption

The good news for most property investors operating through a company (or any other 'non-natural person') is that properties are exempt from these charges if they are being used in a business: including a property rental business.

Hence, in most cases, property investment companies should be exempt from these charges; although it will be essential to ensure properties are being acquired for use in the business, and continue to be held for business purposes thereafter.

The bad news, however, is that any company or other 'non-natural person' eligible for this exemption will need to claim it – whenever they buy property worth more than £500,000 for SDLT purposes; and on an annual basis when they own any property worth more than £500,000 for the purposes of ATED. Hence, even if there is no extra tax, there will still be plenty of extra administration to deal with!

The annual charge under ATED for 2019/20 ranges from £3,650 (for property worth more than £500,000 but not more than £1m) to £232,350 (for property worth more than £20m).

The charges described above apply regardless of where the 'non-natural person' is resident for tax purposes. For further information see the Taxcafe.co.uk guide *Using a Property Company to Save Tax*.

7.19   LAND AND BUILDINGS TRANSACTION TAX

Since April 2015, SDLT has been abolished for property located in Scotland and has been replaced by LBTT. LBTT operates in a broadly similar way to SDLT, subject to a few variations, as noted below.

Residential Property
The basic underlying rates of LBTT on residential property are as follows:

Purchase Consideration	Rate Applying
Up to £145,000	Nil
£145,000 to £250,000	2%
£250,000 to £325,000	5%
£325,000 to £750,000	10%
Over £750,000	12%

Residential property purchases by landlords and other property business owners are, however, also subject to the Additional Dwelling Supplement ('ADS') which we will examine in Section 7.20.

Non-Residential Property
From 25th January 2019, the rates of LBTT on non-residential property are as follows:

Purchase Consideration	Rate Applying
Up to £150,000	Nil
£150,000 to £250,000	1%
Over £250,000	5%

Example
Isla buys a small shop in Inverness for £285,000. She pays LBTT at 1% on £100,000 (£250,000 – £150,000) and at 5% on £35,000 (£285,000 – £250,000), giving a total charge of £2,750.

Key Differences

Apart from the rates applying, LBTT operates in broadly the same way as SDLT. Many of the principles examined in Sections 7.1 to 7.10 continue to apply. Nonetheless, there are a few important differences to be aware of.

LBTT does not apply to the net present value of residential leases. The rates applying to non-residential leases are the same as those for SDLT (see Section 7.9), except that the 2% rate on net present value in excess of £5m does not apply.

Multiple dwellings relief operates differently under LBTT. Instead of taking an average price, LBTT is calculated separately on each dwelling comprised in the purchase. The total LBTT due cannot be less than 25% of the amount due on the total consideration for the whole transaction.

As with SDLT, purchases of six or more dwellings may alternatively be taxed at non-residential rates based on the total consideration for the transaction.

First time buyers purchasing a main residence in Scotland enjoy an increased threshold for the nil rate of LBTT of £175,000, instead of the usual £145,000. All other rates remain the same and, unlike the similar exemption for SDLT described in Section 7.2, the consequent saving (up to £600) is not withdrawn at any point for higher value purchases.

The special rate applying to purchases of residential properties by companies and other 'non-natural' persons described in Section 7.4 does not apply for LBTT.

This is by no means an exhaustive list of all the differences between LBTT and SDLT, so it is essential to take legal advice when purchasing property in Scotland (just as it is when purchasing property anywhere else!)

7.20   THE ADDITIONAL DWELLING SUPPLEMENT

ADS operates in a similar way to the higher SDLT charges examined in Section 7.3. It applies an additional LBTT charge to purchases of residential property in Scotland. From 25th January 2019, the additional charge is 4%.

Purchases for under £40,000 are exempt but, otherwise, the basic rule is that ADS applies to any purchase:

i) Made for the purposes of a property business, including property letting, etc.
ii) By an individual who has a relevant interest in more than one residential property at the end of the day of purchase,
iii) By two or more persons jointly where any of them has a relevant interest in more than one residential property at the end of the day of purchase, or
iv) By a company or other 'non-natural' person.

Heading (i) means **all** purchases of residential property in Scotland by landlords and other property business owners, for use in their business, will be subject to the additional 4% charge under ADS (except purchases for less than £40,000).

Unlike the higher SDLT charges, there is no exemption for transfers between spouses, so the issues discussed in Section 7.7 become all the more important for Scottish property. In effect, where an investment property in Scotland is transferred, spouses are in the same position as other transferees and ADS will be payable whenever the mortgage, or share of mortgage, taken over by the transferee is £40,000 or more.

Replacement of Main Residence

There is an exemption from ADS where the purchaser is buying a property that they intend to adopt as their main residence and is replacing a previous main residence sold within the previous eighteen months.

The exemption also applies where the purchaser's former main residence is sold within eighteen months **after** the new main residence is purchased. However, in this case, ADS will apply in the first place and a refund will have to be claimed later, on the sale of the former main residence.

Where all of two or more joint purchasers are either eligible for this exemption, or will not have any relevant interest in any other residential property at the end of the day of purchase **and** are not buying the property for business purposes, then ADS will not apply (or can be refunded later, as the case may be).

The exemption from ADS is extended to cases where a couple (married or unmarried) are jointly purchasing a new main residence and only one of them owned their former main residence which has been sold within the previous eighteen months, or is subsequently sold within the following eighteen months. (Hence, ADS would **not** be payable in a scenario like 'Jack and Rose' in the example in Section 7.3)

In any other cases involving joint purchasers, ADS will apply.

Relevant Interests in Residential Property

Subject to the points below, any interest in residential property anywhere in the world is a relevant interest for the purpose of ADS. Each individual must also include any relevant interests in residential property held by their spouse, civil partner, co-habitant (i.e. an unmarried partner), or minor children aged under 16 (e.g. property held in trust on their behalf).

An 'interest' means any form of legal right to a share in the property for any period of time.

Leases of more than 20 years are regarded as a relevant interest. Where such a lease exists, the person holding the superior interest in the property (the landlord) is not treated as having a relevant interest.

Where an individual is buying a property for use as their own home, any property to which ADS applied as a consequence of heading (i) above (or would have applied if the property had been in Scotland) can be disregarded.

Tax Tip
An individual who already owns rental property, none of which was purchased before April 2016, can avoid higher charges by buying a home in Scotland. By buying a rental property in England first and then a home in Scotland, you could avoid both sets of higher charges on both properties.

Wealth Warning
If you buy a rental property in Scotland first and then a home in England, you will pay higher charges on both properties.

Caravans, mobile homes, houseboats, and interests in property worth less than £40,000, may also be disregarded for the purposes of ADS.

7.21   SCOTTISH INCOME TAX RATES

The Scottish Parliament has control over Scottish Income Tax rates and thresholds. It may not, however, alter:

- The personal allowance (although it could effectively extend it by introducing a zero-rate tax band)
- The High Income Child Benefit Charge (see Section 3.3)
- The withdrawal of personal allowances where income exceeds £100,000
- Tax rates on dividends, interest, savings income, etc. (see below)
- Capital allowances

Similarly, it has no power over other taxes, such as NI, VAT, CGT, Corporation Tax and IHT. Scottish taxpayers (or their companies) pay all these taxes at the same rates as other UK residents.

The amount of income on which a Scottish taxpayer is liable for tax continues to be computed in exactly the same way as for other UK resident taxpayers: it is only the rates of tax that are different. Hence, the vast majority of the advice in this guide remains equally valid for Scottish taxpayers – it is only the amount of tax that can be saved (or may be suffered) that may vary.

Scottish taxpayers continue to pay Income Tax at normal UK rates on:

- Dividends
- Interest and other savings income
- Income from Real Estate Investment Trusts or Property Authorised Investment Funds

Nonetheless, Scottish Income Tax rates do apply to all of a Scottish taxpayer's property rental or trading income, regardless of where their properties are located.

In other words, a Scottish taxpayer pays Scottish Income Tax rates on income derived from property both within and outwith Scotland.

Other taxpayers continue to pay Income Tax at normal UK rates on all their income, even if it is derived from property in Scotland.

Scottish Income Tax Rates

The Scottish Parliament has set five different Income Tax rates. Combining these with the relevant parts of the UK tax regime means Scottish taxpayers pay Income Tax at the following rates in 2019/20:

Up to £12,500	0%	Personal allowance
£12,500 to £14,549	19%	Starter rate
£14,549 to £24,944	20%	Basic rate
£24,944 to £43,430	21%	Intermediate rate
£43,430 to £100,000	41%	Higher rate
£100,000 to £125,000	61.5%	Personal allowance withdrawal
£125,000 to £150,000	41%	Higher rate
Over £150,000	46%	Top rate

Comparing these rates with the main UK rates in Appendix A, we can see Scottish taxpayers suffer higher rates of Income Tax on all income over £24,944 (except dividends, interest, etc, as detailed above).

Worst of all, while taxpayers in the rest of the UK are now enjoying a higher rate tax threshold of £50,000, Scottish taxpayers are stuck with a threshold of just £43,430. That's **still less than the higher rate threshold** of £43,875 that all **UK taxpayers had ten years ago** in 2009/10!

Most importantly, the lower threshold for Scottish taxpayers means up to £6,570 extra of their taxable income is exposed to higher rate tax.

Not only will this lead to tax increases for those with genuine income in excess of the Scottish higher rate threshold, it will also significantly increase the burden for Scottish landlords whose taxable income is pushed over this level by the restrictions on interest relief examined in Section 4.5.

Practical Impacts

Every Scottish taxpayer effectively has two different sets of tax bands:

- Scottish tax bands that apply to employment, self-employment, rental and pension income, and
- UK tax bands that apply to dividends, interest and savings income and also for CGT purposes

Example 1
In 2019/20, Wallace has total gross rental income of £51,000, allowable interest costs of £8,000 and other qualifying expenses of £1,500. This gives him a taxable rental 'profit' of £47,500 (his deductible interest is restricted to just £2,000 – see Section 4.5). As he is a Scottish taxpayer, he will pay Income Tax on this sum as follows:

£12,500 @ 0%	*£0*
£2,049 @ 19%	*£389*
£10,395 @ 20%	*£2,079*
£18,486 @ 21%	*£3,882*
£4,070 @ 41%	*£1,669*
Less	
£6,000 @ 20%	*(£1,200) basic rate relief on 75% of interest*
Net total due	*£6,819*

Wallace also has a taxable capital gain of £10,000 on a residential property sale (after deducting his annual exemption). His CGT bill will be:

£2,500 @ 18%	*£450*
£7,500 @ 28%	*£2,100*
Total	*£2,550*

*This is because he has £2,500 of his **UK** basic rate band available for CGT purposes.*

If Wallace had been living in a different part of the UK, he would have remained a basic rate taxpayer and his Income Tax bill would have been £1,019 less. However, his CGT bill would still have been the same.

Tax Tip
Scottish taxpayers have the same tax bands for CGT purposes as other UK taxpayers. The CGT planning techniques explored throughout this guide will therefore produce the same savings for Scottish taxpayers.

The interest relief restrictions detailed in Section 4.5 cost Scottish taxpayers more than other taxpayers for a number of reasons:

i) They have a lower higher rate tax threshold (this alone cost Wallace an extra £814 in 2019/20; the cost for other Scottish taxpayers could be as much as £1,314)

ii) The higher and top rates are 1% more (this cost Wallace a further £41 in 2019/20; the cost for other Scottish taxpayers could be considerably more)

iii) Interest relief at the basic rate of 20% does not cover the cost of profits before interest being taxed at the intermediate rate of 21% (Wallace had £1,930 of interest relieved at basic rate where the corresponding profit before interest was being taxed at the intermediate rate: this cost him a further £19; the cost for some Scottish taxpayers could be as much as £185)

The interest relief restrictions imposed by the UK Government cost Wallace an extra £874 because he is a Scottish taxpayer. Without the interest relief restrictions his Income Tax bill would only be £145 more than a non-Scottish taxpayer.

Practical Pointer
Scottish landlords are suffering the 'worst of both worlds'. The higher tax rates and lower higher rate threshold applying to Scottish taxpayers mean they are seeing even greater increases in their tax bills as a result of the UK Government's interest relief restrictions. By 2020/21, Scottish landlords with rental profits before interest of £50,000 or more are likely to be paying over £1,500 more tax than their counterparts elsewhere in the UK.

Generally speaking therefore, the Income Tax planning techniques explored throughout this guide will produce even greater savings for Scottish taxpayers.

Trading Income

Another important point to note is that the upper earnings limit for NI purposes remains at the UK level (£50,000 for 2019/20) for Scottish taxpayers.

Example 2

Gruoch is a property developer based in Dundee. Her taxable profits for 2019/20 are £49,000 and she has interest income of £1,200. She pays Income Tax as follows:

Trading profits		
£12,500 @ 0%	*£0*	*(personal allowance)*
£2,049 @ 19%	*£389*	*(starter rate band)*
£10,395 @ 20%	*£2,079*	*(basic rate band)*
£18,486 @ 21%	*£3,882*	*(intermediate rate band)*
£5,570 @ 41%	*£2,284*	*(excess over Scottish higher rate threshold)*
Interest income		
£500 @ 0%	*£0*	*(personal savings allowance)*
£500 @ 20%	*£100*	*(amount still within UK basic rate band)*
£200 @ 40%	*£80*	*(excess over UK higher rate threshold)*
Total	*£8,814*	

She also has to pay Class 4 NI at 9% on £40,368 (£49,000 – £8,632). The NI rate does not drop to 2% until profits exceed £50,000. Including £156 of Class 2 NI gives her a total tax bill of £12,603, which is £1,334 more than it would have been if she lived in a different part of the UK.

The overall tax rate on the top £5,570 of Gruoch's trading profits is 50%. This rate applies to trading profits made by Scottish taxpayers below state pension age that fall into the gap between the Scottish higher rate threshold and the UK higher rate threshold (i.e. between £43,430 and £50,000 in 2019/20).

Employment income received by Scottish taxpayers below state pension age that falls into this gap suffers an overall tax rate of 53%!

Who Is A Scottish Taxpayer?

You are classed as a Scottish taxpayer if you are UK resident and your main place of residence in the UK is in Scotland. Your main place of residence in the UK must be determined as a question of fact, and it is important to remember that, for *this* purpose:

- It is not possible to elect which property is to be treated as your main place of residence
- Only property in the UK is counted
- It is not necessary to have any legal or equitable interest in the property
- Any type of abode may be counted, including hotel rooms and berths on ships and oil rigs
- Each person must be considered individually (i.e. married couples are not treated as a single 'unit')

Hence, while your 'main place of residence' for this purpose will often be the same as your 'main residence' for CGT purposes, the rules are slightly different and may sometimes lead to a different result.

See Section 6.22 for further guidance on the factors to be considered in determining a main place of residence. Issues such as where your spouse lives or whether you have any legal title in the property are no longer critical for this purpose, but continue to be among those factors.

If you move to or from Scotland during the tax year, you will be classified according to where your main place of residence in the UK is for the majority of the year.

If it is not clear whether your main place of residence is located in Scotland for any given tax year then the question of whether you are a Scottish taxpayer for that year will be based on where you have spent the most days. For this purpose, a 'day' is based on where you are at midnight and you become a Scottish taxpayer if you are present in Scotland at midnight on at least as many days as you are present in any of England, Wales, or Northern Ireland (taking each country separately).

Non-UK residents cannot be Scottish taxpayers.

7.22   LAND TRANSACTION TAX & OTHER WELSH TAXES

From April 2018, SDLT has ceased to apply to property located in Wales and has been replaced by Land Transaction Tax ('LTT'), the first devolved tax for Wales.

Residential Property
The basic underlying rates of LTT on residential property are as follows:

Purchase Consideration	Rate Applying
Up to £180,000	0%
£180,000 to £250,000	3.5%
£250,000 to £400,000	5%
£400,000 to £750,000	7.5%
£750,000 to £1.5m	10%
Over £1.5m	12%

Sadly, the authorities in Cardiff appear to have the same desire to persecute landlords and other property businesses as their colleagues in London and Edinburgh, so there is the usual additional 3% surcharge on most purchases or transfers of second or additional residential properties.

The surcharge also applies to all residential property purchases by, or transfers to, a company.

Non-Residential Property
The rates of LTT on non-residential property are as follows:

Purchase Consideration	Rate Applying
Up to £150,000	0%
£150,000 to £250,000	1%
£250,000 to £1m	5%
Over £1m	6%

The non-residential rates also apply to 'mixed use' property, such as a shop with a flat above it, where both parts are purchased as part of the same transaction.

Important Variations

LTT operates in a broadly similar way to SDLT but there are some important variations, so professional advice is essential when purchasing or transferring property in Wales.

Welsh Income Tax

The Welsh Assembly has the power to vary the Income Tax rates payable by Welsh taxpayers. The main UK rates are each reduced by 10% and the Welsh Assembly decides the Welsh rates to be added. As the Welsh rates are currently all set at 10%, the overall rates paid by Welsh taxpayers remain the same as English or Northern Irish taxpayers at present.

The Welsh Government has committed to not increasing Income Tax rates for Welsh taxpayers during the current Assembly term, so the current overall rates of 20%, 40% and 45% are expected to continue until at least 2021.

As in Scotland, the Welsh Assembly's powers are limited. The UK Government retains control over the personal allowance and the tax rates applying to dividends, interest and other savings income.

Chapter 8

Advanced Tax Planning

8.1   INTRODUCTION TO TAX PLANNING

In previous chapters we have looked at the mechanics of the UK tax system as it applies to the individual property investor. In this chapter we will take a look at some more advanced aspects of UK property taxation and some further useful planning strategies. These strategies relate in the main to those investors who continue to hold their property investments personally.

In many cases, the best tax-planning results will be obtained through the use of a combination of different techniques, rather than merely following any single one.

Each situation is different and the optimum solution only comes through detailed analysis of all the relevant facts. Tax planning should never be undertaken without full knowledge of the facts of the case and the exact circumstances of the individuals and other legal entities involved.

For this reason, the techniques laid out in this chapter, which are by no means exhaustive, are intended only to give you some idea of the tax savings which can be achieved through careful planning. If and when you come to undertake any tax-planning of your own you should seek professional advice from someone fully acquainted with your situation.

Remember also that tax law is constantly changing and a technique that works well now may later be undermined by changes made in Parliament or decisions made in Court.

Bayley's Tax Planning Law

All tax planning should be based on these four guiding principles:

- Hope for the best,
- Plan for the worst,
- Review your position constantly, and
- Expect the unexpected!

The Budgets we have seen over the last few years have provided some of the best arguments for these principles I have ever seen. Especially the last one!

Planning for the Future

In Sections 6.13 and 6.14, we saw the Government is planning to make some major changes to PPR relief and private letting relief. Throughout this chapter, we will assume the changes will go ahead as planned. In particular, therefore, we will assume private letting relief is not available on most property disposals after 5th April 2020. However, the reader should note the proposed changes are not yet certain and the actual provisions, when finally enacted, might be subject to some alteration. There even remains a sliver of hope they might be abandoned altogether: but don't hold your breath!

Nonetheless, my advice remains to 'plan for the worst' and assume the changes will go ahead as planned. Hence, in Sections 8.34 to 8.36, at the end of the chapter, as well as earlier in Section 8.5, we will look at some measures that might be used to mitigate the impact of the changes.

8.2 THE BENEFITS OF JOINT OWNERSHIP

Owning property jointly with one or more other people can be highly beneficial for tax purposes. In this section, we will look at joint ownership benefits available to anyone. In the next section, we will concentrate on married couples.

A number of important tax reliefs, bands and allowances are available on a 'per person' basis, these include:

- The personal allowance
- The annual CGT exemption
- Private letting relief
- Entrepreneurs' relief
- The basic rate tax band
- The £100,000 threshold for withdrawal of personal allowances
- The £150,000 additional rate threshold
- The small earnings exception for NI
- The NI earnings threshold

Furthermore, as discussed in Section 4.9, it is also possible to structure investments so that the AIA effectively operates on a 'per person' basis.

The value of these allowances, bands and reliefs can effectively be doubled in the case of properties held jointly by two people (or tripled for three joint owners, etc.).

How Much Is At Stake?

Sticking with two joint owners, the maximum tax savings that joint ownership can generate in 2019/20 alone are:

- £7,110 on most capital gains on residential property
- £18,310 on capital gains with private letting relief (but see the 'wealth warning' in Section 8.4 and proposed future changes outlined in Section 6.14)
- £1,803,360 on capital gains with entrepreneurs' relief (but see the 'wealth warning' in Section 6.28)
- £20,000 in Income Tax on rental income
- £17,121 in Income Tax and NI on trading profits
- £416,500 in additional Income Tax savings (or even repayments) when claiming the AIA on commercial property, qualifying furnished holiday lets, or assets within 'communal areas' (see Sections 4.9 and 8.17)

The maximum Income Tax savings described above are based on taxpayers with high levels of income such that joint ownership can be used to reduce their taxable income down to £100,000. Most higher-rate taxpayers can still achieve considerable savings, however.

Wealth Warning
Not every tax relief or band is given on a 'per person' basis. Exceptions to be wary of include:

- All SDLT bands
- The VAT registration threshold
- Rent-a-room relief

Additionally, the fact that the upper earnings limit for NI works on a 'per person' basis actually works against joint owners in a trading situation (although this is usually outweighed by Income Tax savings).

Non-Equal Splits

When considering the benefits of joint ownership, remember it is possible to have any split of beneficial ownership you desire, as long as the correct form of joint ownership is in place (see Section 2.14). In this context, it is worth mentioning that a joint tenancy can be changed fairly easily into a tenancy in common. This change is not treated as a disposal for CGT purposes unless at the same time there is also a change to a non-equal split of beneficial ownership.

Changing the Split

Where the joint owners are not married, it is difficult to transfer any share in the property to the other person without incurring CGT or other charges. In Section 8.9 we will look at a possible way around this. Nevertheless, for joint owners other than married couples, it is generally advisable to get your ownership structure right from the outset.

Optimising Rental Income Shares

Joint owners who are not a married couple may agree to share rental income in different proportions to their legal ownership of the property (perhaps because one of the investors is carrying out the management of the jointly held portfolio). The Income Tax treatment should follow the agreed profit-sharing arrangements. It is wise to document your profit-sharing agreement and advise HMRC in order to avoid any dispute.

Sales by Former Joint Owners

For the purposes of calculating PPR relief on any property sale, the seller's period of ownership for their entire interest at the date of sale is treated as commencing on the date they first acquired any interest in the property.

8.3   USING YOUR SPOUSE OR CIVIL PARTNER

Putting property into joint names with your spouse can generate considerable tax savings, just like any other joint owners, as we saw in the previous section. In some cases, an outright transfer of the whole property may even be more beneficial.

The major difference between those who have legally 'tied the knot' and the rest of us, however, is the fact the transfer itself is free from tax (subject to the points made in Section 7.7 regarding SDLT).

Despite this, the transfer is not necessarily free of tax **consequences** and we will look at the impact of transfers to a spouse on PPR relief and private letting relief in Sections 8.4 and 8.5. Note that these consequences are expected to change in many cases where the transfer takes place after 5th April 2020.

The example of George and Charlotte in Section 6.32 demonstrated the potential CGT savings in a simple case where PPR relief did not apply. In such a case (and where the couple are married), it is normally immaterial whether the property was in joint ownership throughout, or was only transferred into joint ownership at a later date, prior to the ultimate sale (often known as a 'pre-sale transfer'). The effect on the couple's final tax liabilities usually remains exactly the same.

As we saw in Section 6.32, the potential CGT saving on a typical investment property is up to £7,110 in 2019/20. However, the position will differ from one couple to another, so investors need to weigh up the costs of any 'pre-sale transfer' against the saving available in their own particular case.

Two key provisos must be made regarding transfers of property to a spouse:

a) The transferee spouse must be beneficially entitled to his/her share of the sale proceeds. Any attempt to prevent this could make the transfer invalid for tax purposes.

b) An interim transfer of property into joint names prior to sale must take place early enough to ensure the transferee spouse genuinely has beneficial title to their share. If it is left until the ultimate sale is a contractual certainty, it may be too late to be effective for tax purposes.

Timing

Where a transfer to a spouse prior to sale is planned, the following guidelines may assist in making it effective for tax purposes. Bear in mind always, though, that the transferee must have beneficial ownership for the transfer to work as intended.

- It is preferable to do the transfer as soon as possible
- Ideally, it should be before the property is put on the market
- A transfer any time after there is a contract for sale to a third party is likely to be ineffective in providing the transferee with the requisite beneficial ownership

But Joint Ownership Is Not Always Beneficial

A transfer into joint names prior to sale is not always beneficial. Sometimes, it is preferable to have the property in the sole name of one spouse at the time of sale. This may arise, for example, if:

- One spouse's annual exemption will be used on other capital gains in the same year, while the other's annual exemption remains fully available,
- Some or all of one spouse's basic rate band is available but the other spouse is a higher rate taxpayer,
- Only one spouse is entitled to PPR relief or private letting relief on the property (see Section 8.4),
- Only one spouse is entitled to entrepreneurs' relief on the property (see Section 6.28), or
- One spouse has capital losses available to set off against the gain on the property

If the best spouse to hold the property at the time of sale is not the one who already holds it, a pre-sale transfer could generate considerable savings. The same provisos as set out above apply equally here.

In summary, when a sale is in prospect, it is well worth assessing whether a transfer into joint ownership, or to the other spouse outright, might result in a significant CGT saving. Always remember that whoever has title to the property at the time of sale must be entitled to the proceeds!

Lastly, it is worth remembering joint ownership does not have to mean equal shares and any other allocation is also possible.

8.4   SAVING MORE TAX WITH TRANSFERS TO SPOUSES

Please note the principles outlined in this section only apply to transfers between legally married spouses or registered civil partners. **Note also that the Government is proposing to change the rules for PPR relief on transfers taking place after 5th April 2020.** We will look at the proposed changes and the relevant consequences at the end of this section.

As we saw in Section 6.11, a lifetime transfer of a property, or share in a property, between spouses usually results in the transferee taking over the transferor's base cost (or an appropriate share). At present, however, it does not necessarily follow that the transferee takes over the reliefs to which the transferor was entitled. Sometimes the reliefs will transfer; sometimes they will not: which could be utterly disastrous, but could also sometimes work in the couple's favour. It's all a question of getting your timing right!

Principal Private Residence Relief: Transfers before 6th April 2020

For the purposes of PPR relief, the position currently depends on whether the property is the couple's main residence at the time of transfer. If it is their main residence at that time then, for the purposes of the relief, the transferee is treated as if they had owned the property since the transferor first acquired it. The transferee spouse is then also entitled to the PPR exemption for the same periods as the transferor.

Example 1
In March 2008 Babur bought a house in London for £500,000 and adopted it as his main residence. In 2014 he married Zainab and she moved in with him. In 2015 Babur put the house into equal joint names. In September 2016 the couple moved out of the house and began to rent it out. In March 2020, the couple sold the house for £1.4m. As Babur put the property into joint names while it was their main residence, Zainab will be entitled to the same periods of PPR exemption as him. Each of them will have the same CGT calculation:

	£
Sale proceeds (half share)	700,000
Less: Cost (half share)	(250,000)

	450,000
PPR relief (10/12 x £450,000)*	(375,000)
Private letting relief **	(40,000)

	35,000
Annual exemption	(12,000)

Taxable gain	23,000

* *The property is exempt for the eight and a half years it was Babur's main residence plus the final eighteen months of ownership (the final period of ownership exemption would only be nine months if the sale was made after 5th April 2020).*

** *Private letting relief is available on a sale before 6th April 2020, but would not be available on a sale made on or after that date.*

If we assume Babur is a higher rate taxpayer and Zainab has enough of her basic rate band available to cover her share of the capital gain then the couple's total CGT liability will be £10,580 (£23,000 x 28% for Babur plus £23,000 x 18% for Zainab).

Example 2
If, instead, Babur had still held the property in his sole name at the time of sale, his CGT calculation would have been:

	£
Sale proceeds	1,400,000
Less: Cost	(500,000)

	900,000
PPR relief (10/12 x £900,000)	(750,000)
Private letting relief	(40,000)

	110,000
Annual exemption	(12,000)

Taxable gain	98,000

Babur's CGT liability would then have been £27,440 (£98,000 x 28%).

Under these circumstances, transferring the property into joint names while it was the couple's main residence has resulted in a CGT saving of £16,860. This saving arises from a number of sources:

- A couple owning a property jointly are entitled to up to £40,000 of private letting relief **each**; meaning up to £80,000 of relief may be available
- Each joint owner has their own annual exemption
- In this particular case, the transferee's basic rate band was available to reduce the rate of CGT she paid from 28% to 18%

The maximum savings arising from each of these sources in 2019/20 are £11,200, £3,360 and £3,750 respectively; making the maximum total saving of £18,310 referred to in Section 8.2. Sadly, the saving for disposals taking place after 5th April 2020 will be considerably less in most cases, due to the proposed changes to private letting relief (see Section 6.14).

> **Tax Tip**
> Where a property has a period of PPR relief built up already, it will currently generally be beneficial to put it into joint names while it is still the couple's main residence.

Under current rules, if the property is **not** the couple's main residence at the time of the transfer then, while the transferee spouse still takes over a share of the transferor's base cost, they are **not** entitled to any historic periods of PPR exemption the transferor has built up and are treated as acquiring their share of the property on the date of the transfer.

Example 3
Let's take the same facts as Example 1, except let us now assume Babur did not put the house into joint names with Zainab until 2017: after the couple had moved out of the property. His CGT calculation remains the same, but Zainab will no longer be entitled to any PPR relief or private letting relief. After deducting her annual exemption of £12,000 from her share of the gain (£450,000), she will be left with a taxable gain of £438,000.

Zainab's CGT liability will now be at least £118,890 (£37,500 x 18% + £400,500 x 28%); bringing the couple's total tax bill up to at least £125,330 (£118,890 + £23,000 x 28%). The transfer into joint ownership has therefore effectively cost the couple at least an extra £97,890 (£125,330 – £27,440).

> **Wealth Warning 1**
> At present, a transfer of a property with a prior period of PPR exemption, that takes place while the property is **not** the couple's main residence, can have disastrous consequences. The transferee is not entitled to the prior period of exemption and, unless the property is re-adopted as their main residence at a later date, they will also not be entitled to the exemption for the final period of ownership and nor will they be entitled to any private letting relief.

Wealth Warning 2

As explained below, the disastrous outcome outlined in Example 3 is not expected to apply where the transfer takes place **after** 5th April 2020. However, this is based on the assumption that the current draft legislation is enacted as it stands. Hence, before acting on this assumption, it is vital to check that the planned changes have indeed gone ahead!

Tax Tip

The easiest way to avoid the disastrous outcome outlined in Example 3 would be to simply transfer the property back into the sole ownership of the original owner.

As explained in Section 8.2, a former joint owner is treated for the purposes of PPR relief as if they had owned the whole property since the date on which they first acquired any beneficial ownership. Hence, in our example, if the property were put back into Babur's sole ownership prior to sale, he would be treated for the purposes of PPR relief as having a single uninterrupted period of ownership of the whole property from 2008 to 2020. This would restore the position outlined in Example 2, where he had a CGT bill of £27,440, a lot better than the disastrous result if the property remained in joint ownership at the time of sale.

Re-adopting the property as a main residence may provide a partial solution in a situation like Example 3, but will not usually be as effective as transferring the property back into the original owner's sole ownership. The benefits of re-adopting a property as a main residence in other cases, following a transfer to a spouse, are examined in Section 8.5.

While the current rules can prove disastrous, they can also be turned to advantage: creating the fabulous **window of opportunity** we will be examining in the next section!

Private Letting Relief: Disposals before 6th April 2020

As explained in Section 8.1, private letting relief is unlikely to be available on most property disposals after 5th April 2020. However, it remains worth looking at the impact of transfers between spouses on earlier disposals.

Where a spouse loses entitlement to any PPR relief, they also lose entitlement to any private letting relief. In addition to this, private letting relief currently operates on a strictly **individual** basis. As a result, a transferee spouse may not be entitled to as much private letting relief as the transferor; or sometimes even none at all.

Example 4

In March 2012, Alex bought a house in Norfolk for £200,000 and began renting it out. In March 2018, she married Eddie and they moved into the house together so that it became their main residence. In July 2018, Alex put the house into equal joint names with Eddie. The couple sold the house for £400,000 in March 2020. Their CGT calculations are as follows:

	Alex £	Eddie £
Sale proceeds (half shares)	200,000	200,000
Less: Cost (half shares)	(100,000)	(100,000)
	-------------	-------------
	100,000	100,000
PPR relief (2/8 x £100,000)	(25,000)	(25,000)
Private letting relief	(25,000)	-
	-------------	-------------
	50,000	75,000
Annual exemption 2019/20	(12,000)	(12,000)
	-------------	-------------
Taxable gain	38,000	63,000

*Eddie is entitled to the same PPR relief as Alex because the property was the couple's main residence at the time he acquired his share; but he is not entitled to any private letting relief because **he** never rented the property out!*

The result is the couple have a total CGT liability of up to £28,280 (£38,000+£63,000 x 28%). If Alex had held on to the property herself, she would have had a maximum CGT bill of £27,440. Hence, the transfer may have cost the couple a little extra tax, although this depends on whether any of Eddie's basic rate band is available.

Private Letting Relief: Disposals after 5th April 2020

While private letting relief will seldom be available on property disposals after 5th April 2020, one benefit of the proposed changes is that a transferee spouse will be entitled to relief in respect of qualifying 'shared occupancy' lettings (see Section 6.14) made by the transferor spouse at any time that is treated as part of the transferee's period of ownership for the purposes of PPR relief.

Hence, this will cover qualifying lettings made by the transferor prior to the date of transfer when:
- The transfer is made after 5th April 2020 (see below), or
- The property was the couple's main residence at the time of the transfer

Principal Private Residence Relief: Transfers after 5th April 2020

Under the current Government proposals outlined in the draft legislation discussed in Section 6.14, for transfers taking place after 5th April 2020, the transferee spouse will **always** inherit the transferor's history for PPR relief purposes.

This change will prevent the disastrous outcome shown in Example 3 (but see Wealth Warning 2 above), but will also prevent taxpayers from turning the current rules to their advantage. Hence, let us now look at the fabulous window of opportunity that remains until 5th April 2020!

8.5   A WINDOW OF OPPORTUNITY

The changes for transfers between spouses outlined in the previous section leave us with a short window of opportunity to use the current rules to wipe out, or reduce, the taxable gain on an existing investment property, or second home.

All you need to benefit from this opportunity is a spouse, and a property that is not currently your main residence, but which you are prepared to adopt as your main residence for a reasonable period before selling. It also works best if the property is currently in your sole ownership (or at least not jointly owned with your spouse), although some savings may still be possible provided it was in your sole ownership at some earlier stage.

A transfer of such a property to your spouse **before** 6th April 2020, and while it is **not** your main residence, can be used to eliminate most, if not all, of your taxable gain.

Example 1
In March 2002, Caleb bought a property in Kensington for £600,000 and began renting it out. In February 2020 Caleb transferred the property to his husband, David. In March 2020, the couple moved into the property and adopted it as their main residence. Two years later, in March 2022, David sells the property for £1.6m. David and Caleb are both higher rate taxpayers for 2021/22. David's CGT calculation is as follows:

	£
Sale proceeds	1,600,000
Less: Cost	(600,000)

	1,000,000
PPR relief (24/25 x £1m)*	(960,000)

Taxable gain	40,000

* - The property was the couple's main residence for 24 months out of David's ownership period of 25 months. Caleb's ownership period is ignored because the property was not their main residence at the time of transfer and the transfer took place before 6th April 2020.

After deducting David's annual exemption for 2021/22 of, say, £12,600, he will be left with a taxable gain of £27,400 and a CGT bill of just £7,672 (at 28%).

If Caleb had held on to the property himself until the sale, his CGT calculation would have been as follows:

	£
Gain before reliefs (as above)	1,000,000
PPR relief (2/20 x £1m)	(100,000)

	900,000
Annual exemption 2021/22 (say)	(12,600)

Taxable gain	887,400

The transfer to David has therefore reduced the taxable gain by £860,000 (£887,400 - £27,400), saving the couple £240,800 (£860,000 x 28%) in CGT.

Although, in the example, David and Caleb moved into the property quite soon after the transfer, this technique will still produce savings on any property that you are prepared to adopt as your main residence at some time in the future. It is only the transfer that needs to take place before 6th April 2020, the periods of occupation as your main residence, and the ultimate date of sale, could both be much later.

Example 2

Maggie bought an investment property in Manchester for £25,000 in April 1985. Some years later, she married Peter and, on 1st April 2020, she transferred the investment property to him. On 1st April 2023, the couple adopted the property as their main residence. Peter sells the property for £185,000 on 1st April 2025.

The gain on the property before any reliefs is £160,000. Peter will be entitled to PPR relief of £64,000 (two fifths) as the property was the couple's main residence for two years out of his ownership period of five years.

If Maggie had held onto the property herself until the sale, she would only have been entitled to PPR relief of £8,000 (two fortieths) as the property would have been the couple's main residence for two years out of her ownership period of forty years.

The transfer on 1st April 2020 has therefore increased the PPR relief on the property by £56,000 (£64,000 - £8,000), giving the couple a CGT saving of £15,680 (at 28%).

Multiple Windows

There is nothing to stop a property investor using this technique on more than one property: the transfers must all take place before 6th April 2020 and the periods of occupation as a main residence need to be different (and cannot overlap). However, in principle, the savings in Examples 1 and 2 could be made by the same couple if they owned both properties.

Opening More Windows (by Election)

A second home, or other suitable property, could also be transferred to a spouse before 6th April 2020 and later 'adopted' as the couple's main residence by way of a main residence election (see Section 6.22). The property would need to qualify as a private residence (see Sections 6.20 and 6.21) and the election would either need to be made within the appropriate time limit, or else within a new two year 'window' created using one of the methods set out in Section 6.22. Even an overseas property might qualify, as explained in Section 6.23.

Re-Glazing (Re-Adopting a Former Main Residence)

Up to now, we have assumed it would not make sense to use this technique on a property with existing historic PPR exemption for an earlier period. Certainly, the type of disastrous outcome illustrated by Example 3 in Section 8.4 should be avoided. But, where a couple intends to re-adopt a former main residence as their main residence once again, the technique may still prove beneficial in some cases.

Example 3
Let's take the same facts as in Example 2, except let us now assume Maggie used the property in Manchester as her main residence for three years, from 1985 to 1988. The transfer on 1st April 2020 took place while the property was still being rented out, so Peter cannot claim any PPR relief for this earlier period of occupation. His PPR relief therefore remains £64,000, as before.

If Maggie had held onto the property herself until the sale, she would have a total of five years' worth of PPR relief. However, this would only amount to £20,000 (£160,000 x 5/40), meaning the transfer to Peter has still increased the PPR relief on the property by £44,000 (£64,000 - £20,000), giving the couple a CGT saving of £12,320 (at 28%).

Maggie could have waited until after 5th April 2020 and then transferred the property into joint names. Subject to Wealth Warning 2 in Section 8.4, this would have meant Peter was treated as if he had acquired his share of the property in 1985 and would be entitled to PPR relief for Maggie's earlier period of occupation. Let's compare the outcomes for the two different approaches:

Date of Transfer: *Owner(s) when sold:*	*Before 6th April* *Peter* *£*	*On or After 6th April* *Maggie & Peter* *£ (Each)*
Gain before reliefs	*160,000*	*80,000*
PPR relief (2/5) / (5/40)	*(64,000)*	*(10,000)*
	96,000	*70,000*
Annual exemption (say)	*(13,500)*	*(13,500)*
Taxable gain	*82,500*	*56,500*

243

The total taxable gain for Peter and Maggie as joint owners would be £113,000 (2 x £56,500), or £30,500 more than for Peter alone. This would cost the couple up to £8,540 more in CGT (at 28%), although this might be reduced to as little as £4,790 if Maggie's basic rate band were available (using 2019/20 rates).

Nonetheless, the transfer into Peter's sole name before 6th April 2020 has proved more beneficial (and both methods are better than if Maggie had held onto the property in her sole name until the date of sale).

In practice, the question of which of the two methods considered in this example is better will depend on the facts of the case. The longer your earlier period of PPR exemption, the less likely it is that a transfer to your spouse before 6th April 2020 will be more beneficial than a later transfer into joint ownership.

A transfer to your spouse before 6th April 2020 will certainly not be beneficial if you do not actually re-adopt the property as your main residence, so it is probably best avoided if you have doubts over whether you will be willing, or able, to do this.

Note that I assumed Maggie would not qualify for any additional relief under the 'temporary absence' rules (see Section 6.18). If she did qualify for any additional relief, this would need to be taken into account and could mean the transfer to Peter on 1st April 2020 was actually disadvantageous.

Half Windows

The technique illustrated in this section will not generally work where a married couple already own a property jointly, due to the rule explained in Section 8.2, whereby a former joint owner is treated, for the purposes of PPR relief, as if they had owned the whole property since the date they first acquired any beneficial ownership.

However, some savings might be achieved if the property has not always been in joint ownership.

Example 4
In February 2007, Mary bought a flat in Chelsea for £750,000 and began to rent it out. In February 2017, she put the property into joint names with her husband, Philip. Later, in January 2020, Mary transferred her share to Philip, so that he became the sole owner. In February 2020, the couple adopted the property as their main residence. They lived there for two years until Philip sold the flat for £2.1m in February 2022.

Due to the 'former joint owner' rule, Philip is treated for PPR relief purposes as if he had held the whole property since February 2017, a total of five years. The gain before reliefs is £1.35m, so Philip is entitled to PPR relief of £540,000

(£1.35m x 2/5) in respect of the two years the couple lived in the property as their main residence.

If the property had remained in joint names until sale, each spouse would have had a gain before reliefs of £675,000 and Philip's PPR relief would have been £270,000 (£675,000 x 2/5). However, as Mary had held the property for fifteen years, her PPR relief would have been just £90,000 (£675,000 x 2/15), giving the couple total relief of £360,000.

Hence, the transfer of Mary's share to Philip in January 2020 has given the couple an extra £180,000 of PPR relief. Philip's sole ownership will mean there is only one annual exemption available (say £12,600), but the total taxable gain will still have been reduced by £167,400, saving the couple up to £46,872 in CGT (at 28%).

Window Summary

There are many ways in which married property owners may be able to benefit from this 'window of opportunity' to eliminate or drastically reduce their taxable gains. But **the key to all these opportunities is to make the transfer before 6th April 2020!**

8.6   MARRIAGE, DIVORCE AND CIVIL PARTNERSHIPS

Getting married alters your tax status dramatically. One major aspect of this for property owners is, from that date onwards, you and your spouse can only have one main residence between you for PPR relief purposes.

If each of you still has your own private residence when the 'happy day' comes, you should elect which one is to be your main residence (see Section 6.22). In these circumstances, the election must be done within two years of the date of marriage. Once an election is made, you can change it at any time, as long as you still have more than one private residence between you.

Once you are married, the tax saving opportunities outlined in Section 8.4 will be available. If you marry before 6th April 2020, it will be important to avoid the disastrous outcome illustrated by Example 3 in that section in respect of the property you have **not** nominated as your main residence, or any former main residence. These problems can be avoided in respect of a second private residence by first changing your main residence election.

Alternatively, it will usually make sense to simply delay transfers of such properties until after 5th April 2020 (subject to Wealth Warning 2 in Section 8.4 and the points made in Section 8.5 regarding re-adopting a main residence).

In some instances (where you marry before 6th April 2020), you may be able to exploit the 'window of opportunity' examined in Section 8.5 in respect of an investment property you intend to adopt as your marital home in the future. This may even include a former main residence, although you will need to 'do your sums' to make sure you are more like Maggie and Peter (Example 3 in Section 8.5) than Babur and Zainab (Example 3 in Section 8.4).

Subject to the points above, it will usually make sense to put properties into joint names in order to maximise the available reliefs on any future sale, but the points made in Section 8.3 should be taken into account and, for disposals after 5th April 2020, the maximum CGT savings in most cases will be just £7,110 (at 2019/20 rates) due to the proposed changes to private letting relief.

Nonetheless, as we saw in Section 8.2, there are also potential Income Tax savings to be made through joint ownership and these may be even greater in some cases, including parents with young children (Section 8.29), and Scottish taxpayers (Section 7.21).

Furthermore, if you don't feel comfortable giving your spouse a joint share in your property, the potential Income Tax savings can still be achieved, at minimal risk, using the method examined in Section 8.7.

Divorce and Separation

Once you get separated or divorced, your married status for CGT purposes ends (see Section 6.7 regarding the end of the exemption for transfers to your spouse).

'Separated' means either legally separated under a court order or separated in circumstances that are likely to be permanent. The good news is, once again, you will be able to have your own individual main residence for PPR relief purposes.

Alternatively, if you have not claimed any PPR relief on another property in the interim, nor made any main residence election in favour of another property, your former marital home may continue to be exempt as long as your ex-spouse continues to use it as their main residence. This extension to the PPR exemption only applies in the case of a subsequent transfer of the former marital home, or a share in it, to the former spouse, as part of a financial settlement.

8.7   HAVE YOUR CAKE AND EAT IT

Income Tax savings can be generated by transferring property into either joint names with your spouse or the sole name of the spouse with the lower overall income. In the right circumstances, moving income from one spouse to another in this way could save a higher-rate taxpayer up to £12,500 in Income Tax in 2019/20 alone. As we saw in Section 8.2, some taxpayers could save up to £20,000.

As explained in Section 8.3, this form of tax planning is not effective unless beneficial title in the property is genuinely transferred. But not everyone trusts their spouse enough to hand over title to their property!

For Income Tax purposes, at least, there is a way to solve this dilemma. Where property is held jointly by a married couple, there is an automatic presumption, for Income Tax purposes, that the income arises in equal shares. This 50/50 split will continue to apply unless and until the couple jointly elect for the income to be split in accordance with the true beneficial title in the property.

Hence, where a married property owner wants to save Income Tax on their rental profits without giving up too much of their title to the property, what they should do is:
- Transfer the property into joint names with their spouse, but
- Retain 99% of the beneficial ownership and transfer only 1%, and
- Simply never elect for the income to be split in accordance with the true beneficial title!

Conversely

Conversely, of course, there will be cases where the actual beneficial ownership split is preferable for tax purposes. In these cases, the election to split the income on an actual basis should usually be made. Beware though that, once made, this election is irreversible.

8.8 INHERITED PROPERTY

In Section 6.11 we looked at the base cost of inherited property and saw this is generally based on the property's value at the date of the previous owner's death. In many cases, this is pretty much all there is to tell and the new owner is treated in every respect as if they had purchased the property on that date.

There are a few areas of complication, however. Firstly, there is the fact that during the period of administration the deceased's estate is treated as a separate legal person, rather like a trust.

Like trusts, estates pay CGT at the higher rates of 20% or 28% (except where entrepreneurs' relief is available). The estate has its own annual exemption equal to the amount given to individuals. The exemption applies for the tax year of death and the following two tax years.

If a property is sold by the deceased's estate, it is treated as if it had been acquired on the date of the deceased's death for its market value on that date. Where 75% or more of the sale proceeds are to go to one or more beneficiaries who occupied the property as their main residence at the time of the deceased's death, the PPR exemption will apply to any gain arising.

Transfers of property from the estate to the beneficiary are exempt from CGT. Once the transfer has taken place, the beneficiary is treated as if they had acquired the property (or the deceased's share of it) for its market value on the date of the deceased's death.

Surviving Joint Owners – Other than Widows and Widowers

Where the new owner of the whole property was already a joint owner prior to the deceased's death, the calculation of PPR relief is based on their whole period of ownership (see Section 8.2). However, a surviving joint owner, other than the deceased's widow or widower (in some cases – see below), cannot claim private letting relief on the deceased's share of an inherited property in respect of lettings made prior to the deceased's death.

Widows and Widowers – Deaths before 6th April 2020

For deaths occurring before 6th April 2020, the position applying where property passes to a surviving spouse depends on whether the property was the couple's main residence at the time of the deceased's death and on whether the survivor was already a joint owner prior to that date.

If the property was **not** the couple's main residence at the time of the deceased's death and the survivor was **not** already a joint owner then they are simply treated as having acquired the property on the date of the deceased's death.

Where the survivor was already a joint owner prior to the deceased's death, and the property was **not** the couple's main residence at that time, then they are in the same position as any other surviving joint owner, as described above.

Where the property **was** the couple's main residence at the time of the deceased's death then, for the purposes of calculating PPR relief, the survivor is in the same position as for deaths occurring after 5th April 2020, as set out below.

For disposals before 6th April 2020, the survivor is not eligible for any private letting relief in respect of a letting made by the deceased alone. Where the survivor had been a joint owner prior to the deceased's death, they are unable to claim private letting relief on the deceased's share of the property in respect of lettings made prior to the deceased's death.

See below regarding proposals expected to apply to disposals taking place after 5th April 2020.

Widows and Widowers – Deaths after 5th April 2020

Under current Government proposals, where a property, or a share in a property, passes to the deceased's widow or widower following a death occurring after 5th April 2020, the survivor will always be treated, for the purposes of PPR relief, as if they had owned the property from the earlier of:

a)   The date they first acquired any interest in it, or
b)   The date the deceased first acquired any interest in it

Widows and Widowers – Disposals after 5th April 2020

Under current Government proposals, for disposals taking place after 5th April 2020, widows and widowers will generally be eligible for private letting relief in respect of any qualifying lettings (see Section 6.14) made by the deceased alone, or both of them jointly, at any time they are treated as owning the property for PPR purposes.

This is subject to the rules in Section 8.4, which will take precedence in respect of any earlier lifetime transfer of an interest in the property made by the deceased before 6th April 2020.

Impact on Base Costs

The rules regarding PPR relief on inherited property do not alter the basic rule regarding the property's base cost. They only act to determine what **proportion** of the gain is covered by PPR relief.

Separated Survivors

If the couple were separated at the date of the deceased's death (see Section 8.6), the survivor is treated like an unmarried partner for all CGT purposes.

8.9   TAX-FREE PROPERTY TRANSFERS

As we have already seen, married couples are able to transfer property from one spouse to the other free from CGT. However, transfers of property, or shares in property, to other people, such as an unmarried partner or adult child, present us with a problem.

In principle, such a transfer must be treated as if the property, or property share, had been sold for its open market value. In many cases, this would produce a significant CGT liability. There are some important exceptions, including the transferor's main residence, qualifying furnished holiday lets, and property used in the transferor's trading business.)

However, where a property owner makes a lifetime transfer of property into a trust, they may elect to 'hold over' the capital gain arising. At a later date, the trust can then transfer the property to the intended recipient and the trustees may again elect to 'hold over' the gain. In this way, CGT may be avoided on both transfers.

The end result is that the transferee is treated as if they had purchased the property for the same price as the transferor.

However, they are **not** treated as if they acquired the property at the same time as the transferor. For all other CGT purposes the date of purchase is the date the property is finally transferred out of the trust.

This technique does not work where the trust is a 'settlor-interested trust' (see Section 6.11) and should not generally be used where PPR relief is available (see Section 6.19). Also, 'hold over' relief is only available for CGT purposes and would not apply to a property classed as trading stock!

Transferring property to a trust has significant IHT implications. Problems can usually be avoided where the property is not worth in excess of £325,000 and the ultimate transfer to the transferee individual takes place within ten years. The tax-saving potential of this technique is examined in the Taxcafe.co.uk guide *'How to Save Inheritance Tax'*.

8.10   SECURING PRINCIPAL PRIVATE RESIDENCE RELIEF

In any planning that places reliance on PPR relief, it is essential to ensure the property or properties concerned genuinely become your private residence. There is no 'hard and fast' rule as to how long you must reside in a property to establish it as your private residence, it is the quality of occupation that counts, not the length.

Hence, it is recommended that you (and your spouse or partner and/or family, if applicable):

- i)   Move into the property for a substantial period
- ii)   Ensure all relevant institutions (banks, utilities, HMRC, employers, etc) are notified
- iii)   Inform family/friends
- iv)   Furnish the property for permanent occupation
- v)   Register on the electoral roll for that address
- vi)   Do not advertise the property for sale or rent until after the expiry of a substantial period

It is not possible to provide a definitive view of what constitutes a 'substantial period'. What matters is that the property genuinely becomes your 'permanent home'. 'Permanent' means it is intended to be your residence, rather than a temporary abode. You must move into the property with no clear plans for moving out again.

As a rough guide only, you should plan your affairs on the basis you will be residing in the property for at least a year, preferably two.

You may see some tax cases reported where taxpayers have successfully claimed the PPR exemption on a property they occupied for much shorter periods. These cases may be helpful but they are very much dependent on their own specific circumstances. They cannot be regarded as setting a minimum occupation period that everyone can rely on.

As already stated, the question will ultimately be decided on quality of occupation, rather than length. Where you are looking to use the PPR exemption on a property, you must embark upon occupying that property wholeheartedly; a mere 'sham' occupation will not suffice.

Main Residence Elections

In some instances, you may be able to establish the desired result merely by electing for the property to be treated as your main residence (see Section 6.22). However, it can only be your <u>main</u> residence if it is indeed your private residence and that still necessitates following at least some of the measures set out above, albeit perhaps adapted a little. You would, for instance, still need to:

i) Use the property as a home for a substantial period (although this could be as a second home or holiday home)
ii) Furnish the property for permanent occupation
iii) Avoid advertising the property for sale or rent until after the expiry of a substantial period (although furnished holiday lettings may be acceptable – see Section 8.17)

8.11 GENERAL ELECTIONS

As explained in Section 6.22, where a taxpayer has two or more private residences, it is possible to elect which is to be regarded as their main residence. In fact, it is not just possible, it is **highly advisable**, even when it seems obvious which property should be the main residence.

Example
Diana owns a house in London purchased in 2014 for £900,000. In July 2018, she bought a cottage in Sussex for £250,000, as her 'weekend retreat'. In early 2022, plans for a new motorway junction to be built only a mile from Diana's cottage are announced. Simultaneously, the value of her property increases

dramatically, while her desire to use the place herself rapidly diminishes. A few months later, in July, she sells it for an astonishing £750,000.

Fortunately for Diana, her accountant had insisted she make a main residence election in January 2020. At the time, she naturally elected that her London house was her main residence, since it seemed far more likely to produce a significant capital gain.

Because of this earlier election Diana was able to make a new election in January 2022, stipulating her Sussex cottage as her main residence.

A week later, Diana made a third election stipulating her London house as her main residence once more. This seemed sensible as the London house still seemed likely to produce a larger capital gain and Diana wished to keep her CGT exposure on that property to a minimum.

Nonetheless, as a result of the Sussex cottage having main residence status for a week, it is covered by the PPR exemption for the last nine months of Diana's ownership. This exempts her from CGT on £93,750 out of her total gain of £500,000 and produces a saving of £26,250 (£93,750 x 28%).

Furthermore, her London house will only lose its PPR exemption for a week.

The moral of the story: always, always, **always** make the main residence election where applicable.

Tax Tip

A property only has to be classed as your main residence for **any** period, no matter how short, for your last nine months of ownership to be exempted under PPR relief (eighteen months for disposals taking place before 6th April 2020). To minimise the impact on the PPR relief available on another property, it is only necessary to elect in favour of the new 'main residence' for a short period. In Diana's case, she was able to preserve most of the PPR exemption on her London house by making another revised 'main residence' election in favour of that property a week after she made the election in favour of her Sussex cottage.

Wealth Warning

Electing for an existing private residence to be your 'main residence' for just a week is fine. Do not confuse this with the need to establish the property as being your private residence in the first place (as explained in Section 8.10 above), where a considerably longer period of occupation is recommended.

Another Wealth Warning

There are restrictions on whether an overseas property can qualify as a private residence for PPR relief (see Section 6.21). See Section

6.23 for some tips on how and when it will still be possible to make main residence elections in favour of homes abroad.

Practical Pointer
If the period for which a property qualifies as your 'main residence' does not fall within the last nine months of your ownership (eighteen months for disposals before 6th April 2020), you will gain a little more PPR relief on that property without increasing the restriction on your main home. For example, if Diana had backdated each of her second and third elections by two years, the effect on her London home would have been the same but she would have gained a further £2,404 of exemption on her Sussex cottage.

8.12   DEVELOPING YOUR HOME

Many people are able to enhance the amount of tax-free capital gain on their home by making improvements to the property. However, where expenditure is incurred specifically for the purpose of realising a profit on the sale of the property, HMRC is able to deny part of the PPR exemption.

Example
Harry bought his house in 1999 and has used it as his main residence ever since. In 2020, the house is worth £500,000. Harry now decides to sell the house and realises he can make more money if he has a swimming pool built. He and his family move out of the house into a new home and he has the pool built at a cost of £40,000.

With its new swimming pool, Harry is able to sell the house for £600,000. He has therefore made an extra profit of £60,000 that will not be covered by his PPR exemption. Deducting his annual exemption (£12,000) will leave him with a taxable gain of £48,000 and a CGT liability of up to £13,440.

In practice, Harry might be able to argue some of the extra £60,000 profit was just down to getting a good offer, or a general increase in property values over the period since work began on the pool. In other words, don't just accept the whole of the extra gain is taxable, take other factors into account.

Many readers will be horrified by this example, but let me reassure you that HMRC generally only uses this power when major capital expenditure is blatantly carried out for no reason other than to make an extra profit on the sale of the property.

If Harry and his family had continued using the property after the pool was built and only sold it perhaps a year or two later, it is highly unlikely there would have been any restriction to his PPR exemption. Hence, in general, homeowners can enhance the value of their property by making capital improvements and still retain their PPR exemption: as long as there is a reasonable delay between those improvements being carried out and the property being put up for sale.

In the more common situation where homeowners carry out minor renovation work in order to prepare a property for sale, there is not usually any restriction in their PPR relief.

Furthermore, in practice, HMRC will not restrict PPR relief simply because a homeowner has obtained planning permission for conversion or improvement work.

Practical Pointer
Where part of the PPR relief on a property is denied as a result of expenditure incurred specifically for the purpose of realising a profit on the sale of that property, the taxable gain arising remains subject to CGT and cannot be treated as a trading profit subject to Income Tax. However, this exemption only applies to the extent the taxable gain would otherwise have qualified for PPR relief or private letting relief.

Home Conversions

Where a property undergoes extensive conversion work, it may no longer remain a single dwelling for tax purposes. This is what HMRC refers to as a 'Change of Use' and it has a far wider-ranging impact than merely letting out part of your home.

Example
David bought a large detached house for £360,000 in December 2007. He lived in the whole house for one year then converted it into two separate, semi-detached, houses. He continued to live in one of these, but rented the other one out. The conversion work cost £60,000, bringing his total costs up to £420,000.

In December 2019, David sold both houses for £450,000 each, making a total gain of £480,000. David's gain must be apportioned between the two houses. As they each sold for the same price, it is reasonable to assume the gain should be split equally between them (but see Section 5.2 for other allocation methods that might be used).
The gain on the house David retained as his own home will be fully covered by the PPR exemption. However, his £240,000 gain on the other house will only be covered by the PPR exemption for one year out of his twelve years of ownership. His PPR exemption on this house thus amounts to only £20,000, leaving a taxable gain of £220,000 (before the annual exemption).

There are two very important differences here to the situation in Section 6.26 where part of the property was let out, both of which occur because the rented house is no longer part of the same dwelling:

i) The PPR exemption is not available for the final period of ownership
ii) No private letting relief is available

Tax Tip
David would have improved his position if he had spent some time living in the other semi-detached property after the conversion.

It may sometimes be more beneficial to treat the gains arising before and after the conversion as two separate gains. In David's case, this would have been preferable if the original property had already increased in value by more than £40,000 before the conversion. This gain would have been completely exempt and half of it would have related to the house that was subsequently rented out. Both approaches are equally acceptable and we will look at this alternative method in more detail later in this section.

Conversion for Sale

David did enough conversion work to create two new 'dwellings' and this altered the amount of PPR relief available. He did, however, retain both new properties long enough for them to remain capital assets in his hands.

Where conversion work is carried out as a prelude to a sale, basic principles would usually dictate the property has become trading stock. The profit arising on the development would then be treated as a trading profit and the principles examined in Chapter 5 would apply.

Nevertheless, there are situations where a homeowner may develop part of their property for sale and still retain the more beneficial CGT treatment.

This is because HMRC cannot deem a former main residence to be trading stock unless they can show the owner has a property development trade. Again, this applies to the extent that the gain arising would have been exempt under PPR relief or private letting relief had the development not taken place.

This means 'one-off' developments that homeowners carry out on their own property may sometimes continue to be subject to CGT instead of Income Tax.

Example
Spencer inherited a large house from his Uncle Charles in March 2014 when it was worth £1.2m. Spencer adopted the house as his main residence and lived there until September 2019, at which point it was worth £1.8m. Spencer then had the house converted into five flats at a total cost of £500,000.

Spencer moved into one of the flats and adopted it as his home. He sold the other flats for £650,000 each in March 2020. Spencer is a higher rate taxpayer and his CGT liability on the sale of the flats is calculated as follows:

	£
Sale proceeds (4 x £650,000)	2,600,000
Less:	
Value prior to conversion (4/5 x £1.8m)	1,440,000
Conversion costs (4/5 x £500,000)	400,000

Gain made on development:	760,000
Less: Annual exemption	12,000

Taxable gain	748,000
CGT at 28%:	£209,440

For the sake of illustration, I have taken a simplistic approach to the allocation of costs by assuming the flats were all equal in size. In reality, a more sophisticated method will usually be appropriate, perhaps based on floor area or, better still, calculations prepared by a surveyor.

Spencer's capital gain is based on the extra value created by the conversion. The property's previous increase in value before conversion work began continues to be exempt because the whole property was his main residence during that period.

In this particular case, Spencer does not appear to have a property development trade. His non-trading status is strengthened by the fact he inherited the property. The situation might be different if he had purchased the property within one or two years before commencing conversion work or had carried out any similar developments in the past. Furthermore, if Spencer already had a property development trade, it is likely this conversion would be seen as part of that business.

In practice, each situation has to be looked at on its own merits and HMRC will frequently argue a trading activity exists.

If Spencer were deemed to have a property development trade, the gain of £760,000 would be taxed as a trading profit and could give rise to Income Tax up to £344,500 and NI between £15,200 and £18,096 (the maximum Income Tax cost arises if he has other taxable income of £100,000). His total tax liability could therefore be increased by up to £153,156.

Furthermore, if Spencer were treated as a developer, HMRC might argue the development profit of £190,000 on the flat he retained should also be taxed as a trading profit, giving him a further tax bill of £89,300!

One drawback to treating the development profit as a capital gain is that Spencer cannot deduct any interest or other overheads: only direct costs.

This seems a small price to pay in Spencer's case but, in some cases, it may be more beneficial if the development is treated as a trading activity.

The New Residence

The flat Spencer retained for personal use has now become his main residence and will continue to be eligible for PPR relief. To see how this works in practice, let's return to the example.

Example Continued
Spencer moves out of the flat in June 2025 and rents it out before eventually selling it in March 2028 for £1.04m. His CGT calculation is as follows:

	£
Sale proceeds	1,040,000
Less:	
Value when inherited (1/5 x £1.2m)	240,000
Conversion costs (1/5 x 500,000)	100,000

Capital Gain before reliefs	700,000
Less:	
PPR relief (£700,000 x 12/14*):	600,000

Gain before annual exemption	100,000

* - March 2014 to June 2025 + last 9 months =12 years out of 14

The new flat is not the same 'dwelling' as the original house, but they were both used as Spencer's main residence. He is therefore able to claim PPR relief on the appropriate proportion of the gain both before and after the conversion.

The calculation set out above is not the only valid method. The law only requires a method that is 'just and reasonable'. An alternative might be to view the gain on the first 'dwelling' from March 2014 to September 2019 as wholly exempt and then compute the gain on the second dwelling (the flat) as follows:

	£
Sale proceeds	1,040,000
Less:	
Value before conversion (1/5 x £1.8m)	360,000
Conversion costs (1/5 x 500,000)	100,000

Capital Gain before reliefs	580,000
Less:	
PPR relief (£580,000 x 6½/8½*):	443,529

Gain before annual exemption	136,471
	======

* - September 2019 to June 2025 + last 9 months = 6½ years out of 8½

This method produces a larger capital gain and is therefore likely to be favoured by HMRC. Nevertheless, the first method may also be regarded as 'just and reasonable'. At this point, I can only advise you to be aware of the alternative methods. Use the one that is best for you, but be prepared for an argument!

Lastly, there is also the possibility discussed above that the development gain on this flat may have been taxed already as a trading profit. In this case, the capital gain would be £390,000 (£1.04m - £650,000), PPR relief would be £292,500 (6/8ths), and the gain before deducting Spencer's annual exemption would be £97,500.

If you're wondering why the PPR relief is 6/8ths in this last calculation when we used 6½ years out of 8½ in the previous one, it's because Spencer was able to treat the flat as his main residence from September 2019 in the earlier calculation (see Section 6.17), but would only be regarded as re-adopting it as a capital asset in March 2020 if it had been treated as trading stock during the development period.

8.13   SOMETHING IN THE GARDEN
(See Section 6.16 for general guidance on PPR relief for gardens and grounds)

It's a common scenario: a homeowner has a large garden, so they sell part of it off for property development. There are the right ways to do this and there are other ways, which are very, very wrong.

The Wrong Ways

DO NOT:
- Sell your house first before selling the development plot
- Fence the development plot off or otherwise separate it from the rest of your garden before selling it
- Use the development plot for any purpose other than your own private residential occupation immediately prior to the sale
- Allow the development plot to fall into disuse

Each of these may result in the complete loss of PPR relief on the plot. Also do not assume the plot is covered by the PPR exemption if the total area of your house and garden exceeds half a hectare.

> ### Practical Pointer
> Fencing off the plot alone may not necessarily lead to the loss of PPR relief; if the plot continues to be used for your own private residential occupation up to the point of sale. Nonetheless, there remains some doubt over this issue, so it is wise to avoid any separation of the plot from the rest of the garden prior to sale.

The Right Ways

First, the simple way: Carefully ensuring you do not commit any of the cardinal sins described above, you simply sell off the plot. This sale will now enjoy the same PPR exemption as applies to your house. (If 90% of a gain on your house would have been exempt, then 90% of the gain on the plot will be exempt.)

The Other 'Right Way'

The drawback to the simple way is you do not get to participate in any of the profit on the development. But what if you hang on to the plot and develop it yourself?

Yes, at first this looks like we've gone the wrong way, but not if you then proceed to move into the new property and adopt it as your main residence. Your old house can safely be sold any time up to nine months after the date you move out and still be covered by the PPR exemption (eighteen months if sold before 6th April 2020). The new house should be fully covered by the PPR exemption as long as you move in within two years of the date development started (but see further in Section 6.17 if the ultimate sale is before 6th April 2020).

Wealth Warning 1
Although the new house will be covered by the PPR exemption, there is an argument that any gain on the land comprised in the development plot arising prior to the point development commenced is not covered. For example, if the cost of the land were £20,000 (based on an allocation of the original house's purchase price) and it was worth £30,000 immediately prior to commencement of the development, there would be a gain of £10,000 that was not covered by PPR relief. Such a small gain would probably be covered by the owner's annual exemption, but larger gains could lead to a CGT liability.

Wealth Warning 2
More worryingly, some commentators suggest the gain on the new house would have to be calculated on a 'time apportionment' basis, with PPR relief only applying to the period of occupation. For example, if the land originally cost £20,000 in 2010; the development took place in 2020 and cost £160,000; and the house was then occupied as a main residence until sold for £255,000 in 2025; the PPR relief would be restricted to just £25,000, leaving a taxable gain of £50,000.

At present, it is not clear which of the above interpretations is correct. Personally, I would argue strongly in favour of either full PPR exemption or the 'just and reasonable' allocation under 'Wealth Warning 1', as permitted by the relevant legislation.

What is beyond doubt is if the newly developed property were sold straight away, this would give rise to a trading profit (see Chapter 5). Well, almost beyond doubt, as it depends on your intentions when the development commenced: see Section 2.9.

8.14 STUDENT LOANS

Each unmarried adult is entitled to their own main private residence exempt from CGT. Once your children reach the age of 18 therefore, it is possible to put some tax-free capital growth into their hands. (They don't actually have to be students by the way – it works just as well if they are in employment or even just living a life of leisure at your expense, as many teenagers seem to do!)

The basic method is straightforward: all you need to do is buy a property in their name which they move into and adopt as their main residence.

Financing can be achieved in a number of ways, but the important point is that they must have legal and beneficial title to the property. (Hence this simple technique should only be used if you are prepared to pass wealth on to the children.)

The purchase of the property has possible IHT implications but these are avoided simply by surviving for seven years.

> **Wealth Warning**
> You should be careful not to make any use of the property yourself, since, if you have provided the funds for its purchase, any subsequent occupation by you or your spouse may give rise to an Income Tax charge under the 'pre-owned assets' regime.

Alternatively, if you would prefer to keep the wealth yourself for the time being, you may want to use the trust method set out in the next section.

8.15 USING A TRUST FOR EXTRA PRINCIPAL PRIVATE RESIDENCE RELIEF

As explained in Section 6.19, a trust is exempt from CGT on a property occupied as a main residence by one of the trust's beneficiaries.

Although this exemption does not apply where a capital gain on a property has been held over on transfer into the trust, there is no problem where the property is purchased by the trust in the first place (or is transferred to the trust with no hold over claim). Hence, it is possible to obtain PPR relief on an additional property using the following method:

i)   Set up a trust with another person (or persons) as the beneficiary (but not your spouse)
ii)   Purchase a residential property through the trust
iii)   The beneficiary adopts the property as their main residence (remember, like everyone else, they can only have one main residence and the usual rules apply if they are married)

You retain the reversionary interest in the trust. This means the trust assets will ultimately revert to you. As explained in Section 6.11, this means the trust is a 'settlor-interested' trust and hold over relief is not available on any transfer of property into the trust. This is not a problem – you don't want hold over relief anyway!

Some years later, but within nine months of when the property ceases to be the beneficiary's main residence, the trust can either sell the property or transfer it to you. Either way, the gain arising will be exempt from CGT and you can either retain the property or enjoy the tax free sale proceeds.

Wealth Warnings

This method has potential IHT implications, which are explained in detail in the Taxcafe.co.uk guide *'How to Save Inheritance Tax'*. In general, however, it is usually possible to avoid any problems by restricting the value of property held in the trust to no more than the amount of the IHT nil rate band (currently £325,000). A couple can effectively double this amount as long as they structure their investments carefully.

Once again, you should be careful to ensure that neither you nor your spouse makes any use of the property while it is held by the trust, as this may give rise to Income Tax charges under the 'pre-owned assets' regime.

8.16   PLANNING WITH ABSENCE PERIODS

In Section 6.18, we saw that some periods of absence from a main residence may be included as a period of occupation for the purposes of PPR relief where certain conditions are met.

Where those conditions apply, it is only any period for which the owner actually **claims** PPR relief on another property that must be excluded.

This may sound like good news, but it may actually be disadvantageous in some cases. This is because, technically speaking, PPR relief is not actually **claimed**. Where the appropriate conditions are met, it applies automatically, leaving the property owner with no control over how it applies: or which property it applies to!

Example

In October 2011, Aisha bought a house in Sheffield for £120,000 and adopted it as her main residence. In January 2016, she was transferred to her employer's London branch, where she bought a flat for £550,000 and adopted it as her new main residence. She then began renting out her house in Sheffield. In January 2020, she returned to Sheffield and resumed occupation of her original home. She then began to rent out her London property.

A short time later, Aisha decided to sell her Sheffield property and eventually sold it for £183,000 in October 2020, giving her a gain of £63,000.

Because Aisha has not claimed PPR relief on any other property for the period from January 2016 to January 2020, her Sheffield property is treated as her main residence for this period and is fully exempt from CGT.

BUT, the consequence of this is that her London property cannot be treated as her main residence for this period. This leaves this more expensive property fully exposed to CGT with no PPR relief available. When Aisha sells this property for £1m in 2024, her CGT bill could be up to £126,000!

To avoid this outcome, Aisha needs to make a PPR relief claim on her London property first: before any claim on her Sheffield property. She therefore needs to trigger a disposal of the London property before she sells the Sheffield property. She could do this by:

- Actually selling the property
- Transferring the property to a connected person (other than her spouse) (see Appendix B for a list of connected persons)
- Transferring the property into a company or trust

Transfers of property subject to a mortgage may give rise to SDLT costs (see Section 7.7). Transfers into a company or trust give rise to many other tax implications, which are examined in the Taxcafe.co.uk guides *'Using a Property Company to Save Tax'* and *'How to Save Inheritance Tax'* respectively.

If the London property is disposed of before the Sheffield property then it will be treated as Aisha's main residence for the period from January 2016 to January 2020 and will be fully exempt from CGT (she will have sold it within less than nine months after this period).

Meanwhile, the Sheffield property will no longer be treated as Aisha's main residence for this period. However, she will still be eligible for PPR relief for the first four years and three months of her ownership (when the property was her main residence) plus the last nine months. This exempts five years out of her total ownership period of nine years, giving her PPR relief of £35,000 (£63,000 x 5/9). Deducting her annual exemption of £12,300 (say) would leave her with a taxable gain of £22,700 and a maximum CGT liability of just £6,356.

As we can see, the temporary absence rules mean there could be some periods where a property owner is potentially eligible for PPR relief on more than one property. The relief will automatically apply to the first property to be disposed of, so it is important to ensure the property attracting the most valuable relief is disposed of first!

Alternatively, it may be sensible to simply avoid moving back into the original property so the PPR relief entitlement on the more expensive property can be preserved. In our example, Aisha could have saved herself a lot of trouble if she had never moved back into the Sheffield property: and still had the same amount of CGT to pay on its sale.

8.17 FURNISHED HOLIDAY LETS

Furnished holiday lets enjoy the best of all worlds. They continue to be treated as investment properties whenever that is more beneficial, but get treated like a trade when many trading reliefs are up for grabs. They qualify as private residential accommodation, yet still get many of the advantages generally reserved for commercial property.

Getting one of your properties to qualify as a furnished holiday let is the property tax equivalent of winning the lottery!

In essence, properties qualifying as 'furnished holiday lets' enjoy a special tax regime, which includes many of the tax advantages usually only accorded to trading properties. At the same time, the profits derived from furnished holiday lets are still treated as rental income.

The taxation benefits of qualifying furnished holiday lets include:

- Entrepreneurs' relief
- Rollover relief on replacement of business assets
- Holdover relief for gifts
- Capital allowances for furniture, fixtures, fittings and integral features (see Section 4.9)
- No restriction on tax relief for interest and finance costs
- Despite its 'trading-style' advantages, NI should not usually be payable in respect of income from furnished holiday lets (but see Section 7.17)
- Nonetheless, profits derived from a furnished holiday letting business qualify as 'earnings' for the purpose of pension contributions

The letting of holiday accommodation is, however, standard-rated for VAT purposes (whether or not the qualifying conditions set out below are met). The landlord must therefore register for VAT if gross annual income from UK holiday lettings exceeds £85,000. Foreign VAT registration will also often be required in respect of holiday lettings elsewhere within the European Union.

Occasionally, a furnished holiday letting business might be exempt from IHT, but this requires a far more substantial level of activities than simply meeting the conditions set out below (see the Taxcafe.co.uk guide *'How to Save Inheritance Tax'* for further details).

The available reliefs extend to any property used in a furnished holiday letting business. This will include not only the holiday accommodation itself but also any office premises from which the business is run.

Loss Relief

Losses arising in a furnished holiday letting business may only be carried forward for set off against future profits from the same furnished holiday letting business. For this purpose, all of a landlord's UK furnished holiday lets are regarded as one business but furnished holiday lets elsewhere in the EEA are regarded as a different business. (All furnished holiday lets within the EEA but outside the UK are regarded as the same business)

Qualifying Conditions

To qualify as a furnished holiday let, the property must meet the qualifying conditions for the relevant period. The relevant period is normally the tax year, but when the property begins or ceases to be let out fully furnished, then it is the first or last twelve months for which it is so let (see below for the definition of 'fully furnished').

The qualifying conditions are that the property must be:

i) Situated in the UK or the European Economic Area (see Section 1.5)
ii) Fully furnished (see below)
iii) Let out on a commercial basis with a view to the realisation of profits
iv) Available for letting as holiday accommodation to the public generally for at least 210 days
v) Actually let as holiday accommodation to members of the public for at least 105 days
vi) Not in 'longer term occupation' for more than 155 days

'Longer term occupation' means any period of more than 31 consecutive days during which the property is in the same occupation, unless this arises due to exceptional circumstances (e.g. the tenant falls ill, or their flight home is delayed). Periods of longer term occupation cannot be counted towards the 105 days required under condition (v).

A taxpayer with more than one furnished holiday let may use a system of averaging to determine whether they meet condition (v).

Landlords can elect for properties that qualified in the previous year (including those qualifying by using averaging, as above) to stay within the regime for up to two further tax years, despite failing to meet condition (v). In effect, this means properties generally only need to meet this test once every three years. The property must meet the other qualifying conditions and the landlord must have had a genuine intention to meet condition (v) each year.

Other Qualification Issues

While the property need not be in a recognised holiday area, the lettings should strictly be to holidaymakers and tourists in order to qualify.

Where a property qualifies as a furnished holiday let, it generally qualifies for the whole of each tax year: subject to the special rules for the years in which fully furnished letting commences or ceases, as explained above.

Where, however, there is some other use of the property during the year, the available CGT reliefs will be restricted accordingly. Nevertheless, it remains possible for the taxpayer and their family to use the property privately as a second home during the 'off season' and still fit within the qualifying conditions set out above.

Some years ago, there was a concern that such private use could lead to accusations that the furnished holiday lets were not being undertaken on a commercial basis and the property would therefore fail to meet condition (iii).

However, it is now understood that the property can still qualify as long as the holiday letting business is run on a commercial basis, rather than the property as a whole.

Example
Arthur has a second home in Cornwall called 'Camelot' that he rents out as furnished holiday accommodation during the spring and summer. The property's running costs amount to £50 per day.

Arthur spends 120 days at Camelot himself each year and advertises it as a holiday rental for the rest of the year at a price of £120 per night. His advertising costs, and other overheads relating to the letting, amount to a total of £750 per year.

He normally expects to rent the property for an average of around 140 nights but, in 2019/20, he only manages to rent it for 110 nights, giving him income of £13,200, and leaving him with an overall net cost for the property over the year of £5,850 (£13,200 − 366 x £50 − £750).

However, his running costs for his rental season of 246 days only amount to £12,300 (£50 x 246). If he had rented out the property for the expected 140 nights, he would therefore have had income of £16,800 (£120 x 140) and a rental profit of £3,750 (£16,800 – £12,300 – £750).

Arthur is therefore letting out the property on a commercial basis with a view to making a profit. The fact that the property gives rise to an overall net cost for the year is irrelevant. What matters is that his letting business is run on a commercial basis. The other qualifying conditions are also satisfied, so Camelot qualifies as a furnished holiday let.

Note that Arthur's private use of the property means he has to exclude part of his running costs when calculating his rental profit for Income Tax purposes. In 2019/20 for example, he will have a taxable profit of £150 (£13,200 – £12,300 – £750).

Arthur will also be subject to some restrictions in the applicable CGT reliefs for Camelot.

What Is a Fully Furnished Letting?

To be classed as a 'fully furnished letting', the landlord must provide sufficient furnishings so the property is capable of 'normal residential use' without the tenant having to provide their own. Typically, this will include beds, chairs, tables, sofas, carpets or other floor coverings, curtains or blinds, and kitchen equipment.

The key phrase here is whether the property is capable of 'normal residential use' and the level of furnishings and equipment required must be considered in this context. In essence, the landlord must provide the tenant with some privacy, somewhere to sit, somewhere to sleep, somewhere to eat, and the facilities required to feed themselves.

Interaction with Other Reliefs

A property that qualifies as a furnished holiday let and has also qualified as the owner's main residence at some time during their ownership will currently be eligible for private letting relief. For disposals prior to 6th April 2020, this produces a quite remarkable combination of tax reliefs.

Example
In Section 6.20 we met Bonnie who had a small cottage on Skye that, for ten years, she rented out as furnished holiday accommodation for 48 weeks each year and occupied herself for the remaining four weeks. The property also qualified as Bonnie's main residence (perhaps by election).

When, on 1st April 2020, Bonnie realised a capital gain of £104,000 on her sale of the property, we saw she obtained PPR relief of £22,400 and private letting relief of £22,400, reducing her gain to £59,200. But it doesn't end there!

Bonnie would then be entitled to entrepreneurs' relief (see below) on 48/52nds of this gain, i.e. £59,200 x 48/52 = £54,646. This leaves only £4,554 exposed to CGT at normal rates. However, as Bonnie can allocate her annual exemption in the most beneficial way, she can exempt this amount altogether.

The taxable gain of £47,200 remaining after deducting her annual exemption of £12,000 is therefore wholly eligible for entrepreneurs' relief, giving Bonnie a CGT bill of just £4,720 (£47,200 x 10%), or a mere 4.5% of her total gain.

Bonnie's entrepreneurs' relief claim is restricted due to her private use of the property for four weeks per year (although the restriction did not actually affect her in this case). A similar restriction would apply if she attempted to claim rollover relief on replacement of the property or holdover relief on a gift of it. These restrictions apply whenever the owner makes any private use of the property, whether it qualifies as their main residence or not.

In the case of entrepreneurs' relief, however, it could be fairly easy to avoid any such restriction, as we shall see in Section 8.20.

Entrepreneurs' Relief on Furnished Holiday Lets

In the above example, I assumed entrepreneurs' relief would be available on Bonnie's sale of her cottage.

As explained in Section 6.28, entrepreneurs' relief is available when a qualifying business or part of a qualifying business is sold or when assets used in a qualifying business are sold within three years of that business's cessation.

As also explained in Section 6.28, a 'part' of a qualifying business must be capable of being run as a going concern in its own right in order to qualify for these purposes.

In my view, most furnished holiday lets must be a 'part' of a business capable of being run independently of any other part of the business. Hence, my interpretation of the entrepreneurs' relief legislation is that a capital gain on the sale of a qualifying furnished holiday let should generally qualify for entrepreneurs' relief as long as:

a)   The property is still being used as a qualifying furnished holiday let at the time of sale, or
b)   The property was being used in a qualifying furnished holiday letting business at the time of cessation of that business and is sold within three years thereafter

And the business was run for the requisite 'qualifying period' prior to the sale or cessation (see Section 6.28).

However, I am aware that HMRC is applying the entrepreneurs' relief legislation in a more restrictive manner, arguing that the sale of a single furnished holiday let does not constitute the sale of a qualifying 'part' of a business when the owner also continues to operate other furnished holiday letting properties.

HMRC's view seems to be that advertising the properties together (e.g. through the same website) makes them a single business.

This is a developing area of tax law, so it is difficult to provide any definitive guidance until we see a suitable case in court. In the meantime, each case will have to be argued on its own merits. The more steps the owner takes to separate the way the different properties are run, the better their chances are likely to be. Useful steps may include:

- Advertising each property separately
- Ensuring each property has its own website
- Keeping separate sets of books and records for each property
- Using different cleaners, gardeners, etc.
- Using significantly different names for each property

Naturally, the commercial impact of these steps needs to be weighed against the potential CGT savings: which may be remote and uncertain when no sales are anticipated in the foreseeable future.

> **Tax Tip**
> A more certain approach might be to separate out the property that is intended for sale by initially transferring it into different ownership, such as the owner's spouse or adult child, or a trust. As long as the property is a qualifying furnished holiday let at the time of the transfer, it should be possible to carry this out free from CGT. The new owner would then need to operate the property as a furnished holiday let for at least two years, but could then sell it with the certainty of obtaining entrepreneurs' relief (provided they did not have any other furnished holiday lets themselves!)

Subject to the uncertainty created by this issue, a property investor might be able to realise total capital gains of up to £10m on qualifying furnished holiday lets at a maximum effective CGT rate of just 10%. As explained in Section 6.28, a couple investing in property jointly may be able to benefit from this rate on total gains of up to £20m.

8.18   TAX-FREE HOLIDAY HOMES

There is a fairly easy way to shelter the entire capital gain on a qualifying furnished holiday let. If the property has never been used for any other purpose then the entire capital gain arising on a gift of the property can be held over where a joint election is made by the transferor and transferee. If the transferee then adopts the property as their main residence, any capital gain arising when they sell it, including the original held over gain, will be fully exempt.

It may sometimes even be possible for the transferee to establish the property as their main residence by way of election. However, the transferee must still retain the property for a long enough period to ensure it is treated as a capital asset in their hands and qualifies as a private residence.

The transferor should avoid any personal use of the property after the transfer, as this could give rise to an Income Tax charge.

In view of the restrictions on private residences overseas (see Section 6.21), this strategy may be difficult to apply to an overseas furnished holiday let within the EEA: although Section 6.23 contains some pointers on how such properties might still become the transferee's main residence for PPR relief purposes.

This technique cannot be used on a transfer to a spouse although, for the time being, the technique in Section 8.5 can be used instead.

8.19   HOTELS AND GUEST HOUSES

Small hotels and guest houses that continue to be the owner's main residence, despite also being a business property, are currently in a rather special situation.

Hotel or guest house accommodation counts as private residential accommodation for the purposes of private letting relief. Hence, in many cases, where a disposal takes place before 6th April 2020, up to £40,000 (per person) of any gain arising as a result of the business use of the property can be relieved. HMRC accepts this approach in respect of any part of the property that has had some private use by the owner.

Many commentators also argue that private letting relief should currently extend to parts of a hotel or guest house that have only ever had exclusive business use and I have successfully argued this point myself on more than one occasion.

Sadly, as explained in Section 6.25, private letting relief will no longer be available for disposals of properties of this nature taking place after 5th April 2020, due to the proposed exclusion for lettings in the course of a trade.

However, since the 'business use' element of a hotel or guest house qualifies for entrepreneurs' relief (see Section 6.28), rollover relief (Section 8.27), and 'hold over' relief on a gift (Section 6.11), these properties will remain quite versatile from a CGT perspective, even after they lose their qualifying status for private letting relief.

Live-in owners with small hotels and guest houses may claim rent-a-room relief (see Section 4.11) where appropriate.

8.20 ENTREPRENEURS' RELIEF ON INVESTMENT PROPERTY

As explained in Section 6.28, entrepreneurs' relief is available on the disposal of a property used in a qualifying business carried on by the property's owner for a 'qualifying period' prior to:

a) The disposal of the property as part of the sale of the business (or a part of the business capable of operating as a going concern in its own right), or

b) The cessation of the business (in this case, the property must be sold within three years of the cessation)

The 'qualifying period' referred to above is generally two years where the disposal takes place after 5th April 2019 (but see Section 6.28 for further details).

In Section 6.28, we also saw there were restrictions on entrepreneurs' relief for a property used by the owner's 'personal company', or a partnership in which they are a partner, where the property was not so used throughout their ownership. However, no such restrictions apply where the property is used in the owner's own qualifying business, such as a trade, profession, or as a qualifying furnished holiday let, and full relief is available provided the property is in the appropriate use at the time of disposal, or cessation of the business, as the case may be.

Where the owner has an existing qualifying business, it appears there is no minimum period the property must be used in that business, provided the owner runs the business itself for at least the 'qualifying period'.

For those without an existing qualifying business, it will be necessary to set one up and run it for at least the 'qualifying period' in order to benefit.

Example
In 1982, Abdul bought a shop as an investment property for £30,000. It is now worth £330,000 and he would like to sell it. Before selling the property, Abdul adopts it as his own trading premises for just over two years. He then ceases trading and sells the property, making a gain of £300,000.

Because Abdul used the property in his own trade, he will be entitled to entrepreneurs' relief, reducing the CGT due on his sale from £60,000 to £30,000 (ignoring the annual exemption and assuming Abdul is a higher rate taxpayer).

He still gets the relief despite the fact the entire gain arose before he adopted the property as his trading premises!

Abdul would need to use the property in his own qualifying trade – e.g. as a shop with him as sole proprietor. Using it as the office for his investment business will not suffice. He can, however, employ a manager to run the shop for him if he wishes.

A similar approach might work with residential property by adopting it as a furnished holiday let for two years or more. Where the owner already has an existing furnished holiday letting business, it might even be possible for them to obtain entrepreneurs' relief on a residential investment property by letting it out as a qualifying furnished holiday let for a shorter period before sale, although the qualifying criteria set out in Section 8.17 would need to be met.

As explained in Section 8.17, it is not clear whether this would work when the owner does not also either sell their other furnished holiday lets or cease their furnished holiday letting business altogether.

8.21   ENTERPRISE INVESTMENT SCHEME SHARES

CGT liabilities can be deferred by reinvesting some or all of a capital gain in Enterprise Investment Scheme shares. To obtain relief, the investment must take place within the period beginning a year before, and ending three years after, the date of the disposal that gave rise to the gain.

Furthermore, CGT reinvestment relief is still available even when the investor is connected with the company issuing the shares. Hence, it may even be possible to defer CGT on your property gains by investing in your own trading company!

Unfortunately, companies engaged in any form of property business are generally ineligible to issue Enterprise Investment Scheme shares.

Alternatively, products are available that enable taxpayers to utilise a 'portfolio' approach when investing in these intrinsically risky investments. This does not totally eliminate the risk, but it certainly improves the odds!

There is no limit on the amount that can be invested in Enterprise Investment Scheme shares for CGT deferral purposes.

Gains held over on reinvestment into Enterprise Investment Scheme shares become subject to CGT when those shares are sold.

Qualifying investments of up to £1m per year in Enterprise Investment Scheme shares issued by an unconnected company also carry an Income Tax credit of up to 30%. Investments may be carried back to the previous tax year for Income Tax credit purposes. From 2018/19 onwards, the qualifying investment limit is increased to £2m, but any amount in excess of £1m must be in 'knowledge-intensive companies'.

Combining the Income Tax credit with the CGT deferral gives a potential for total tax savings of up to 58% of the amount invested.

8.22   SWEET SHOP COMPANIES

The 'sweet shop principle' is a method that enables property investors to defer CGT using Enterprise Investment Scheme shares. The idea is you find a simple, low risk trading business, like a sweet shop, which requires business premises. Then you set up 'Sweet Shop Company Limited' to run the shop. This company issues Enterprise Investment Scheme shares to you in exchange for the cash proceeds of a property sale. The company then uses this cash to buy its retail premises.

In this way, you are effectively able to roll over any capital gain into the purchase of the business premises, via the medium of the sweet shop company. This is probably the least risky way to secure a CGT deferral with Enterprise Investment Scheme shares.

It doesn't necessarily have to be a sweet shop, but it must not be any type of trade or business that is specifically excluded in the legislation and, as I explained in the last section, this covers most types of property business. Even hotels and guest houses are excluded.

8.23   THE SEED ENTERPRISE INVESTMENT SCHEME

The Seed Enterprise Investment Scheme provides Income Tax relief at 50% to individuals investing up to £100,000 per tax year in qualifying companies. Qualifying investments may also be carried back to the previous tax year for Income Tax relief purposes.

Capital gains that are reinvested in Seed Enterprise Investment Scheme shares are given a 50% exemption from CGT. This compares well with the Enterprise Investment Scheme, where capital gains are only deferred until the shares are sold, although half the gain does remain exposed to CGT.

The combination of Income Tax and CGT reliefs provides the opportunity to obtain up to 64% tax relief on reinvested gains – leaving only a small part of the amount invested exposed to the inherent commercial risk of investing in small businesses.

Furthermore, since Income Tax loss relief would be available on 50% of the investment should the Seed Enterprise Investment Scheme company fail, the ultimate amount at risk may be as little as 16% for a higher rate taxpayer or just 13.5% for an additional rate taxpayer with annual income over £150,000.

The scheme is targeted at small 'start-up companies'. This brings several restrictions, including the fact that the company issuing the shares must have total assets of no more than £200,000 before issuing the shares.

Investors must not be employees of the issuing company (but may be directors) and, together with their 'associates', must not hold, nor be entitled to acquire, an interest of more than 30% in the share capital. 'Associates' are broadly the same as 'connected persons' (see Appendix B.

There are many further restrictions so professional advice is essential!

8.24   THE BENEFITS AND PITFALLS OF RE-MORTGAGING

If you have a property that has risen significantly in value since you bought it, you can realise the 'profit' by re-mortgaging and thus obtain the cash value of your equity by different means. When you re-mortgage a property, you have not actually made a disposal. Hence, you cannot be charged any CGT.

Where the funds generated by re-mortgaging are used to purchase new investment properties, the interest on the new borrowings can be claimed against the income from the new properties. This applies even if the re-mortgaged property is the borrower's own home. The interest relief remains available as long as the funds are invested for business purposes.

It is also vital to remember that Income Tax relief for interest paid by residential landlords is at basic rate only from 2020/21 (see Section 4.5).

Sometimes the borrower will re-mortgage a property for other reasons – perhaps simply to provide living expenses. While this will still produce the CGT benefit described above, only interest on borrowings against a rental property up to the value of the property when first rented out (plus other capital invested in the business) will be eligible for Income Tax relief under these circumstances (see Section 4.4 for further details).

When re-mortgaging it is vital to borrow responsibly, taking account of your potential CGT liabilities, the restrictions in Income Tax relief for interest, and the impact of changes in market conditions.

8.25   NON-DOMICILED INVESTORS

A UK resident but non-UK domiciled taxpayer may opt to only pay UK tax on income or capital gains from foreign properties if and when these sums are remitted back to the UK. This is known as the 'remittance basis' and, while it can be useful, it often comes at a price.

Furthermore, as explained in Section 3.8, an individual resident in the UK for 15 or more of the previous 20 UK tax years is generally deemed UK domiciled for all UK tax purposes. Individuals born in the UK who have emigrated but later return may also be treated as UK domiciled.

Those falling foul of the 15 year rule may still claim the remittance basis to exempt the element of a gain on overseas property arising before 5th April 2017. The Remittance Basis Charge (see below) will still apply and will be increased to £90,000 if they have been UK resident for 17 or more of the last 20 UK tax years.

Apart from this, anyone deemed UK domiciled under the above provisions is now unable to claim the remittance basis.

For a detailed explanation of 'domicile' and the provisions described above, see the Taxcafe.co.uk guide 'How to Save Inheritance Tax'.

The Remittance Basis Charge

Any adult resident in the UK for seven or more of the previous nine UK tax years who opts to use the remittance basis must pay an annual charge (the 'Remittance Basis Charge') unless their total unremitted overseas income and gains for the year are less than £2,000.

The charge is currently £30,000, increasing to £60,000 for an adult resident in the UK for 12 or more of the last 14 UK tax years.

Taxpayers paying the Remittance Basis Charge are subject to CGT at the higher rates of 20% or 28% on any gains that remain taxable, regardless of their level of income (unless entrepreneurs' relief applies). Furthermore, taxpayers claiming the remittance basis lose entitlement to their personal allowance and CGT annual exemption if they have unremitted overseas income and gains of £2,000 or more.

Despite these charges, some non-UK domiciled individuals may still be able to make considerable tax savings by investing in foreign property and retaining their income and gains overseas.

8.26 USING LEASE PREMIUMS TO GENERATE TAX-FREE RECEIPTS

As we saw in Section 6.34, the granting at a premium of a lease of between two and fifty years' duration gives rise to a capital receipt equal to 2% of that premium for each whole year by which the lease exceeds one year. For example, 12% of the premium charged for a seven-year lease will be treated as a capital disposal. Clever investors might consider this a good way to use their annual CGT exemption.

Example
Bob owns a small workshop that Terry wants to lease for 20 years. If Bob charges a premium of £31,580, 38% of this (£12,000) will be treated as a capital disposal. If Bob has no other gains this year, his 2019/20 annual exemption will cover any capital gain, meaning £12,000 of the premium is received tax free. Bob and Terry then simply negotiate a level of rent that takes suitable account of the premium Terry has paid.

For simplicity I have ignored Bob's deductible base cost (see Section 6.34).

8.27 ROLLOVER RELIEF

The capital gain arising on the sale of a property used in your own trading business may be rolled over into the purchase of a new trading property within the period beginning one year before, and ending three years after, the disposal of the original property. This defers any CGT liability on the original property until such time as the new property is sold.

Property qualifying under the furnished holiday letting regime is treated as trading property for the purposes of this relief (see Section 8.17).

Full relief is available only if the old property was used exclusively for 'trading purposes' throughout your ownership, or at least since 31st March 1982, if it was acquired earlier. Furthermore, for rollover relief purposes, it is the sale ***proceeds*** of the old property that must be reinvested and not merely the capital gain. Any shortfall in the amount reinvested is deducted from the amount of gain eligible for rollover.

If there is less than full trading use of the property then an appropriate proportion of the gain arising may be rolled over.

Example
Stavros sells an office building in March 2020 for £600,000, realising a capital gain of £240,000. He has owned the building since March 2010 and, up until March 2015 he rented all of it out. From March 2015 until the date of sale he used two thirds of the building as his own premises from which he ran a property development business.

Stavros is eligible to roll over £80,000 (£240,000 x 5/10 x 2/3) of his capital gain into the purchase of new trading premises. The eligible amount has been restricted by reference to both the time the property was used for trading purposes and the proportion used for trading purposes.

In August 2020, Stavros buys a small gift shop in Cornwall for £180,000 and begins to use it as his trading premises. He is able to claim rollover relief of £60,000. He cannot claim the full £80,000 that was eligible, because he has only reinvested £180,000 out of the £200,000 qualifying portion of his sale proceeds (£600,000 x 5/10 x 2/3 = £200,000). The amount reinvested fell £20,000 short of the qualifying sale proceeds, so £20,000 must be deducted from the amount eligible for rollover.

The new property does not need to be in the same trade or even the same kind of trade. It could even be a furnished holiday let.

There is no minimum period for which the new property needs to be used for trading purposes, although it must be acquired with the intention of using it for trading purposes. In our example, Stavros could run the gift shop for, say, two years then convert it into residential property. His CGT rollover relief would not be clawed back, although he would have a reduced base cost for the property when he eventually came to sell it.

Tax Tip
Where you have a capital gain eligible for rollover relief, it is only necessary to use the replacement property for trading purposes for a limited period. This might include initially running the new property as a guest house or qualifying furnished holiday let before later converting to long-term letting or even adopting it as your own home.

What Kinds of Properties Can Qualify?

Rollover relief is generally only available to property investors for:

- Furnished holiday lets (see Section 8.17)
- The trading premises of a property development, property dealing or property management business
- Property where the owner provides significant additional services

The latter case would generally require a level of services akin to a guest house, although the owner need not reside there themselves.

Gains on other rental properties may be eligible for rollover relief in certain limited circumstances, such as a compulsory purchase of commercial property, or residential property purchased by a tenant under the Leasehold Reform Act 1967.

8.28   USING YOUR BASIC RATE BAND TO SAVE CGT

The rate of CGT applying to most gains depends on the level of your taxable income. Savings can be achieved by ensuring capital gains fall into a tax year in which you have a lower level of income. The savings are generated by the 10% difference between the rates of CGT applying to gains falling into your basic rate band (10% or 18%) and the rates applying once the basic rate band has been exhausted (20% or 28%). Applying this difference to the whole basic rate band of £37,500 creates the maximum potential saving of £3,750 (at 2019/20 rates).

Where you are also able to utilise your annual CGT exemption, the total saving available could be up to £7,110 (£3,750 + £12,000 x 28%). For a couple, the savings could be as much as £14,220.

How Can Property Investors Use These Savings?

Utilising your annual exemption is simply a question of ensuring each property disposal falls into a different tax year.

To utilise your basic rate band, you may need to defer disposals until a tax year in which your taxable income has reduced. One good way to do this, where you are in employment or self-employment, is to wait until you retire.

Example
Edwina has a residential investment property that will yield a capital gain of £60,000 when she sells it. She has a salary of £40,000 but is due to retire in March 2020. She is also currently making a rental profit of £1,000 per month.

If Edwina was to sell her property shortly before 5th April 2020, she would be subject to CGT at 28% on a gain of £48,000 (£60,000 less her annual exemption of £12,000), giving her a bill of £13,440.

If, however, she was to delay her sale until 6th April 2020, or shortly afterwards, she would pay CGT at just 18% on the first £37,500 of her taxable gain, reducing her tax bill to just £9,606 (see notes below).

Notes to the Example
i)   The annual CGT exemption for 2020/21 is estimated at £12,300
ii)   I have assumed Edwina's total income for 2020/21 will be less than her personal allowance. A retiring taxpayer can usually achieve this by deferring their pension entitlement. Even if Edwina had some investment income that used up part of her basic rate band, she would still make a considerable saving by waiting until after she retires to sell her property
iii)   I have assumed CGT rates remain the same in 2020/21
iv)   Remember the date of sale for CGT purposes is the date on which there is an unconditional sales contract (see Section 6.6)

The example also demonstrates the fact that selling an investment property early in a tax year means there is less income from that property to use up your basic rate band, thus potentially producing a CGT saving.

There are many other situations where property investors may be able to reduce their CGT liability by selling property in a tax year in which their taxable income is at a lower level. Examples include:

- Self-employed taxpayers making large capital allowances claims
- Employed taxpayers on career breaks
- Company owners who are able to refrain from taking income out of their company that year
- Furnished holiday let owners with big capital allowance claims
- Investors reducing their taxable income by making tax-advantaged investments, such as investment bonds

Remember, however, there is no guarantee that CGT rates will not be increased in the future.

Wealth Warning
Don't forget that deferring residential property disposals until after 5th April 2020 will mean the disposal must be reported, and the CGT paid, within 30 days (see Sections 6.30 and 6.31). Furthermore, in view of the proposed changes to PPR relief and private letting relief (see Sections 6.13 and 6.14) it will generally be unwise to defer the sale of a property that is currently eligible for these reliefs.

Extending the Basic Rate Band

The basic rate band can be extended through the payment of pension contributions or gift aid donations. While it is generally more beneficial to use this as a means to save Income Tax, it can also be used to save CGT. Furthermore, where a property owner is unlikely to ever have income in excess of the higher rate tax threshold, this may be their best opportunity to make tax savings through these payments.

Example Revisited
In Section 6.4, we met Boudicca who had a taxable gain of £38,000. She had taxable income of £35,000 for 2019/20, leaving £15,000 of her basic rate band available which reduced her CGT bill to £9,140.

Let us now assume Boudicca makes a net pension contribution of £2,880 in March 2020. This is grossed up for basic rate tax relief given at source and treated as a 'gross' pension contribution of £3,600, thus extending Boudicca's basic rate band to £41,100 (£37,500 + £3,600) and giving her a higher rate tax threshold of £53,600 (£50,000 + £3,600).

This means there is now £18,600 (£53,600 – £35,000) of Boudicca's basic rate band available and her CGT calculation will be as follows:

£18,600 x 18%	*£3,348*
£19,400 x 28%	*£5,432*
Total	*£8,780*

Boudicca's pension contribution has saved her £360 in CGT.

Combining the tax relief of £720 given at source with her £360 CGT saving gives Boudicca a total benefit of £1,080: increasing the value of her net pension contribution by 37.5%.

A gross pension contribution of £3,600 (or £2,880 net) is the maximum for which an individual with no taxable earnings is able to obtain tax relief. 'Earnings' for this purpose generally means employment income or self-employment or partnership trading income, but also includes profits from furnished holiday lets. Those with earnings of more than £3,600 can generally obtain tax relief for gross contributions up to the lower of £40,000 or the total amount of their earnings for the year.

8.29   AVOIDING THE HIGH INCOME CHILD BENEFIT CHARGE

Many parents are suffering the draconian HICBC on income between £50,000 and £60,000. This creates the truly horrendous tax rates set out in the table in Section 3.3. Some property investor couples may, however, be able to avoid the HICBC by redistributing their income.

Example
Cherilyn and Salvatore are a married couple with a portfolio of rental properties yielding total annual profits of £90,000. Cherilyn owns more properties than Salvatore, so she receives £60,000 of this profit.

The couple also have three young children and are therefore eligible to claim £2,501 per year in Child Benefit (at current rates). However, Cherilyn's profit share means she will effectively have to repay the Child Benefit by way of an additional Income Tax charge of £2,501.

The answer to this problem is simple: Cherilyn should transfer some of her properties to Salvatore. If, as a result, Cherilyn's share of the couple's profits is reduced to £50,000 or less, she will not be subject to the HICBC – thus saving the couple £2,501 per year (at current rates).

Ideally, it would generally be best if the couple owned all their properties jointly. As their rental profits (hopefully) increase, this will protect them from both higher rate tax and the HICBC for as long as possible.

If a married couple isn't comfortable with this idea, the method set out in Section 8.7 could be used instead, and the optimum position for Income Tax purposes could often still be achieved.

As a result of the restrictions on Income Tax relief for interest paid by residential landlords, many more property investor couples are likely to be caught by the HICBC. The advice given above remains sound, but these couples will need to reduce their taxable 'profit' (under the rules set out in Section 4.5) to £50,000 per person, or less, in order to avoid the HICBC.

Unmarried Couples

For unmarried couples, the solution may not be so simple, as a direct transfer of properties from one partner to the other, or into joint names, will generally lead to a CGT charge. This can often be avoided by using the technique set out in Section 8.9.

Where property is already held jointly, however, a simple solution is to alter the couple's rental profit shares in such a way that neither partner has income over £50,000. See Section 8.2 regarding rental profit shares for unmarried joint owners.

Joint Income over £100,000

A couple with total joint taxable income over £100,000 may not be able to avoid the HICBC altogether but, if your total joint taxable income is less than £120,000, you could still minimise the impact by equalising your income. Alternatively, you could avoid the HICBC by transferring properties into a trust or company. These strategies have many further tax implications and require professional advice.

8.30   PARTNERSHIP PROBLEMS AND OPPORTUNITIES

Some of the legal background to property partnerships was covered in Section 2.14. Most of the rules outlined throughout this guide apply equally to partnerships, including individuals who are members of corporate or limited partnerships.

> **Wealth Warning**
> Profit shares attributed to a partner that is not subject to UK Income Tax (typically a company) may, under certain circumstances, be allocated to individuals, who are members of the partnership, for tax purposes.

In many ways, a property partnership simply combines joint ownership with a more sophisticated profit sharing agreement. However, a partnership is considerably more flexible, as, subject to the terms of the partnership agreement, partners may join, leave or change their profit share at any time.

Each partner is taxed on his or her share of rental income, trading profits or capital gains, as allocated according to the partnership agreement (subject to the 'Wealth Warning' above).

There are, however, restrictions on any 'non-active' partners claiming relief for their share of partnership trading losses. Broadly speaking, a partner is usually classed as 'non-active' if they spend an average of less than ten hours per week engaged in the partnership's trading activities.

Firstly, the total cumulative amount of loss that a non-active partner may claim is restricted to the amount of capital they have invested in the partnership. Capital contributions may be excluded if the investment was made primarily to secure extra loss relief.

Secondly, there is an annual limit of £25,000 on claims for partnership trading loss relief by non-active partners. This limit applies to the total claims made by any individual each tax year in respect of all partnerships in which they are a non-active partner and any trade in which they are a so-called 'non-active sole trader' (see Section 5.11).

The restriction of relief for partnership trading losses is of particular concern to 'husband and wife' property trading partnerships where one spouse is not actively involved. Getting the less active spouse to work in the business for at least ten hours a week may therefore be advisable.

A partner's share of partnership rental losses can only be set against their share of future rental profits from the same partnership.

Interest Relief

Partnerships investing in residential rental property are subject to the same restrictions on relief for interest and finance costs as individuals (see Section 4.5).

A partner who borrows funds to invest in the partnership is entitled to tax relief for interest on those borrowings but this, again, is subject to the restrictions set out in Section 4.5 (to the extent the partnership is investing in residential rental property) and also to the tax relief 'cap' explained in Section 3.20.

Treatment of Partnership Property

For both CGT and SDLT purposes, each partner is effectively treated as if they individually own a share of the partnership properties. This means tax may be charged whenever a partner:

a) Introduces property into a partnership,
b) Takes property out of a partnership, or
c) Changes their share in the partnership properties

Additional SDLT may also be charged where a partner withdraws capital from a partnership within three years of introducing property.

For CGT purposes, a partner's share in partnership properties is determined according to the first item on this list the partners have entered into:

i)   An agreement as to how capital assets are allocated
ii)   An agreement as to how capital profits are shared
iii)   An agreement as to how income profits are shared

If there is no agreement falling under any of (i) to (iii) above, the partners' shares are deemed to be equal. By having a fixed agreement as to how capital assets or capital profits are allocated, partners can change their income profit shares without giving rise to any CGT charges. Sadly, the same cannot be said for SDLT.

Stamp Duty Land Tax

For SDLT purposes, a partner's share in partnership properties is based on their share of income profits. Furthermore, the deemed consideration for SDLT on transactions between business partners and the partnership is based on market value. This makes any changes in profit shares a potentially costly exercise.

Example Part 1
Dave is in a property investment partnership with Dozy, Beaky, Mick and Tich. Each partner has a 20% profit share. Dave would like to retire and leave the partnership. The partners agree that, by way of consideration for giving up his partnership share, Dave should take the property known as 'Dee Towers' with him. Dee Towers is an office building worth £1m.

Dave already had a 20% share in Dee Towers through the partnership, so he is treated as acquiring an 80% share, worth £800,000, when he leaves. He will therefore face a SDLT charge of £29,500! (See Section 7.5)

Example Part 2
As a result of Dave's departure, each of the continuing partners increases their profit share by 5%, from 20% to 25%.

After Dee Towers is transferred to Dave, the partnership is left with a commercial property portfolio with a total gross value of £15m and borrowings of £11m. While the partnership's net assets are only £4m, each of the continuing partners is treated as having acquired an additional 5% interest in property worth £15m. Worse still, as these are 'linked transactions' (see Section 7.8) the SDLT arising is calculated on a total value of £3m (£15m x 5% x 4) and amounts to £139,500 (see Section 7.5), giving Dozy, Beaky, Mick and Tich a charge of £34,875 each!

As we can see, the transfer of one property worth £1m has given rise to SDLT charges totalling £169,000 (£29,500 + £139,500), or 16.9% of the property's value.

If the continuing partners had paid Dave in cash instead, he would have had no SDLT to pay but they would each have acquired a 5% interest in commercial property worth a total of £16m, giving rise to SDLT based on deemed consideration of £3.2m (£16m x 5% x 4), resulting in a total charge of £149,500, or £37,375 each.

The cash route is better overall, but we're still looking at a charge equal to almost 15% of the actual transaction value.

By and large, therefore, anyone using a property investment partnership should try to get their profit shares right in the first place and do their utmost to avoid changing them at a later stage.

Note, however, that a straightforward cash investment into the partnership will not incur any SDLT charge if there is no change in the partnership profit shares.

It is striking to note that neither the net asset value of the partnership, nor the amount actually paid to purchase a partner's profit share, has any bearing on the amount of SDLT payable, which is based instead on the gross value of the partnership's property portfolio. It is worth contrasting this with the position that would have existed if the partners had set up a property investment company instead.

Subject to some anti-avoidance rules, shares in a property investment company can change hands for a Stamp Duty charge of only 0.5%. This represents a considerable saving compared to the rates applying to property investment partnerships. Furthermore, the charge on company shares is based on the actual consideration paid and not on the gross value of the underlying properties.

Example Revisited
As above, Dozy, Beaky, Mick and Tich decide to buy out Dave's 20%share of a property investment business that owns a property portfolio with a gross value of £16m, but has net assets of only £5m. This time, however, they are purchasing shares in a property investment company. They each pay £250,000 to buy an extra 5% shareholding, giving each of them a Stamp Duty charge of just £1,250, or £5,000 in total between them.

Using a company instead of a partnership has saved the investors a total of £144,500 (£149,500 – £5,000) on the transaction. (This is compared with buying Dave's partnership share for cash. For details of the tax arising when a property is taken out of a company by a shareholder, see the Taxcafe.co.uk guide *'Using a Property Company to Save Tax'*, although it is not generally recommended!)

The lesson is clear – if you and your colleagues are likely to change profit shares at any time, a company is likely to be much better than a partnership.

> **Wealth Warning**
> The SDLT rules for partnerships apply not only to property held by the partnership, but also to property held by one or more partners for the purposes of the partnership business. This would not generally apply to the partnership's own business premises, but would usually apply to property rented out by the partnership.

Profit Shares in Trading Partnerships

There is no SDLT charge on the purchase of profit share in most trading partnerships, including a property management partnership. Sadly, this relaxation does not apply to property investment, property development, or property dealing partnerships and, this time, furnished holiday lets don't escape either.

Land and Buildings Transaction Tax/Land Transaction Tax

Partnerships investing in property in Scotland or Wales will be subject to LBTT or LTT on those properties rather than SDLT. Most of the principles outlined above continue to apply, although the rates are different (see Sections 7.19 and 7.22).

The position for purchasing shares in a property investment company is not affected by the location of the company's properties. Hence, in 'Example Revisited', the continuing partners would still have paid a total of £5,000 in Stamp Duty if the company's properties had been in Scotland or Wales.

Other Partnership Restrictions

The annual investment allowance (see Section 3.15) is not available to a partnership where one or more members of the partnership are a company.

The trading income allowance (see Section 5.13) is not available on partnership trading income.

Partnership Benefits

Property can generally be transferred into a partnership free from both CGT and SDLT if the partnership shares in the property following the transfer match the individual partners' shares in the property prior to the transfer. Partnership shares in property for this purpose are determined under the rules outlined earlier in this section, which are different for each tax.

Furthermore, the proportion of a property deemed to be transferred for SDLT purposes is reduced not only by the partnership share held by the transferor, but also by any partnership shares held by 'connected persons' (as per Appendix B, but with heading (vi) disregarded). (The transferor must be one of the partners.)

Hence, a transfer of property into a partnership made up of yourself and your spouse, or other close relatives (as per headings (ii) to (v) in Appendix B), will be completely exempt from SDLT. This could be a good way to avoid the problems described in Section 7.7 regarding property subject to an outstanding mortgage.

Property transferred into a partnership made up of yourself and your spouse will also be exempt from CGT.

Transfers of property from a partnership to a company controlled by the same individuals are usually exempt from SDLT, and may also be exempt from CGT.

For further details of the tax position on both transfers into a partnership, and from a partnership to a company, see the Taxcafe.co.uk guide *Using a Property Company to Save Tax'*.

8.31   LIMITED LIABILITY PARTNERSHIPS

Like a Scottish partnership, a limited liability partnership ('LLP'), is a legal person and may own property directly. The rules described in the previous section apply equally to LLPs, subject to the further points set out below.

Interest on funds borrowed to invest in, or lend to, a property investment LLP is not eligible for Income Tax relief.

Members of an LLP whose profit share is mostly fixed without reference to the overall performance of the business may, under certain circumstances, be treated as employees for Income Tax and NI purposes.

8.32 EMIGRATING TO SAVE CAPITAL GAINS TAX

As explained in Sections 2.15 and 6.3, non-UK residents are now liable to UK CGT on all UK property. Despite this, there are still opportunities for long-term investors to make significant CGT savings by emigrating. However, merely going on a world cruise for a year will not be sufficient, as it is usually necessary to become non-UK resident for more than five years in order to avoid paying UK CGT in full on all your capital gains.

In this section, I will provide an overview of what is required to successfully achieve non-UK resident status for CGT purposes and the benefits arising. The main points worth noting are:

- Emigration must generally be permanent, or at least long-term (a period that covers at least five complete UK tax years is usually required)
- Disposals should be deferred until you are non-UK resident. In most cases, you will need to wait until the next tax year after you have left the UK
- Limited return visits to the UK are permitted (see below)
- Resuming UK residence before the expiry of the required period may result in substantial CGT liabilities

Finally, it is essential to ensure there is no risk of inadvertently becoming liable for some form of capital taxation elsewhere. There's no point 'jumping out of the frying pan and into the fire!'

Emigration to avoid UK CGT is a strategy that is generally only worth contemplating when the stakes are high. Professional advice is essential.

Example

Eleanor has been a highly successful property investor for many years. By April 2015, she already had a UK residential property portfolio worth £12m and would have faced potential CGT liabilities of over £2m if she were to sell it. By April 2019, she also had a portfolio of UK commercial property investments worth £15m that would give rise to a further £1m of CGT if disposed.

Eleanor decides to emigrate and on 3rd April 2020 flies to Utopia where she starts a new life. In the 2020/21 UK tax year, she sells all her UK properties.

Her UK residential property portfolio sells for a total of £15m. As a non-UK resident, she is only liable for UK CGT on the portfolio's increase in value after 5th April 2015: £3m. Her UK commercial property portfolio sells for a total of £15.5m. As a non-UK resident, she is only liable for UK CGT on the increase in value after 5th April 2019: £500,000.

For the sake of illustration, I will assume Eleanor is a higher rate taxpayer for UK Income Tax purposes, and will ignore her annual exemption. Hence, she has a UK CGT bill of:

£3m x 28%	*£840,000*
£500,000 x 20%	*£100,000*
Total:	*£940,000*

Eventually, Eleanor decides to return home and, on 8th April 2025, she comes back to the UK to live. As Eleanor was non-UK resident for over five years, she will remain exempt from UK CGT on the remaining, more substantial, part of the capital gains realised in 2020/21.

Emigrating has saved Eleanor more than £3m in UK CGT: all the tax that would have arisen on her residential properties if she had sold them for their market value on 5th April 2015, and all the tax that would have arisen on her commercial properties if she had sold them for their market value on 5th April 2019.

Remember, however, Utopia does not exist. Real countries have their own tax systems and may tax immigrants like Eleanor on their UK capital gains. It is therefore always essential to take local professional advice in the destination country.

Becoming Non-UK Resident

Special rules apply to individuals working full-time overseas and individuals who maintain a home in the UK without having a home overseas. Individuals working full-time in the UK for even part of the tax year may also be deemed UK resident.

Apart from individuals working full-time overseas, you will usually remain UK resident for the whole of the tax year in which you depart (e.g. 2019/20 in Eleanor's case) and become UK resident again for the whole of the tax year in which you return (e.g. 2025/26 in Eleanor's case).

Subject to these points, to achieve or maintain non-UK resident status you simply need to limit your visits to the UK. The maximum number of days a non-UK resident may spend in the UK is determined by the number of 'ties' they have. The 'ties' for this purpose are:

i) The Family Tie: The individual has a spouse, common-law partner, or minor child who is resident in the UK. A minor child need only be counted if the individual sees them on more than 60 days in the tax year. Separated spouses do not need to be counted.

ii) The Accommodation Tie: The individual has a home or other accommodation available to them in the UK for at least 91 consecutive days during the tax year and spends at least one night there during the tax year (or spends at least 16 nights there if the available accommodation is the home of a close relative).

iii) The Work Tie: The individual works in the UK for more than three hours on at least 40 days during the tax year.

iv) The 90-Day Tie: The individual spent more than 90 days in the UK in either of the two previous tax years.

v) The Country Tie: There is no other country where the individual was present at midnight on more days during the tax year than in the UK.

The maximum permitted visits to the UK depend on whether the individual was UK resident in any of the three previous tax years. The middle column below applies if they **were** UK resident **in any** of those years. The right-hand column applies if they were **not** UK resident in any of those years and, in this case, the country tie is disregarded.

Maximum Return Visits to UK

No. of Ties	Res in last 3 Years	Not Res last 3 Years
0	182 Days	182 Days
1	120 Days	182 Days
2	90 Days	120 Days
3	45 Days	90 Days
4 or 5	15 Days	45 Days

The general rule is that any day on which you are present in the UK at midnight is counted for the purpose of these tests. In other words, we actually count nights rather than days!

8.33   YEAR END TAX PLANNING

Rental Income
For individuals with rental income, it is generally necessary to draw up accounts for the tax year, rather than any other accounting period. Hence, for these property businesses, 5th April is twice as important since, not only is it the end of the tax year, it is generally also the end of their accounting period. Where I refer in this section to 'your year end', those with property rental businesses should therefore generally read this as meaning 5th April.

Property Trades
As we saw in Chapter 5, those with property trades may choose their own accounting date. Where I refer in this section to 'your year end', those with property trades should read this as meaning their own accounting date, rather than the tax year end.

The Tax Year End
Where I refer to 'the tax year end' this means 5th April whatever kind of business you have!

Timing Is Everything

For businesses using the 'accruals' basis (see Section 3.9) income and expenditure must be recognised when it arises, or is incurred, rather than when it is received or paid. Hence, whenever you need to make some business expenditure in the near future, it may make sense to ensure it takes place by your year end, in order to get tax relief in an earlier year, rather than having to wait another twelve months.

Obviously, this does not mean it is worth incurring expenditure just for the sake of it. It is seldom wise to make uncommercial decisions purely for tax reasons! What it does mean is that it can often be worth accelerating some of the expenditure that is going to be taking place in any case, so that it falls into an earlier accounting year.

Conversely, those who are basic rate taxpayers this year, but expect to be higher rate taxpayers next year, may be better off delaying business expenditure so that it falls into next year and provides tax relief at 40% instead of just 20%.

In some cases, those expecting total taxable income between £100,000 and £125,000, or over £150,000, next year may also be better off delaying business expenditure so that it falls into that year and provides tax relief at 45% or 60% (see Section 3.3 and Appendix A). The same may apply to those who expect to be subject to the HICBC next year (see Section 3.3).

Businesses on a Cash Basis

For businesses operating on a cash basis (see Sections 4.18 and 5.12) the tax-planning objective will usually be to accelerate the actual *payment* of any necessary expenditure to before the accounting year end.

Landlords on the cash basis might also do well to consider setting the due dates for rent receivable to fall shortly after the tax year end. Property traders using the cash basis may want to consider deferring sales until after their accounting year end if possible. As before, the position may differ if the taxpayer expects to be paying a higher rate of tax next year.

Capital Allowances

Where capital allowances are available (see Sections 3.14 to 3.18), the full allowance is usually given for the year in which expenditure is incurred. Where expenditure is eligible for capital allowances, therefore, consider making your purchase by your year end.

However, where you have already incurred qualifying expenditure in excess of the AIA (see Section 3.15) this year, it may be better to defer any further expenditure to get full tax relief in your next accounting period rather than a writing down allowance of just 6% or 18%.

Any assets bought on Hire Purchase must actually be brought into use in the business by your year end to qualify for capital allowances.

Cars

Capital allowances may be available on a car used in your property business. The allowance is usually restricted by reference to the private use of the car, but nevertheless it is worth noting that:

- A balancing allowance is usually available on the sale of an old car previously used in your property business, and
- A full year's allowance will be given on any new car brought into use in the business by your year end

Sales of old cars and purchases of new cars before your year end will often save tax if they are used in your business. Sales of old cars can give rise to a balancing charge, although a balancing allowance is more common.

8.34   BEATING THE CHANGES TO PPR RELIEF & PRIVATE LETTING RELIEF

As explained in Sections 6.13 and 6.14, the Government is proposing to make major changes to the CGT reliefs available on a former main residence disposed of after 5th April 2020, namely:

- The extension to PPR relief for the final period of ownership is to be reduced to nine months
- Private letting relief is to be restricted to periods of shared occupancy and not available for lettings in the course of a trade

Example

Megan and Harry are higher rate taxpayers. They bought their flat in Norwich for £50,000 on 6th April 2000 and lived there as their main residence until 6th October 2006, when they started renting it out. By early 2020, the flat is worth £250,000 and they are ready to sell it. Let's look at the difference it will make to their capital gain of £200,000 if they sell the flat on 5th or 6th April 2020:

	Sale on 5th April	*Sale on 6th April*
Capital gain	*£200,000*	*£200,000*
PPR relief for:		
8 years out of 20*	*(£80,000)*	
7 years and 3 months out of 20 years**		*(£72,500)*
Private letting relief (£40,000 each)	*(£80,000)*	*-*
Annual exemptions (£12,000 each)***	*(£24,000)*	*(£24,000)*
Taxable gain	*£16,000*	*£103,500*
CGT at 28%:	*£4,480*	*£28,980*

* Six and a half years of actual occupation plus last eighteen months
** Six and a half years of actual occupation plus last nine months
*** Assumed unchanged from 2019/20 for the sake of illustration

As we can see, a single day's delay in the sale would cost Megan and Harry an additional £24,500 in CGT.

The loss of private letting relief in most cases will cost higher rate taxpayers up to £11,200; or £22,400 for couples owning property jointly. The reduction in the final period of ownership exemption cost Megan and Harry a further £2,100, although its impact will vary immensely from case to case.

Planning for the Changes

To beat these changes, it will be necessary to trigger a disposal of the property before 6th April 2020. There are a number of methods of doing this, including:

i)   Selling the property
ii)   Entering an unconditional contract for sale by 5th April 2020 (see Section 6.6)
iii) Transferring the property to a connected person (see Appendix B) other than your spouse
iv)   Transferring the property to your unmarried partner
v)   Transferring the property to your spouse and re-adopting as your main residence at a later date (see Section 8.5 for the potential savings, but beware of the potential downside illustrated by Example 3 in Section 8.4)
vi)   Transferring the property to a trust without holding over the gain (see further in Section 8.35)
vii) Transferring the property to a company (see further in Section 8.36)
viii) Transferring the property to a partnership made up of yourself and connected persons (see Appendix B) other than your spouse

The drawback, of course, is that all these methods may trigger a CGT liability, except for method (v). Hence, they are generally only worth contemplating where the liability on a disposal before 6th April 2020 is nil, or small; or you had been intending to dispose of the property in the near future in any case.

Having said that, in a case like Megan and Harry's, it could be worth triggering a CGT liability now, in order to make savings in the long term. Furthermore, where a sale in the near future is in prospect, triggering a disposal before 6th April 2020 will give you until 31st January 2021 to pay the CGT, rather than just 30 days (see Section 6.30).

Transfers under any of methods (iii) to (viii) can be made as a gift, or for any price up to the property's market value. This will not alter the CGT position, but charging a price for the transfer could give rise to SDLT liabilities under methods (iii) to (vi). Transfers of property subject to a mortgage under any of those methods may also give rise to SDLT costs (see Section 7.7), even if the lender allows it.

SDLT can be avoided using method (viii) but you will have to retain some share in the property, so you will only be able to trigger the necessary disposal for a part interest, although this could be up to, say, 90%.

Transfers for less than market value under methods (iii), (iv), or (viii) could give rise to IHT liabilities if you die within the following seven years. See the Taxcafe.co.uk guide 'How to Save Inheritance Tax' for details.

8.35   USING A TRUST TO BEAT THE CHANGES

A transfer of property into trust (with no holdover relief) could fit well with the planning outlined in Section 8.15. Alternatively, since you do not want 'hold over' relief in any case, a settlor-interested trust (see Section 6.11) could be used to enable you to retain beneficial entitlement to the income from the property and/or the ultimate sale proceeds.

Example
Let's take the same facts as the example in Section 8.34, except let us now assume Megan and Harry transfer the property into a trust on 5th April 2020, with themselves as beneficiaries. Five years later, on 5th April 2025, the trust sells the property for £350,000. The trust has a gain of £100,000. After deducting its annual exemption of, say, £6,750 (see Section 6.19), it will have a taxable gain of £93,250 and a CGT liability (at 28%) of £26,110. The net proceeds of £323,890 can then be distributed to Megan and Harry and the total CGT they have suffered will amount to £30,590 (£4,480 personally plus £26,110 in the trust).

If Megan and Harry had kept the property in their own names until 2025, their CGT liability would have been as follows:

Capital gain	*£300,000*
PPR relief for 7 years, 3 months out of 25 years	*(£87,000)*
Annual exemptions (say £13,500 each)	*(£27,000)*

Taxable gain	*£186,000*
CGT at 28%:	*£52,080*

As we can see, using the trust has led to an eventual overall saving of £21,490 (£52,080 – £30,590). This is slightly reduced from the saving arising from a simple sale before 6th April 2020 but it must be remembered that Megan and Harry had an extra five years' worth of income and growth on the property.

Transferring property into a trust has IHT implications, even when it is a settlor-interested trust. However, transfers worth no more than £325,000 per person will not usually give rise to any problems if the property remains in the trust for less than ten years, and the transferors survive at least seven years after making the initial transfer. Income arising in the trust is also subject to a different Income Tax regime, although any negative effects can usually be avoided by using an 'interest in possession trust'. See the Taxcafe.co.uk guide *'How to Save Inheritance Tax'*.

8.36 USING A COMPANY TO BEAT THE CHANGES

A transfer of property into a company may also be a useful method for restoring tax relief for interest costs (see Section 4.5), although the SDLT arising on the transfer would need to be taken into account. The SDLT will usually be based on the property's market value, except when property is transferred from a partnership into a company controlled by the same individuals.

Example

Let's take the same facts as the example in Section 8.34, except let us now assume Megan and Harry transfer the property into a company on 5th April 2020. This gives rise to SDLT of £10,000 (see Section 7.3). In April 2025, the company sells the property for £350,000, realising a gain of £90,000 (£350,000 – £250,000 – £10,000).

Assuming the Corporation Tax rate remains 19% (as per the latest Government proposals) the company will have a tax bill of £17,100. Hence, the total tax suffered will amount to £31,580 (£4,480 CGT on the initial transfer plus £10,000 SDLT and £17,100 Corporation Tax).

At this stage, Megan and Harry are £20,500 better off than if they had kept the property in their own names (see Section 8.35 for the CGT they would have paid: £52,080 – £31,580 = £20,500).

However, winding up the company and distributing its overall net profit of £72,900 (£90,000 – £17,100) to Megan and Harry would give rise to further CGT liabilities of £9,180 (assuming their annual exemptions of, say, £13,500 each, are available and they remain higher rate taxpayers); leaving them only £11,320 (£20,500 – £9,180) better off in the end.

As we can see, this method produces greater savings where the eventual sale proceeds are retained in the company, but still has some benefit where the company is ultimately wound up. Nonetheless, the savings are again less than those arising from a simple sale before 6th April 2020.

It must again be remembered, however, that Megan and Harry have had an extra five years' worth of income and growth on the property. They will also have benefitted from a lower tax rate on their rental income within the company, plus full relief for any applicable interest costs.

Using a company to hold investment property gives rise to many other tax implications, which are examined in detail in the Taxcafe.co.uk guide *'Using a Property Company to Save Tax'*.

Appendix A

UK Tax Rates and Allowances: 2018/19 to 2020/21

	Rates	2018/19 £	2019/20 £	2020/21 £
Income Tax (2)				
Personal allowance		11,850	12,500	12,500
Basic rate band	20%	34,500	37,500	37,500
Higher rate/Threshold	40%	46,350	50,000	50,000
Personal allowance withdrawal				
Effective rate/From	60%	100,000	100,000	100,000
To		123,700	125,000	125,000
Additional rate/Threshold	45%	150,000	150,000	150,000
Starting rate band (3)	0%	5,000	5,000	5,000
Personal savings allowance (4)		1,000	1,000	1,000
Dividend allowance		2,000	2,000	2,000
Marriage allowance (5)		1,185	1,250	1,250
National Insurance				
Threshold	9%/12%	8,424	8,632	8,788(1)
Upper earnings limit	2%	46,350	50,000	50,000
Employment allowance		3,000	3,000	3,000
Class 2 – per week		2.95	3.00	3.05(1)
Small profits threshold		6,205	6,365	6,475(1)
Pension Contributions				
Annual allowance		40,000	40,000	40,000
Lifetime allowance		1.030m	1.055m	1.075m(1)
Capital Gains Tax				
Annual exemption		11,700	12,000	12,300(1)
Inheritance Tax				
Nil rate band		325,000	325,000	325,000
Main residence nil rate band		125,000	150,000	175,000
Annual Exemption		3,000	3,000	3,000
VAT Threshold		85,000	85,000	85,000

Notes
1. Forecast based on inflation (per the CPI) of 1.7%
2. Different rates and thresholds apply to Scottish taxpayers (except on interest, savings and dividend income, and on capital gains)
3. Applies to interest and savings income only
4. £500 if higher rate taxpayer; unavailable to additional rate taxpayers
5. Available where neither spouse/civil partner pays higher rate tax

Appendix B

Connected Persons

The definition of 'connected persons' differs slightly from one area of UK tax law to another. The definition applying for CGT, SDLT and Corporation Tax purposes is set out below, and also forms a reasonable guide to the definition for other purposes.

An individual's connected persons include the following:

i)   Their husband, wife or civil partner
ii) The following relatives:
   o   Mother, father or remoter ancestor
   o   Son, daughter or remoter descendant
   o   Brother or sister
iii) Relatives under (ii) above of the individual's spouse or civil partner
iv) Spouses or civil partners of the individual's relatives under (ii) above
v)   Spouses or civil partners of an individual under (iii) above
vi) The individual's business partners and their:
   o   Spouses or civil partners
   o   Relatives (as defined under (ii) above)
vii) Trusts where the individual is:
   o   The settlor (the person who set up the trust or transferred property, other assets, or funds into it), or
   o   A person 'connected' (as defined in this appendix) with the settlor
viii)Companies under the control of the individual, either alone, or together with persons under (i) to (vii) above
ix) Companies under the control of the individual acting together with one or more other persons

Short Leases

(See Section 6.34)

Proportion of the original cost of a lease of 50 or more years' duration allowed as a deduction for CGT purposes on a disposal of that lease.

Years Remaining	%	Years Remaining	%
50	100	25	81.100
49	99.657	24	79.622
48	99.289	23	78.055
47	98.902	22	76.399
46	98.490	21	74.635
45	98.059	20	72.770
44	97.595	19	70.791
43	97.107	18	68.697
42	96.593	17	66.470
41	96.041	16	64.116
40	95.457	15	61.617
39	94.842	14	58.971
38	94.189	13	56.167
37	93.497	12	53.191
36	92.761	11	50.038
35	91.981	10	46.695
34	91.156	9	43.154
33	90.280	8	39.399
32	89.354	7	35.414
31	88.371	6	31.195
30	87.330	5	26.722
29	86.226	4	21.983
28	85.053	3	16.959
27	83.816	2	11.629
26	82.496	1	5.983

Appendix D

Abbreviations Used in this Guide

ADS	Additional Dwelling Supplement
AIA	Annual Investment Allowance
ATED	The Annual Tax on Enveloped Dwellings
CGT	Capital Gains Tax
CIS	Construction Industry Scheme
CPI	Consumer Prices Index
EEA	European Economic Area
GAAR	General Anti-Abuse Rule
HICBC	High Income Child Benefit Charge
HMRC	HM Revenue and Customs
IHT	Inheritance Tax
LBTT	Land and Buildings Transaction Tax
LLP	Limited Liability Partnership
LTT	Land Transaction Tax
MTD	Making Tax Digital
NI	National Insurance
PAYE	Pay As You Earn
PPR	Principal Private Residence
SBA	Structures and Buildings Allowance
SDLT	Stamp Duty Land Tax
SIPP	Self-Invested Personal Pension Scheme
UK	United Kingdom
UTR	Unique Taxpayer Reference
VAT	Value Added Tax

Lightning Source UK Ltd.
Milton Keynes UK
UKHW020615211219
355800UK00008B/264/P